Copyright Questions and Answers for Information Professionals

From the Columns of
Against the Grain

"Lolly Gasaway is an expert in the field of copyright law and practice and is widely known for her ability to explain the law in a way that is understandable to all. This book, with its 336 questions and Lolly's accurate, comprehensive, and understandable answers, should be on every information professional's desk."

—*Marybeth Peters, Register of Copyrights, 1994–2010*

• • •

"Lolly Gasaway is a pioneer in the field of copyright education for information professionals. Both her commitment to the profession and her extensive knowledge are reflected in this comprehensive and detailed book, which addresses a wide range of topics that will enable the reader to understand the practical application of copyright. *Copyright Questions and Answers for Information Professionals* is an invaluable resource, and I highly recommend it to anyone, from beginner to expert, who grapples with understanding and applying the complex law of copyright."

—*Donna L. Ferullo, Director, University Copyright Office, Purdue University*

• • •

"Lolly Gasaway's compilation of copyright questions and answers for information professionals is a unique and needed resource. Copyright questions abound, and information professionals often have similar, recurring questions. However, finding a single, organized resource that covers a variety of complex scenarios is difficult at best. Lolly's very practical book solves this problem and will likely become a 'go to' reference book for many years. *Copyright Questions and Answers for Information Professionals* supports and enhances copyright literacy and fluency for information professionals."

—*Kimberly M. Bonner, Executive Director, Center for Intellectual Property, University of Maryland University College*

"Few professionals can rival the depth of experience and seasoned perspective that Lolly Gasaway brings to the challenge of understanding copyright for libraries. Her Q&A style will inform, provoke, and at times even entertain readers who need to grasp the law's practical implications."

—*Kenneth D. Crews, Director of the Copyright Advisory Office, Columbia University Libraries, and faculty member in the Columbia Law School*

• • •

"Lolly Gasaway's pioneering columns on copyright and education provide an unparalleled view of the evolution of copyright in the late twentieth century and trace the growing influence of technology on that law through her always insightful and helpful responses to reader questions. The questions are invariably complex, but Lolly's answers are inevitably accessible to all, not just copyright practitioners. This book provides a solid foundation for understanding the increasingly complex social conversations about copyright law in the twenty-first century."

—*Dwayne K. Buttler, Evelyn J. Schneider Endowed Chair for Scholarly Communication, University of Louisville*

• • •

"What a gift our copyright guru has given us in this treasure house, which contains hundreds of practical, complicated, and timely copyright scenarios. No longer must you face those twisted conundrums alone, with a colleague like Lolly an arm's length away with exactly what you need, exactly when you need it. If you have anything to do with copyright on your campus and you don't snap up this book, you need to get a new day job."

—*Peggy E. Hoon, Scholarly Communications Librarian, University of North Carolina, Charlotte*

Copyright Questions and Answers for Information Professionals

From the Columns of *Against the Grain*

Laura N. Gasaway

PURDUE UNIVERSITY PRESS
West Lafayette, Indiana

Library of Congress Cataloging-in-Publication Data

Gasaway, Laura N.
  Copyright questions and answers for information professionals : from the columns of against the grain / Laura N. Gasaway.
    p. cm. -- (Charleston insights in library, archival, and information sciences)
  Includes bibliographical references and index.
  ISBN 978-1-55753-639-6 (pbk. : alk. paper) -- ISBN 978-1-61249-253-7 (epdf) -- ISBN 978-1-61249-254-4 (epub) 1. Fair use (Copyright)--United States. 2. Copyright--United States. 3. Photocopying--Fair use(Copyright)--United States. I. Title.
  KF3030.1.G375 2013
  346.7304'82--dc23
                    2012032276

Note to Readers

This publication is designed to provide accurate and authoritative information in regard to the subject matter covered. It is based upon sources believed to be accurate and reliable and is intended to be current as of the time it was written. It is sold with the understanding that the publisher is not engaged in rendering legal, accounting, or other professional services. If legal advice or other expert assistance is required, the services of a competent professional person should be sought. Also, to confirm that the information has not been affected or changed by recent developments, traditional legal research techniques should be used, including checking primary sources where appropriate.

  (Based on the Declaration of Principles jointly adopted by a Committee of the American Bar Association and a Committee of Publishers and Associations.)

Contents

Foreword

Laura N. "Lolly" Gasaway is the Paul B. Eaton Distinguished Professor of Law at UNC-Chapel Hill. Copyright is her métier, and she is nationally known. From 2005 to 2008 she was co-chair of an elite nineteen-person task force appointed by the U.S. Copyright Office and the Library of Congress to study section 108 of the Copyright Act and suggest needed changes.

I first encountered this amazing woman when I attended one of her famous "copyright for librarians" seminars. I came home with a spiral-bound book full of information about copyright and all kinds of books and articles to read. I also had Lolly's handy chart, "When U.S. Works Pass into the Public Domain" (http://www.unc.edu/~unclng/public-d.htm), which she updates as needed. I still have that spiral-bound book filled with all sorts of useful notes.

It was several years later that my husband and I began *Against the Grain (ATG)*, the periodical which is an outgrowth of the Charleston Conferences. Bruce is a lawyer, but whenever I asked him a question related to copyright he would tell me to ask the real copyright expert, Lolly Gasaway. With all the new happenings in collection development and the emergence of the Internet, more and more questions kept coming up. So, why not ask Lolly to answer a few questions about copyright for *ATG* readers? She graciously agreed and she has never missed a column since she began writing one over fifteen years ago!

I remember the feeling of empowerment I had when people on or off the job would ask me a copyright question. As *ATG* editor, I would suggest they ask Lolly. A neighbor wanted to know if recipes were copyrightable. A faculty member wanted to know if a facsimile copy of an old work was still under copyright. What about a translation of an ancient work? What about copies of library materials made with a patron's digital camera? Are e-mail messages protected by copyright? Is it infringement for a library to loan a Kindle with e-books on it? Can a U.S. academic institution allow access to its home institution's materials for students in a study abroad program? Can a faculty member with a Netflix account show movies to students? Can we digitize old masters theses without permission from the author? Could we embed links on our websites? These are just a few of the hundreds of questions that Lolly answers in this essential volume.

For nearly two decades Lolly Gasaway has taken the time to answer queries of this nature in her column with untiring knowledge, dedication, energy, organization, and expertise. As Bruce and I looked at the growing body of information, we thought of the need for a book compilation. Again, Lolly graciously agreed. We are excited to offer Lolly's book as the very first volume in the Purdue University Press Charleston Insights in Library, Archival, and Information Sciences series.

Katina Strauch
Editor, *Against the Grain*
Founder, Charleston Conference

Preface

For almost 15 years I have authored the "Copyright Questions and Answers" column for *Against the Grain (ATG)*. It has been a labor of love, and I very much enjoy responding to the questions that librarians, publishers, teachers, and authors raise in my copyright law workshops, submit to me over the telephone, and increasingly—today almost exclusively—send to me via e-mail. I was delighted when Katrina Strauch asked me to turn questions from this column into a book that the journal would publish as the first in a series of books evolving from *ATG*. She was fortunate to strike an agreement with Purdue University Press to publish the series.

I have always felt a responsibility to respond to questions, hoping that I could help fellow librarians and faculty members who struggle to comply with copyright law and have nowhere to go for help. Who knew that these questions would lead to, first of all, the creation of the *ATG* column, and now this book.

My own interest in copyright for librarians and teachers is long and deep. I completed my MLS in 1968 and worked as a librarian in the University of Houston Law Library while I simultaneously attended law school there. In 1973, as I was about to receive my JD degree, *Williams & Wilkins Co. v. United States*,[1] was affirmed in a per curiam opinion from an evenly divided U.S. Supreme Court. The first library photocopying case involved a medical publisher suing the National Library of Medicine for photocopying for medical researchers from the publisher's journals. I felt as if my eyes had been opened, and I knew how I would spend my career—educating librarians, college faculty, and K–12 teachers about copyright. The *ATG* column is a part of this outreach.

---

1   487 F.2d 1345 (Ct. Cl. 1973).

Over the years I have consulted on copyright law with educational institutions and libraries of all types. Recognizing that practicing librarians want guidance and often appreciate bright-line rules, I have tried to strike a balance in my advisement. Guidelines on fair use and best practices are both somewhat controversial, and I believe that both should play a role in helping information professionals, teachers, authors, and publishers make decisions about fair use. Guidelines are not the law, but instead provide guidance as to what in 1976 Congress thought constituted fair use in the classroom, with the educational uses of music, and for interlibrary loan. Two courts have cited the Guidelines on Multiple Copying for Classroom Use with approval and one has rejected them. These opinions are discussed in this text. Other guidelines have been neither the subject of nor mentioned in litigation to date, and best practices have been rejected by one court.

In 2009 I was appointed as the only librarian on the Board of Directors of the Copyright Clearance Center (although there have been other librarians on the board in the past). I take this role seriously, speaking up for libraries and the concerns of librarians and library users on that board.

• • •

This book is arranged by topical chapter, each with a short introduction that defines what the chapter addresses. The introduction is followed by questions and answers grouped by subject within the chapter topic. Chapter 13, "Miscellaneous Issues," contains questions and answers on subjects that do not fit neatly into any of the other topics. The content of the answers in each chapter has been updated.

This book contains an extensive subject index designed to facilitate readers' access to the answers they seek. As such, it can be used in two major ways: (1) readers are invited to read the entire book, and (2) the book can serve as a reference work for readers to obtain answers to specific questions through use of the table of contents and index.

In this book I often refer to the chart I developed many years ago and have updated as the statute changes, "When U.S. Works Pass into the Public Domain" (http://www.unc.edu/~unclng/public-d.htm), a copy of which appears in the appendix to this book. Another useful chart is Peter Hirtle's "Copyright Term and the Public Domain in the United States," which can be found at http://copyright.cornell.edu/resources/publicdomain.cfm.

• • •

I am grateful to the many librarians, faculty members, authors, and publishers who have supplied these questions to me over the years. After all, this is your book! I owe thanks to Charles Watkinson and Purdue University Press for agreeing to publish not only this book but also the *Against the Grain* series. Katina Strauch has been endlessly supportive of me and the copyright column over the years and I appreciate her so much. Finally, thanks to Joan Blazich, my outstanding research assistant, for her help with editing and Ashley Arthur, member of the Faculty Administrative Services staff at the University of North Carolina School of Law for her assistance with manuscript preparation.

CHAPTER 1
Copyright Basics

Librarians and others have asked a large number of fundamental copyright questions over the years that deal with basic copyright issues rather than with library copying, Internet use of copyrighted works, and so forth—questions such as, what does it take to create a copyrighted work? who owns the copyright in a specific work? and, what happens to the copyright in a work when the author is an employee or is now deceased?

Section 102(a) of the Copyright Act of 1976 states that copyright attaches when an author creates an original work that is fixed in a tangible medium of expression. Works in which there is no copyright are in the public domain. Not all works can qualify for copyright, and section 102(b) details some exclusions from protection, including facts, processes, formulae, ideas, and procedures. The exclusive rights of the copyright holder are listed in section 106: reproduction, distribution, adaptation, public performance, public display and, for sound recordings, public performance by digital means. The statute dictates that the author of the work is the initial owner of the copyright, but the author may transfer one or more of these rights to a publisher or someone else. If a work is a work made for hire, then the employer is the author. There are significant copyright ownership issues concerning faculty authors in colleges and universities, as well as corporate employee authors.

Copyright ownership is separate from copyright registration, and one may own a copyright without registering it. Although registration of the work with the U.S. Copyright Office is not mandatory, it does provide important remedies for the owner. Moreover, an owner may bring suit only for registered works. Further, the owner may receive statutory damages and attorneys' fees if the work was registered before the infringement occurred. In order to register a work, the owner completes a form and pays a one-time fee to the U.S. Copyright Office, which then provides a certificate of registration. One may use the records at the U.S. Copyright Office to determine whether a work produced after 1978 was registered (*see* http://www.copyright.gov/records/). Although earlier records may be searched year by year, it is not easy to do. The University of Pennsylvania also has early records, and they are somewhat easier to search (*see* http://onlinebooks.library.upenn.edu/cce/).

Many of the questions in this chapter center on the ability to copyright works such as legal briefs and translations of existing works. Formalities of copyright, including registration, duration of copyright, and notice, are also addressed. This chapter also contains questions concerning derivative works and the copyright status of works published in other countries.

While most of the issues deal with the current Copyright Act,[1] the previous statute, the 1909 Copyright Act[2] is still relevant, especially for the term of copyright. The 1976 Copyright Act became effective January 1, 1978, and the term of copyright is life of the author plus 70 years for works with a personal author and for other works, 95 years after the date of first publication or 120 years after creation, whichever expires first. Under the 1909 Act, only published works received federal copyright protection, as opposed to those created and fixed. The term of copyright was 28 years and could be renewed for a second 28 years. Today, a work is eligible for copyright protection from the time it is created and fixed in a tangible medium of expression, whether or not it is published. In contrast, under the 1909 Act, unpublished works were protected by common law copyright, which meant

---

1   17 U.S.C. §§ 101–1332 (2006) (*see* http://www.copyright.gov/history/1909act.pdf).

2   Pub. L. 60–349, 35 Stat. 1075 (Mar. 4, 1909; *repealed* Jan. 1, 1978).

that they had an indefinite term of copyright and never entered into the public domain.

The variety of questions in this chapter is indicative of the degree of concern that librarians, faculty members, authors, and publishers have about copyright and the wide range of their interests.

• • •

Q1 *What does it take to create a copyrighted work? Does it have to be registered for protection?*

Under the current law, the Copyright Act of 1976, to create a copyrighted work, all one has to do is to create an original work (one that is not copied from someone else) that has at least a modicum of creativity and then fix it in a tangible medium of expression now known or later developed.

Registration is not required for copyright protection but instead is voluntary. If a copyright owner wants to sue infringers, however, the work must be registered prior to filing suit in federal court. Because copyright is a federal matter, infringement suits must be brought in federal court. Registration also provides some other important benefits to owners. For example, if the work is registered before the infringement occurs, the owner may recover statutory damages, as opposed to having to prove actual damages and profits. Further, if the litigation is successful, the owner may recover attorneys' fees.

• • •

Q2 *What is the public policy reason for awarding copyright to the authors of letters? For example, if a famous author sends a letter to a breathless admirer or even a lover, why does the recipient of the letter not own the copyright? Could the letter not be considered a gift to the recipient?*

The U.S. Constitution, in article II, section 8, clause 8, states that Congress may enact legislation to provide exclusive rights to authors for their writings. A letter is clearly a writing, and the writer of the letter is the author. In most types of works, when the author creates the work, it is then reproduced as multiple copies, such as with books, articles, music recordings, and so forth. But this is not always the case. Major exceptions are works of art and private letters, of which only a single copy may exist. It is a constitutional matter to recognize the letter writer as the author, who is also the initial owner of the copyright.

There is a difference between the copy and the copyright that confuses most people, including librarians of institutions that hold manuscript collections. The author of the letter owns the copyright in the literary work, that is, the letter; the recipient of the letter owns the only copy of the letter, or the recipient may have donated the original copy of the letter to a library or museum. The institution seldom actually holds the copyright, but it may still restrict access to the copy that it holds. In exchange for the right access, the institution may establish a variety of requirements that a user must satisfy before being permitted to access the letter. The donor of the letter (who may be either the author or the recipient) also may place restrictions on the availability or use of that letter, to which the institution must agree at the time of transfer. For the library to own the copyright, the author would have to transfer the copyright to the library in writing.

Issues such as invasion of privacy also must be considered with letters since a letter was intended as private correspondence between two parties. One could argue that either party should have the right to make the letters public. Under copyright, however, the law protects the right of first publication so that the author or heirs have the first right to publish the text of letters for the duration of the copyright. No copyright rights belong to the letter's recipient.

• • •

Q3 *A narrative by a woman slave from the 1840s was discovered and published in 2000. Since it has now been published, it is in the category of works that existed as an unpublished work on January 1, 1978, but which was published before the end of 2002. Therefore, it will not enter the public domain until the end of 2047. Who owns the copyright in this newly published work?*

The heirs of the author would hold the copyright in the work even though it was published 60 years after it was written. If the author has no heirs or they cannot be identified, then the editor may hold the copyright based on what the editor contributed to the work. The new material that the editor produced must be original and have at least minimum creativity in order to be eligible for copyright protection.

• • •

Q4 *A faculty member in the university has produced a song cycle based on the poetry of Gustavo Adolfo Becquer, a nineteenth century Spanish poet. The library has not been able to find any answers concerning his copyrights. It has contacted publishers, but has received no response. Becquer died in 1870; could his work still be under copyright?*

His poetry is in the public domain. Even in Spain where the copyright term was life of the author plus 50 years, the copyrights would have expired in 1920. Thus, the faculty member is free to prepare a derivative work based on Becquer's poems. If the faculty member contributes enough original work, which it sounds as if he or she may have, then the derivative work is eligible for copyright protection even though the underlying work is in the public domain. No one can copy the faculty member's song cycle, but others are free to write their own song cycles based on Becquer's poetry.

• • •

Q5 *Are facsimile copies of public domain works still under copyright?*

No. Facsimile copies are simply reproductions that do not create a new copyright in the work. So, a microform copy of a public domain work is also in the public domain. If, however, the facsimile copy has new material that was added, such as a new preface or an index, that new material may be protected by copyright. The material that is in the public domain work remains in the public domain. Often the publishers of these facsimile copies of works produce a collection of several titles and claim copyright in the collection. The individual titles may be reproduced, but not the entire collection.

• • •

Q6 *When someone produces a genealogical transcription, is that transcription copyrightable?*

A genealogical transcription may be defined as a readable version of a document in which the original handwriting is difficult to read. Any copyright would exist in the original document and would belong, at least initially, to the original author. In all likelihood, the work was not published but remained in manuscript format or was a handwritten document. So, the work was protected by common law copyright if it was created before January 1, 1978. This means that the work was ineligible for federal copyright protection because it was not published, but it also means that it never entered the public domain. When the Copyright Act of 1976 was enacted, Congress set a date at which unpublished works would enter the public domain. Works that existed on January 1, 1978, but remained unpublished through the end of 2002 entered the public domain at the end of 2002, or life of the author plus 70 years, whichever is greater. Works that were published between 1978 and the end of 2002 do not enter the public domain until the end of 2047, or life of the author plus 70 years, whichever is greater.

Even though the transcription is very useful, it does not create a new copyright in the work. On the other hand, a compilation of transcriptions, as long as it is not a total universe of documents (such as all of the letters of a particular writer), might qualify as a copyrightable compilation. The compilation itself has to be original, and sufficient creativity must be found from among the following factors: the selection of items, the indexing, the organization, or value added to the material.

Q7 *Is it true that nothing will enter the public domain until the year 2019? Why? Who initiated and pushed for such change in the copyright law?*

It is unfortunately true. The Sonny Bono Copyright Term Extension Act was signed into law on October 27, 1998, as an amendment to the Copyright Act of 1976. It basically extended the term of copyright for works published in the United States from life of the author plus 50 years to life plus 70 years, and it applied retroactively to works still under copyright. Because of the retroactivity provision, this means that only works published before 1923 are clearly in the public domain; works published from 1923 through 1963 may be in the public domain if they were not renewed for copyright at the expiration of the first 28-year term. If they were renewed, these works received an additional 67 years after the initial 28 years of protection. Therefore, it will be January 1, 2019, before anything else goes into the public domain. Works published from 1964 through 1977 were given a total of 95 years of protection by the same amendment, and the need to renew a copyright was eliminated.

It was predominantly the movie studios that pushed for term extension in this country. The European Union had gone to life plus 70 years a couple of years earlier, and the argument was made that U.S. law should be harmonized with that of the EU. Book publishers were actually not in favor of the extension, but did not formally object. The motion picture industry did most of the lobbying and funding of the effort to enact term extension.

• • •

Q8 *A librarian found my 1998 chart, "When U.S. Works Pass into the Public Domain" (see Appendix; also available at http://www. unc.edu/~unclng/public-d.htm) reproduced on a website and asks the following: The chart states that works published before 1923 are now in the public domain. (1) Does it mean that in 2008 one can count that date as 1933? (2) If something is published before this date and* *then the copyright is renewed, does the renewal apply only to publications since the copyright renewal? For example, a U.S. publication dated 1906: is it in the public domain even if later publications have a renewed copyright notice in them?*

(1) No, the year does not move as it did in the past; it is still 1923 for works first published in the United States. It will be 2019 before the works from 1923 enter the public domain. If the copyright term remains life plus 70 years, then beginning in 2019 works will enter the public domain year by year as in the past.

(2) The 1906 work is in the public domain. Even if the 1906 work were renewed for copyright, it would have received only an additional 28 years, so the first term would have expired in 1934. The renewal of 28 years would have expired in 1962, so it is now in the public domain. If new editions of the original 1906 work are published, only the new material gets a new copyright date, and the term for that new material is measured from the publication date of the new edition, if there is no personal author or, if there is a personal author, life plus 70 years.

• • •

Q9 *A library wants to distribute the public domain chart mentioned in Q8 to users on its campus. May the library do so? The library would like to change "published before 1923" to "published more than 75 years ago." This will obviate the need to change the chart every year.*

I always grant permission to use my public domain chart (*see* Appendix; also available at http://www.unc.edu/~unclng/public-d.htm) if the requester does two things: (1) uses my name with it and (2) includes the website address so that the user will have a source for any future changes to the statute. But I do not permit changes to the chart. The "published more than 75 years ago" was correct until October 27, 1998, when the Sonny Bono Term Extension Act was signed into law. Now, that is not correct. It will be 2019 before anything else goes into the public domain. So, the "published before 1923" will remain in effect until 2019 when the chart can begin to say "published more than 95 years ago."

Q10 *A university faculty member is publishing a textbook. She is planning to use samples of folktales, poetry, and the like and is in the process of getting permissions. Should she be unsuccessful in obtaining permission, she wants to substitute works that are in the public domain. The library has located some examples of fairy tales and poetry that were published well before 1923, but the anthologies in which they appear were published later, some as far back as the 1940s but many in more recent compilations. Is the date of the anthology the relevant date?*

No. The critical date is the date of first publication of the poem or tale. Republication in a new anthology does not change the underlying copyright date for the individual piece. Anthologies are copyrighted, but the copyright is in the compilation and not in each individual piece. Additionally, the anthology copyright covers any new materials added such as a new preface, editorial comments and the like. Note that some anthologies include new translations of folk tales from original languages, and the translation may be copyrighted as a derivative work.

• • •

Q11 *Does "publishing" include mimeographed reports, memos, and leaflets that are distributed to group or organization members?*

The concept of publication has much less import today than it did under the 1909 Copyright Act, the previous statute. Today, if a work is published, even widely, without a notice of copyright, the copyright is not lost. Under the 1909 Act, however, the author could lose rights through failure to place a copyright notice on a published work.

Because of the harshness of this law, courts developed the concept of limited publication (not relevant for works published since 1978). For works published in 1977 or earlier, however, limited publication was an important concept. If only a few copies were distributed, and/or those that were distributed had restrictions on use and distribution, then failure to include a copyright notice on these copies did not result in loss of copyright to the author. These restrictions on use typically were printed on the copies themselves. Whether the mimeographed reports, memos, or leaflets were published under the 1909 Act depends on the number of copies actually distributed and whether there were restrictions on further use and distribution.

• • •

Q12   *What is the copyright status of state court briefs? An attorney believes that briefs are copyrightable and that Lexis and Westlaw infringe when they include briefs in their databases without permission. The library maintains that state court briefs are public information and not subject to copyright. Is there a difference in U.S. government works and state government documents?*

Section 105 of the Copyright Act says that works produced by the federal government are not copyrightable. Because the Act is a federal statute, it is silent as to the status of state documents. Many states claim copyright in their documents or at least in some of them. *The Compendium II of Copyright Office Practices*, available at http://www.copyrightcompendium.com/, says that state statutes and court reports are not copyrightable. The question, of course, is whether briefs filed in a state court are government documents.

If the brief is for the state as a party to the litigation, and the brief is prepared by attorneys who are state employees, the brief is likely to be a government document, so the answer as to whether it is copyrighted or not will depend on whether the state claims copyright in its documents. If, however, the brief is one written by a private attorney for a private party to the litigation, then the brief may well be copyrighted. Some attorneys and law firms do claim copyright in their briefs and are particularly unhappy with services such as Lexis and Westlaw that sell copies of their briefs.

Legal authorities seem to say only that there *may* be copyright in briefs. Another possibility, of course, is that in filing the brief with a court, that brief becomes public domain as a part of the court record. Public domain is certainly the best argument from an open government–type of argument, however. But consider the following: A songwriter has not published a particular song, but it is introduced into evidence in a court case concerning the ownership of the copyright.

Clearly, introducing the song into evidence in court is not copyright infringement and is excused; however, this does not put the song into the public domain. Analogizing to briefs would mean that they do not become public domain just because they are filed in court. Unfortunately, this is one area in which currently there is no clear answer, but there soon may be. In 2012 two lawyers sued Lexis and West for including their briefs in their databases (see http://title17.net/2012/02/lawyers-sue-west-and-lexis-for-selling-lawyers-briefs-without-permission/).

• • •

Q13 *If there is no copyright notice on a government document, should a library assume that it is not copyrighted?*

If the work is published by the Government Printing Office, yes. If it is produced by a federal agency, section 105 of the Copyright Act says that the federal government may not own copyright in works it produces. This was an absolute until about 1978, when the National Science Foundation began to offer grants to researchers that permitted the researcher to publish research results and claim personal copyright in that work. Today, some federal agencies contract out various studies and reports and may permit the contractor to hold copyright. For these, one must hope that they contain a notice of copyright. The problem is that notice of copyright is now optional.

As a rule of thumb, if the author of the work is a federal agency itself, or a federal official acting in his official capacity, the work is public domain. The terms of the grant or contract determine whether a government contractor may hold copyright.

• • •

Q14 *A school is in the process of publishing an environmental science lab manual with lesson plans created by teachers from five different school systems working as a consortium under a grant. Teachers used information from the Internet, encyclopedias, and other sources for the manual. (1) Is it possible to copyright the manual with these materials included? (2) What if the school wishes to* *sell copies of this manual to other schools? (3) Can the school sell the manual if it is not copyrighted? (4) If copies are sold, how should the profits be divided?*

(1) Certainly, the school may claim copyright in the manual unless the terms of the grant dictate otherwise.

(2) Whether the manual may be sold really does not depend on whether the school claims copyright in the manual. The real issue is whether including these materials in the manual infringes the copyright of the encyclopedia or materials on the Internet. One would apply the fair use test to make this determination: what is the purpose of the use, what is the nature of the works copied, how much is used, and what effect did this have on the market for the work. (*See* section 107 of the Copyright Act of 1976.) There is no problem with selling the manual per se. However, uses that may be considered fair use even when there is a commercial advantage may not hold up as fair use if the manual is sold. If the amount used is more than a fair use portion, the school should seek permission if the manual is to be sold.

(3) The manual is protected by copyright whether or not it is registered. The Copyright Act says that copyright subsists from the time an original work of authorship is fixed in a tangible medium of expression. One can certainly sell an uncopyrighted work too, but this work would meet the requirements for copyright.

(4) The group producing the manual may divide the profits in whatever manner it chooses. Profits could be shared equally among the five school systems, or the schools could reach an agreement about how much each institution contributed to the work and develop a different formula for sharing the proceeds. Another alternative is to put any proceeds into a pool to be used to develop future works.

• • •

Q15 *When a university faculty member creates material while employed by the university, who owns the copyright?*

The first step in answering this question is to consult the university's copyright ownership policy. In the absence of a policy, generally, faculty members own the copyright in works they create with a few exceptions: (1) Works directed by the institution (e.g., the head of the biology department requires several faculty to collaborate and produce a lab manual for the introductory biology course) are generally owned by the university. (2) Works that made exceptional use of university resources may be owned by the institution, or the faculty member may have to reimburse the school. (3) Works produced by faculty under an external grant or contract are usually owned by the institution, but the external funding authority controls who owns the copyright. If the faculty member has an employment contract that specifies copyrighted works produced by faculty are works made for hire, then, for copyright ownership purposes, the university is the author. Such a contract is outside the norm since the tradition is faculty ownership in higher education.

For staff, the answer is just the opposite. The university normally owns all works produced by a staff member within the scope of employment. So, if a computer programmer develops a program for the university, the institution will own the copyright. Web pages produced by a librarian as a part of the job are owned by the school. Some universities occasionally permit staff ownership of the copyright, but by prior written agreement only.

Why are faculty works treated differently? By tradition, faculty have owned the copyrighted works they produce. Perhaps this was viewed as a reward or to compensate for low salaries. Moreover, few faculty-produced works have generated enough income for universities to have much of an interest. The only exception is online courses a faculty member creates, but often what the university really needs is a "shop right" to use the work within the institution rather than ownership.

• • •

Q16 *Are student works submitted for courses considered to be owned by the institution that is awarding course credit? If not, would a blanket policy on reproduction of student works by the college, published in the college catalog, substitute for individual language to that effect in each course syllabus? What about student newspapers and alumni publications?*

The student is the author and owns the copyright in works the student creates for courses. The fact that the institution is awarding credit is immaterial. If the institution wants to own the copyrights, it must obtain a written transfer of copyright from each of the students. A policy that permits the institution to reproduce student works does not affect copyright ownership but is instead in the nature of a license. Publishing a policy in the catalog likely would suffice to give the institution permission to reproduce the work, but it may not cover making the work available electronically since the U.S Supreme Court, in *New York Times Co. v. Tasini*, 533 U.S. 483 (2001), held that an author's electronic rights must be specifically transferred.

Typically, an educational institution owns the copyright in any of its official publications, whether they are printed works or websites. This includes catalogs, view books, histories of the institution written at the behest of the school, official web pages, and the like.

Works generated by groups such as student groups, faculty groups, and alumni organizations are most likely owned by the group. An academic institution may be able to claim copyright ownership of certain works by student groups that are generated at the request of the institution. For example, if the college or university asks the student government association to draft a code of conduct, the college or university might have some claims to the work. The same is true of faculty governance group work products. Student newspapers may also be owned by the university, but not definitely so.

Some alumni organizations are loosely governed by the academic institution; others are totally separate entities. Academic institutions have no claim of ownership on works generated by alumni associations that are separate entities.

• • •

Q17 *What rights does an individual researcher who is an employee have to own the copyright in works she produced if the research is conducted, and resulting report or article created, in house?*

The phrasing of this question leads one to assume that the copyrighted work is being created within a corporate environment. The

Copyright Act states that copyright belongs to the author, but if the work is a work made for hire, the employer is the author according to the Act. A work made for hire typically is one produced within the scope of someone's employment. Most corporations have internal employment policies that dictate that any copyrighted work produced by a corporate employee within the scope of his or her job belongs to the company. Even without such a policy, "scope of employment" likely means that any work produced (1) during work hours, (2) using any company resources, or (3) that is part of the job regardless of where and when it is developed, belongs to the company.

If "in house" in the question refers to a nonprofit organization, the copyright in any work created by an employee may belong to the organization, but not necessarily so. Many nonprofit libraries, such as public libraries, permit their employees to hold the copyright in works created, even within the scope of employment, as long as the library itself has the unfettered right to use the work.

• • •

Q18 *A librarian has been asked to present a paper at a conference. The association that sponsors the conference has asked her to bring 25 copies of the paper to sell. What copyright symbol should be placed on the copies?*

Although notice of copyright is no longer required, it is a good idea to include notice on such papers. As the author the librarian, not the association, owns the copyright. A notice alerts anyone who purchases the paper that the librarian holds copyright in the work. The notice is more than the "symbol." It consists of three elements: (1) the "C" in a circle (©), the word "copyright," or the abbreviation "copr."; (2) the name of the copyright holder; and (3) the year of first publication.

• • •

Q19 *The editors of an academic volume that will be published in October 2010 ask why the publisher wants to include in the copyright notice the year 2011 rather than 2010. The publisher says that* *it is normal practice for volumes published in the second half of the year to have a copyright date of the following year. Is this a problem? What happens if someone plagiarizes from the work in the two months before the copyright date?*

Actually, this is a common practice, and it does not make much difference for copyright protection. The copyright notice really has nothing to do with protecting the work. The Copyright Act of 1976 protects works from the time they are "created" and fixed in a tangible medium of expression. Thus, the individual chapters or articles are protected from the point of fixation. Assuming that the work is a compilation or collective work (such as a journal issue with separately authored chapters or articles), it is protected for 95 years after date of first publication or 120 years after creation, whichever comes first. Using the date of 2011 rather than 2010 actually gives one additional year of protection for the compilation or collective work since the copyright does not expire until the last day of the year 95 years after 2011, or 2106. However, with such a long term of protection, whether the copyright expires in 2105 or 2106 does not make much difference.

Plagiarism is not a copyright issue, but reproduction is. If an author reproduces portions of an article written by another author and incorporates the reproduced material into another work, that is copyright infringement. If a publisher registers a work for copyright within three months after publication, then not only can the publisher sue any infringers, but it may recover statutory damages and attorneys' fees.

Thus, there is no disadvantage to authors when publishers use a copyright date that is a little later than the actual publication date. It is a common practice.

• • •

Q20 *Is there sufficient creative content in cataloging records to make them eligible for copyright protection?*

Unfortunately, no. This is not to say that catalogers are not incredibly creative in what they do! But for copyright law purposes, a work must be original, and originality requires that the work originate with the creator (i.e., not be copied from someone else), and have a least a bit of creativity. Some works are simply excluded from copyright protection according to section 102(b) of the Copyright Act. Ineligible works include concepts, systems, procedures, principles, or discoveries, no matter how they are explained, illustrated, or embodied in a work. Cataloging records consist almost entirely of facts, and facts are not copyrightable. So, cataloging records themselves are not copyrightable. A collection of such records may be copyrightable as a compilation, however.

The same is true for metadata, the term often used when the record is electronic. A metadata record may be described as a set of attributes, or elements, necessary to describe the resource in question, such as records that describe a book or other item. Examples of metadata records are author, title, date of creation or publication, subject coverage, and the call number specifying location of the item on the shelf. Metadata in libraries typically consists of facts, and facts are not copyrightable. A compilation of metadata records could be copyrightable as a compilation if the compilation contains sufficient originality, such as section of items, indexing, arrangement, and organization.

• • •

Q21 *Why is it okay for people to use quotes from others in their e-mail signature lines? Is it because quotes are brief, and not a full representation of someone's work?*

Whether it is "okay" to use a quote in a signature line may depend on more than copyright law. For example, there may be institutional or company policies that prohibit attaching quotations to an e-mail signature. Additionally, the user of a quotation should cite the source so there is no issue of plagiarism.

For copyright purposes, short phrases are not copyrightable according to section 102(b) of the Copyright Act. Usually, however, a quotation comes from a longer work. If the work is in the public domain, use of the quotation is no problem, of course. If it comes from a copyrighted work, one would apply the four fair use factors—purpose and character of the use, nature of the copyrighted work, amount and substantiality used, and market effect—to determine whether use of the quotation is permissible; the third factor, the amount and substantiality used, is the most critical. So, a one-sentence quotation from a longer work likely is fair use. A one-sentence quotation from a four-line poem may not be, however.

• • •

Q22 *From an institutional point of view, should universities encourage faculty to register their copyrighted works?*

This question assumes that the institution has some interest in the faculty member's copyrighted works. Only the copyright owner can register the copyright; if it is the institution that owns the copyright in the work, then only the university may register it. Registration of the work gives the owner the ability to file suit in federal court, as well as access to certain remedies. If the faculty member owns the copyright, then why the university should care about registration is unclear, other than wanting its faculty members to be able to enforce their rights.

• • •

Q23 *How can an author modify copyright transfer agreements with journal publishers to reserve some individual rights? What sorts of changes are most often needed?*

It depends on the exact language of the publisher's transfer agreement, of course. At a minimum, the publisher will need the reproduction and distribution rights to publish the work in its journal. Other rights depend on what the author actually envisions doing with the work. In general look for: (1) the right to reuse the article in a later work (such as a chapter in a book the author will write), (2) the right to reproduce copies of the work for distribution to classes or post in course management software, (3) the right to reproduce and distribute a limited number of copies to professional colleagues, (4) the right to post the article on the author's home page after the article appears in the print publication, and (5) the general electronic rights. Does the author wish to grant all other electronic rights to the publisher or retain them? What the author wants also may depend on the work itself, as well as any uses the author contemplates.

The "how to" is easy. The author should just mark out undesirable terms and write in new ones. The publisher may or may not be willing to negotiate terms, but it is certainly worth a try!

• • •

Q24 *If a scholar translates an ancient Greek or Roman work, or one from the Renaissance, are there any copyright issues?*

A translation is a derivative work, and authors of copyrighted works own the right to prepare derivative works. The works mentioned, however, are in the public domain, so creating the translation without permission does not infringe. In fact, the translator may claim copyright in the translation of the work. The copyright in the translation makes the copying of that translation actionable as infringement, but since the original work is in the public domain, it does not prevent others from also translating the same work and publishing another translation.

• • •

Q25 *When does the estate of the author come into the picture for the expiration of copyrights?*

The term of copyright is tied to the death of the author and expires 70 years after the author's death. Copyrights are property, and after the death of the author, copyrights pass through the author's will to whoever is designated as the beneficiary. Should the author die intestate (without a will) then copyright passes to the author's heirs as governed by the laws of the state where the author is domiciled. The Copyright Act of 1976 intended that the copyright exist not only for the life of the author but also for two generations of heirs. Whether the author, a beneficiary of the will, or an heir owns the copyright, the term remains the same and is measured by the life of the author, not by the life of subsequent owners of the copyright.

$$\cdots$$

Q26 *In taking care to reproduce the copyright notice as now required, a library has encountered the following statement several times. "All rights reserved. This book is protected by copyright. No part of this book may be reproduced in any form or by any means, including photocopying, or utilized by any information storage and retrieval system without written permission from the copyright owner." Does this mean no copies whatsoever, or does fair use apply, regardless of this statement?*

The good news is that librarians may ignore those restrictive warnings; they have no effect unless the library signed a license agreement accepting those terms when it acquired the work. The library may still reproduce the work, not only under fair use but also under the section 108 library exceptions.

$$\cdots$$

Q27 *How are international publications covered under U.S. law? Are they protected?*

The first determination is what is meant by "international publications"? Are these publications by international organizations such as the United Nations, or are they works published in a foreign country? If the work is published by the United Nations, any of its agencies, or the Organization of American States, it is protected under U.S. copyright law according to section 104(b)(5) of the Copyright Act. Works by other international organizations are not subject to U.S. copyright.

Foreign works are protected under U.S. copyright if they are published in a country that is a party to a copyright treaty to which the United States is a signatory. (*See* section 104(b)(2) of the Copyright Act.) This would include all of the signatory countries to the Berne Convention or any bilateral or multilateral treaty to which the United

States is a party. Additionally, under section 104(b)(6), the President may by proclamation extend U.S. copyright to works published in another country if that nation extends copyright to U.S. authors on virtually the same basis as that nation extends to its own authors.

CHAPTER 2

Copies for Users

The Copyright Act contains a series of exceptions to the section 106 exclusive rights of the copyright holder. One of these exceptions, section 108, applies specifically to libraries and archives. This section permits libraries that satisfy certain criteria to make copies for the library itself (covered in chapter 11, "Preservation and Archiving"), and for users. Libraries also have general fair use rights,[1] as do users themselves. Fair use requires courts to analyze the copying, evaluate it on the basis of the four fair use factors, and weigh these factors to determine whether a particular use is a fair use. The four fair use factors are (1) purpose and character of the use, (2) nature of the copyrighted work, (3) amount and substantiality of the portion used in comparison to the copyrighted work as a whole, and (4) market effect.

Section 108(a) of the Copyright Act applies to all of the copying activity detailed in the remainder of that section. In order to qualify for the exception, libraries and archives must meet three criteria: (1) the copying a library does must not have a direct or indirect commercial advantage, (2) the library must be open either to the public or to researchers conducting research in a specialized field, and (3) each copy reproduced must contain a notice of copyright.

---

1   17 U.S.C. § 107(f)(4) (2006).

Libraries are permitted to make a single copy of one article from a periodical issue, chapter of a book, and so forth, to satisfy a user request under section 108(d). But the copy must become the property of the user, the library must give the user a warning of copyright,[2] and the library must have no notice that the reproduction provided will be used for other than fair use purposes. Section 108(g)(1) relates to the copying in section 108(d) and limits the copying so that it is neither concerted nor systematic.

Section 108(e) expands the copying that libraries may do for users under section 108(d). Section 108(e) applies to a single copy of a substantial portion of a work, or even an entire work, upon the request of a user. The same three requirements from section 108(d) apply to 108(e), but 108(e) has the additional requirement that the library must first make a reasonable effort to obtain a copy of the work at a fair price.

Copying for users includes multiple copying for the classroom in academic and school libraries (e.g., preparing course packs, providing copies requested by distance education students, copying handouts for meetings, and so forth). Users also may reproduce their own copies under fair use. When a user makes copies, whether by photocopying or by using a digital camera or scanner, the user is liable,[3] but the library is not if it posts a notice on equipment that advises users that making a copy may be subject to the copyright law.[4]

Section 108 of the Copyright Act is primarily an exception for the reproduction of text. Section 108(i) excludes from library copying musical works, pictorial, graphic, and sculptural works, and audiovisual works other than those pertaining to the news. For preservation and replacement, however, this exclusion does not apply, and nonprint works may be preserved and replaced under the conditions detailed in sections 108(b), (c), and (h); this is covered in chapter 11, "Preservation and Archiving." The section 108(i) exclusion is for photographs and graphic works that are part of a textual work reproduced under sections 108(d) and (e).

---

2   37 C.F.R. § 201.14 (2011).

3   17 U.S.C. § 108(f)(2) (2006).

4   17 U.S.C. § 108(f)(1) (2006).

Q28 *When making copies for users, does it make a difference if the library is part of a for-profit entity?*

This is not absolutely clear in the statute. Certainly, the answer is easier if the library is in a nonprofit organization. The question of whether a library in the for-profit sector copies for commercial advantage has never been litigated. In *American Geophysical Union v. Texaco, Inc.*, 37 F.3d 881 (2d Cir. 1994), the courts, especially the district court, seemed to say there is a commercial advantage, although the *Texaco* case was a section 107 fair use and not a section 108 library exceptions case. The librarian should consult corporate counsel to assist the library in making the decision about whether and how Texaco applies to the particular corporation.

• • •

Q29 *How often may a library copy from the same journal title and what restrictions apply?*

The restriction on copying for users is found in section 108(d) of the Copyright Act, which states that only one article from a journal issue may be reproduced for a user. Under section 108(e), larger portions may be reproduced for the user, but the library must first make a reasonable effort to purchase a copy for the user, and this includes even a used copy. Section 108(g)(1) states that libraries may copy the same material on separate occasions. This means that if several users request the same article, each user is treated as an individual and the library may make a copy for each of them. So, there is no such restriction.

• • •

Q30 *A number of public library patrons each day ask for a copy of that day's New York Times crossword puzzle. Is it permissible to photocopy the number of copies projected to be needed and make them available at the circulation desk for the patrons?*

While it likely is fair use for patrons themselves to make a photocopy of the puzzle for personal use, and even for the library to reproduce a copy of the puzzle for a patron upon request, there are re-strictions on what a library can do. Section 108(d) allows libraries to make a single copy of an article, book chapter, and the like, for a user upon request, but the library must provide a warning of copyright, the copy must become the property of the user, and the library must have no notice that the copy will be used for other than fair use purposes. This subsection is further restricted by section 108(g), which states among other things that the copying under section 108(d) cannot be systematic. Making multiple copies of the crossword puzzle each day is certainly systematic. The library could seek permission from the *New York Times* to make these copies in advance each day, or continue to make single copies for users upon request.

$$\bullet \ \bullet \ \bullet$$

Q31 *A public library has acquired two new sewing books, both of which come with a packet of sewing patterns. Is it infringement for the library to place a note on the packets asking patrons not to cut the patterns but to trace them for their personal use instead? Or would it be preferable for the note to ask users not to cut the patterns and to leave them to their own devices to figure out what to do after that?*

Under the first sale doctrine in section 109(a) of the Copyright Act, after anyone (including a library) obtains a copy of a work in its collection, it may choose to lend these materials to others. Instructing users not to deface the work, which is what cutting the patterns would do, is not infringement. Fashion design is not protected under U. S. copyright law, but patterns are graphic works and typically are protected. Thus, duplicating dress or crafts patterns via tracing or by another method likely is infringement. There is some possibility that it is a fair use for an individual who copies the pattern for personal use, but the library should not advise tracing as it may encourage infringement.

$$\bullet \ \bullet \ \bullet$$

Q32 *A library is building a significant collection of scores and anthologies of music, mostly Broadway music, movie tunes, and*

popular music. Librarians from other libraries and patrons use the
library because it has copies of these works. In the past, the library
viewed it as good customer service to fax copies of the music when
someone needed a copy in a hurry. Is there a problem with repro-
ducing sheet music? Why is it any different than when the library
lends the sheet music or the published anthology that contains the
particular musical work?

Yes, reproducing copyrighted sheet music is a problem. The exceptions provided for libraries under the library provision, section 108 of
the Copyright Act, do not apply to musical works, according to section
108(i), except for the sections 108(b) and (c) exceptions, which cover
preservation and replacement. So, libraries may not photocopy or fax
copyrighted sheet music for patrons.

This is different than lending the sheet music or the anthology
that contains the work. Under section 109(a), the first sale doctrine,
libraries are permitted to lend materials from their collection. Reproducing the work either by photocopying or by scanning infringes the
reproduction right of the copyright holder. On the other hand, it may
be fair use for the patron to make a copy, but the library should not
make the copy for the user.

• • •

Q33 *Should a library be concerned that researchers are using*
digital cameras to make reproductions of both published and un-
published works from their collections? This would not seem to be
substantially different than allowing a photocopy to be made. Could
it be interpreted to fall under section 108(b) or (c) of the Copyright
Act that restricts a library from making a digital copy of such ma-
terial available to the public outside the premises of the library or
archive? What are the implications of using scanners as opposed to
photocopiers?

If a researcher makes a copy of a work or a portion thereof with
his or her own digital camera, it is no different than copying the
work by hand or making a photocopy. It may well be a fair use for

the individual user. Because of the volume and scope of copying that libraries do, they are governed by a special section of the Copyright Act that limits library copying. Sections 108(b) and (c) generally permit library preservation copying of unpublished works and replacement copies for published material. The "on premises" restriction relates only to library copying and not what a user may do for research.

If the library provides public use scanners, then the section 108(f)(1) notice should be placed on or near that equipment just as is done for photocopiers. If the researcher is using either his or her own or the library's camera or scanner, the researcher may be liable if the activities are not fair use, but the library is not (*see* section 108(f)(2)).

• • •

Q34 *If an academic librarian is preparing a presentation for students and colleagues, may she incorporate content from a blog without infringing copyright?*

Blog content is copyrighted just as are other literary works. So, there are no special rules for blog content. A fair use portion of blog content may be used, just as a fair use portion of anything may be used. No permission is required to use a fair use portion, but for more than that, the librarian should contact the blog author and ask permission to use the material.

• • •

Q35 *A library is interested in PDF documents on the web that are available at no charge, such as dissertations made freely available by a particular higher education institution. What can an academic library do with respect to these documents from other institutions? (1) May the catalog point to the website of the institution that posts these PDF documents? (2) May paper versions be printed and added to the library's collection? (3) May the library save local electronic versions of documents and point to them?*

The desire to make these materials accessible to the users of a library makes sense, but some of these proposed alternatives are infringement and some are not.

(1) Pointing to the PDF on the web is no problem at all. A link is a cross-reference, and placing a link in the library online catalog is a very good option. However, the library should make sure that the file has been placed on the web by someone who has the authority to do so. In other words, anyone could take a dissertation and put a PDF version on the web without permission of the author. That person is certainly infringing, and libraries should not link to infringing sites. If the institution that granted the degree hosts the PDF file, then that institution is doing so with permission; often graduate students must agree to make dissertations available electronically, and the institution has the right to post them on the web. The official website for dissertations at a particular school would not be an infringing site, so linking to it is no problem.

(2) Printing a copy and adding it to the collection without permission is infringement. Just because the work is posted on the web does not mean that there is no copyright in the work. In fact, most doctoral students retain the copyright unless and until they assign it to a publisher. Posting the PDF makes the dissertation available to users at other institutions, but it does not give another library the reproduction right. A link does not reproduce the work, but copying it for the collection on paper does.

(3) Saving a local electronic version of a document and pointing to it rather than to the institutional site on which it is posted creates the same reproduction problems as stated in (2).

• • •

Q36 *A faculty member at the college wants to compile a number of journal articles on a particular topic and put them on a CD to distribute to other faculty members. Is this permissible?*

Not unless the faculty member either has permission from copyright owners or the articles are from journals to which the institution holds a license that permits reproduction and distribution in electronic form to others in the school.

Q37 *A for-profit service sells and distributes, via the web, a course pack of journal articles for college courses. Most of the articles the service distributes are contained within databases to which the service has subscribed, so copyright should be covered in their contract agreement with publishers. Occasionally an article is not available in one of these databases, and the for-profit service has requested that the library provide it with a copy. The service then obtains copyright clearance from the CCC (Copyright Clearance Center) before making the work available online in the course pack. Is there any problem with a library providing the service with a copy? Should the library require an official request? What does the for-profit service need to do to be compliant with the copyright law?*

There is no problem in providing the service with a copy. The for-profit service is handling the copyright permissions and royalties. Under section 108(d) of the Copyright Act, a library may provide a copy to a user upon request. If royalties are due because of the use the patron will make of the material, either the supplying library or the requesting entity must pay them. In this instance, the for-profit service is paying the royalties. It is unclear what is meant by an "official request." Does this mean an interlibrary loan request?

The only responsibilities of the library that supplies the copy upon request are to provide the section 108(d) warning to the patron and to make sure the copy contains the real notice of copyright. It is the for-profit service that must ensure its own compliance. In general, the university library should not be concerned about the for-profit service's compliance but instead should worry about its own.

• • •

Q38 *In a government agency, staff members prepare an alert service that consists of items taken from news stories and articles on the web (from Reuters, Associated Press, and various newspapers), news stories posted on other listservs, e-mails from colleagues, and so forth. Because this is disseminated as an internal list, is it permissible to reproduce the news stories in these e-mails? What about disseminating the updates to a much wider audience outside the or-*

ganization? What are the copyright concerns with circulating these internal e-mails containing the full text of articles? If only citations are distributed, what happens when employees then request copies of the articles?

If any of these sources are licensed products, the license agreement controls the redistribution of this content by an employee. If the organization has a Copyright Clearance Center Annual Copyright License, then redistribution within the organization is permitted. If the organization is not a CCC licensee, and redistribution of full text is done more than very occasionally, permission is required, and often there is a fee, even for a nonprofit organization. As an alternative, the employee could prepare a brief description of the contents and distribute it along with a link to the item on the web. Or the headline could be distributed, since headlines are not copyrightable in the United States, in contrast with many European countries. Distribution outside the organization other than headlines and links is even more likely to be infringement since licenses usually cover only employees.

Under section 108 of the Copyright Act, libraries are permitted to make single copies for users under certain conditions. No multiple copying is permitted, however. Section 108(d) allows a library to make a copy of an article from a journal issue for a user. One of the conditions that the library must meet in order to qualify for this exception is that the copy must become the property of the user. Another condition, found in section 108(g)(1) is that the copying may not be systematic, and it is certainly arguable that distributing the list of citations, accepting requests for the articles, and making multiple copies in anticipation of demand is systematic copying since it is neither isolated nor spontaneous. But it is equally likely that a court would consider this to be simply functioning under section 108(d); further, many libraries traditionally provide such service.

• • •

Q39 *When a for-profit company files for approval from the Federal Drug Administration, for either a new drug or a medical device,* *the company must provide copies of all articles and other literature, along with the filing. Now, in Europe, there is a medical device directive, MEDDEV.2.7.1 Rev.3—Guidelines on Medical Devices, that requires all manufacturers that want to sell product in European Union countries to provide a clinical evaluation of their product. Part of the evaluation is a literature search, along with copies of the articles and other materials that support their evaluation. Must copyright royalties be paid for these copies provided in response to a government directive?*

If the company has a Copyright Clearance Center Annual Copyright License (often called a blanket license), the library can provide copies of these articles to accompany federal and international filings without concern, including digital copies. If the company does not have a CCC license, then it should look at its various license agreements for full-text journals to see if this activity is covered by the license agreement. Otherwise, royalties should be paid.

Paul Goldstein, in his multi-volume treatise, *Goldstein on Copyright*, has long posited that supplying copies as required by a government agency as part of an application process or other regulation is a fair use. In January 2012 the U.S. Patent and Trademark Office (PTO) issued a written report concerning the use of copyrighted articles and books in the process of patent application examinations. Although the PTO has many license agreements that cover the use of journals, occasional copies of non-licensed journal articles are necessary. The report states that the fair use doctrine provides protection for the use of copyrighted non-patent literature in the prosecution of a patent (application through the PTO). For a fee the PTO provides certified copies of the files, including these articles, to the public, and it believes that this is fair use.

• • •

Q40 *A faculty member has received 36 microfilm reels containing the Papers of Charles Sumner, 1811–1874, through interlibrary loan to use for research for a work he is writing. How much may he copy under fair use?*

These papers could now be in the public domain. Works that existed as of January 1, 1978, but which were never published passed into the public domain at the end of 2002, or life of the author plus 70 years, whichever is greater. For these papers, it is the publication date that would determine whether the work is still under copyright. It is possible that the microform is the first publication of these papers. If this microfilm was published between 1978 and 2002, the copyright will extend to 2047 or 70 years after the death of the author, whichever is greater.

• • •

Q41 *One of the departments in a company is preparing for an upcoming tradeshow and has compiled a CD that includes the publications of staff members in that department. The department manager believes that first authors on articles can get permission from journals to share copies of their articles as long as copies are not for sale. Is this true or does the department need to purchase reprints from the publisher to distribute? Do the rules change if one changes the format from print to digital?*

If the authors assigned the copyright to the publisher (which is most often the case), then even the authors must have permission from the publisher in order to reproduce copies of the articles, regardless of whether the reproduction is in print or digital format on a CD. A change of format does not alter the copyright issues with regard to permissions. So, if the publisher owns the copyright, it determines whether the articles may be reproduced and distributed or whether reprints must be purchased in order to distribute them. It is the original copyright transfer from the author(s) to the publisher that controls. If the authors of an article did not transfer the copyright, then any of the authors can give permission for the reproduction.

• • •

Q42 *The university has an extensive distance learning program, and the library is asked to serve the needs of these students. How can the library provide copies of materials to these students?*

Library service to distance learners is treated the same as service to on-campus students. Consider two traditional services provided by libraries: (1) providing access to reserve collections and (2) assisting students with research projects. Services to distance education students can be offered on a similar basis. The difference, of course, is that students are unable to reproduce their own copies of works from the library's print reserves or from the collection. So, the library must act for the student in many instances.

The library may send copies of print reserve materials to distance learners upon request of the user. If the works are included in the electronic reserves system, then the student may access the materials directly and whatever permission or royalty arrangements the institution has for those works typically covers all enrolled students. For research projects, remote students may access online catalogs and periodical indexes and use those to identify needed materials. When the student forwards a request for these materials, the library should treat the request as a section 108(d) or (e) transaction and reproduce a copy of the article or book chapter and send it to the student either as a photocopy or electronically. It is not an interlibrary loan. Another alternative is to check out the bound volume to the student and send it.

• • •

Q43 *What liability does an individual librarian or library have when a student or patron needs help using the copy machine?*

If the library has posted the requisite notice on unsupervised reproduction equipment and follows the other requirements of section 108 of the Copyright Act, it is not liable for the infringing activities of users. This question relates to patrons who are unable to operate the copy equipment due to age or disability or because they do not understand how to do so. Rendering assistance to help a patron use equipment is not the same thing as making the copy for the user under sections 108(d) and (e). The library is not liable should the copies be infringing copies, but the patron still is liable under section 108(f)(2).

Q44 *What if someone wants to write a cookbook, and although the work uses strictly original recipes, it is later discovered that a similar recipe was previously published? Is it infringement?*

The good news is that individual recipes are not copyrighted. Copyright does not extend to ideas or facts, and recipes generally have standard lists of ingredients and directions, so they have been viewed as lacking sufficient originality to qualify for copyright under section 102(a) of the Copyright Act. Cookbooks, on the other hand, are copyrighted as compilations. What is protected is the selection, arrangement, and indexing of the recipes, along with any material such as a preface, descriptive instructions, photographs, and so forth. So, all recipes in a cookbook do not have to be original. Therefore, there is no concern about using a recipe that is similar to a later discovered one.

• • •

Q45 *The Classroom Guidelines state that they are minimum standards. If no maximum standards exist, how do libraries know where to draw the line? The campus attorneys have advised the strictest possible interpretation, for example, no more than nine instances of multiple copying for the students in a class per term without permission from the copyright holder.*

University counsel are basically doing what content providers hoped would happen. They are converting minimum guidelines into maximums. The few courts that have cited and discussed the Guidelines on Multiple Copying for Classroom Use (Classroom Guidelines) have tended to do the same. Yet, the Classroom Guidelines clearly were intended to define the minimum of what constitutes fair use. Many other institutions refer faculty members to the four fair use factors (purpose and character of the use, the nature of the work copied, amount used, and market effect) to assist them with making the decision about the maximum use, and they recognize that the numerical limits and portion limitations are indeed minimum guidelines. Librarians should encourage university attorneys to take a broader view of what is permitted under the Classroom Guidelines.

•••

Q46 *For a no credit keyboarding course for which there is no textbook, may the professor make copies of handouts directly from a single textbook to distribute to the class?*

The Guidelines for Multiple Copying for Classroom Use (Classroom Guidelines) provide safe harbor guidelines for reproducing handouts, such as a chapter from a book, and distributing them to students in a class. For the Classroom Guidelines, it makes no difference whether or not the course is for credit, as long as it is offered by a nonprofit educational institution. Although the Guidelines are minimum rather than maximum, among the tests that must be met under the Guidelines is "cumulative effects." This test states that no more than three chapters from a book may be reproduced and distributed to a class during the term. More than three chapters means that either the students should purchase the textbook or that the school should seek permission and pay royalties for the reproduction if requested. The Guidelines also state that the material may be used for only one term without permission, and thereafter the school should seek permission.

•••

Q47 *Teachers in a middle school want to reproduce workbook pages and literary texts. Why is this problematic since the school is poorly funded and serves primarily students from immigrant families? To conduct the English as a second language courses, the teachers have relied on photocopied stories from other books as the school cannot afford to buy classroom copies of stories for this particular group of students. The school is now discouraging this type of copying, using the justification that the copying of texts fails to teach the children the importance of avoiding plagiarism. Unfortunately, this logic seems to ignore the sad fact that unless the children learn to read, they will never be able to appreciate plagiarism for good or* *evil. Why is it wrong to assist immigrant children by copying stories to help them learn to read?*

While the described situation seems grossly unfair from a moral perspective, from a copyright perspective, the only possible excuse for such copying is fair use, and whether the copying is fair use is not quite so clear. The Guidelines on Multiple Copying for Classroom Use (Classroom Guidelines) were negotiated by publishers, authors, and educational associations in 1976. They were presented to Congress and published in the House Report that accompanied the 1976 Copyright Act (House Report 94-1476). They are not the law, but have a pretty good stamp of Congress on them. Further, they have been cited with approval by several courts. The Classroom Guidelines apply only to nonprofit educational institutions and provide a safe harbor, so even if the copying for students exceeds the limitations contained in the Guidelines, a court might still find that the use is a fair use. One would apply the four fair use factors (purpose and character of the use, nature of the copyrighted work, amount and substantiality used, and market effect) to try to determine whether the use is fair.

The Classroom Guidelines state that no copying from workbooks, standardized tests, and so forth is permitted because these works are meant to be consumed. Schools are supposed to purchase one copy for each student. While this is very difficult for many school districts, consider what constitutes the market for workbooks. The publisher has only one market for workbooks, and that is schools. Therefore, the effect of such copying on the market is that the copies substitute for the purchase of a workbook. This is not to say that single copies of very small portions of a workbook might not be fair use, but multiple copying of workbooks, even for immigrant children, likely is not. Perhaps the school can obtain permission from the copyright holders for the copying.

• • •

Q48 *A professor wants to make multiple copies of several cases handed down by the U.S. Supreme Court. Since U.S. government documents are fair use, how does this apply if he is copying the cases* *from a textbook, not the Supreme Court Reporter? Does that make any difference?*

Actually, U.S. government documents are public domain rather than fair use, which means that the works may be copied, edited, and so forth without seeking permission from the copyright owner or applying the four fair use factors. The official *U.S. Reports*, available from the GPO (Government Printing Office), is a government publication and therefore may be freely reproduced, edited, or translated. The *Supreme Court Reporter*, published by West Publishing Company, is a commercially published law reporter, and it contains features that make the volume copyrightable as a compilation, such as the headnotes, the editorial features, and the like. However, if the faculty member copies only the case itself without the headnotes, he is reproducing only public domain material.

Taking a court opinion from a textbook presents a different issue since most textbooks or casebooks contain edited versions of cases. Has the editor done enough work to qualify the cases as derivative works that would be separately copyrightable? Perhaps. The faculty member then has several alternatives to stay within the law: (1) reproduce the opinion from the *U.S. Reports*, (2) reproduce the opinion minus the headnotes from the *Supreme Court Reporter*, (3) create a web page and link to the full-text version of the opinion online, (4) download the opinion from a website that uses the official version, or (5) seek permission from the editor of the casebook to use the edited version. It usually is not difficult to obtain free permission when the use of the copies made is for teaching purposes in a nonprofit educational institution.

• • •

Q49 *Instructors and students copy the same course materials semester after semester. Whose responsibility is it for setting copyright policies and following copyright guidelines: the administration, the library, or faculty?*

It is the institution's responsibility to develop a copyright policy and to see that it is followed. The institution bears the ultimate responsibility, but the faculty member may also be liable if he or she is violating the institution's policy about reproducing course materials. The question implies that the copying is being done without paying royalties or seeking permission from the copyright owner. Most institutions have policies about paying royalties for course packs, even though the course pack litigation to date has involved for-profit copy centers that reproduced course packs and not colleges or universities themselves. A student making a copy for research or scholarship may be a fair use.

• • •

Q50 *(1) May a teacher scan and display a short story or poem in its entirety for students enrolled in a course in a nonprofit educational institution to read prior to an upcoming class session? (2) May that material—or any material posted in the course management system for the course—be accessed at any time during the duration of the course other than during scheduled class sessions (i.e., can students review the material at any time prior to the end of the course)?*

(1) Yes, if it is typically the amount of material that would be displayed to a class in a face-to-face situation (the old "put it on transparencies or slides" idea). So, if the work is a book-length poem, probably not, but a two-page poem, yes. The same is true for a brief short story. If it is more than a few pages, though, it likely would not be permissible under section 110(2) of the Copyright Act (known as the TEACH Act), but it would be covered by section 107 (fair use) and should follow the Guidelines on Multiple Copying for Classroom Use (Classroom Guidelines).

(2) Text materials placed in the course management system under fair use can be accessed at any time, but performances and displays under the TEACH Act are restricted to access during the class session. Under the Classroom Guidelines, text materials such as articles may remain in the course management system for only one semester, but there is no limit on downloading or retention during the course term. For performances and displays, there is not a one-semester limit, but student access is limited to the "class session" and the works may not be downloaded.

Q51 *The school choir director is under the impression that a work of music can be reproduced for each member of the choir for a college choir performance without penalty as long as the photocopies are collected and destroyed within 45 days. This sounds like flagrant infringement. Is it?*

It is pretty suspect. The Guidelines for Educational Uses of Music (Music Guidelines), which were developed in 1976 and published in House Report 94-1476, allow photocopying sheet music for performance but for emergency purposes only. For example, if one of the performers has lost his or her copy of the music and the performance is imminent. According to the Music Guidelines, even after the performance the school still must purchase the music. In order to protect the school from liability, the faculty member should be required to produce some proof of an agreement from music publishers before committing the school to such a practice. The Music Guidelines are available at http://www.unc.edu/~unclng/music-guidelines.htm.

• • •

Q52 *A teacher in a nonprofit educational institution music therapy program is interested in the use of sheet music and printed scores in that program. She asks whether fair use, the TEACH Act, or other statutes and regulations apply. What are the guidelines for students who routinely download sheet music to learn and bring into lessons and music therapy clinical sessions?*

If these music therapy sessions are for teaching students to be music therapists in a nonprofit educational institution, then the Guidelines for Educational Uses of Music apply. The Music Guidelines cover both the reproduction of music recordings as well as sheet music for educational purposes, but typically for study, not for performance. General fair use also applies. For performance and display of nondramatic music in a face-to-face classroom in a nonprofit educational institution, the section 110(1) exception applies and permits the performance of a nondramatic musical work if the purpose is for instruction and the other conditions are met. It the class is a transmitted or online class, then the TEACH Act permits the performance. Neither of these sections apply to reproducing sheet music, though. If the music is to be performed, it is a good idea to ask students to make sure that they examine the copyright notice on the sheet music on the web and ensure that there is no restriction on downloading for performance.

• • •

Q53 *A state agency library is often used by attorneys general (AG) who argue cases on behalf of the agency. Sometimes they need a copy of an industry standard for their case. They ask the librarian to copy the entire standard, which can cost from $40 to over $200 each, depending on who created it (e.g., American Ladder Institute, American Society of Safety Engineers). May the library reproduce industry standards for the AG? If not, then is it permissible to check out the library's copy of the standard to the AG and let them do what they will as long as the library gets its copy back? Is there any exception to copyright law that allows attorneys to make photocopies for court cases without the restrictions of copyright?*

According to the standard legal treatise, *Nimmer on Copyright*, if the material is going to be introduced into evidence in a court proceeding, reproducing it for this purpose is fair use. But if the standard is used only for preparation for the trial and will not be introduced into evidence, it may be fair use or it may be infringement to reproduce the entire standard. Lending the standard to the AG is no problem. If the AG staff rather than the library reproduces the standard, it may be infringement, but the library has avoided liability. The state has not, however, and will still be liable for any infringement.

• • •

Q54 *What are the copyright issues regarding copying an assessment tool that was published in 1960 and reproduced many times in various texts? Is it infringement to reproduce the tool?*

The first question is whether the assessment tool is protected by copyright or whether it is in the public domain. If published in 1960, the copyright would have expired in 1988 (28 years after the date of publication). The copyright would have had to be renewed in 1988; if it was not renewed, the work is in the public domain today. If it was renewed, then the work would have received an additional 67 years of copyright protection. Assuming the renewal occurred in a timely fashion, copyright protection would last until 2055. If the work is still under copyright, whether permission is required depends on the use that will be made of the reproduction of the assessment tool. Reproducing it or a portion of it for scholarship or research is likely to be fair use. Reproducing it for use in teaching in a nonprofit educational institution may be fair use. Making copies for other purposes, such as using the assessment tool for students, probably requires permission. The fact that the assessment tool has been reproduced many times in textbooks does not necessarily mean that it was done without permission or paying royalties.

• • •

Q55 *A professor of communication studies has written an article that analyzes critiques of and comments upon advertising appearing in a popular computer magazine. The article quotes from several of the ads, and the professor wants to reprint six of the advertisements in the article. Would this qualify as a fair use? If not, from whom should she seek permission?*

Quoting from the advertisements, with proper attribution, is likely to be a fair use. The purpose of using the quotations is to produce a critique of them, the amount used is small, and there is likely to be no market effect. To reproduce some of the ads in their entirety, she does need permission since each advertisement is an entire copyrighted work. It is the same as including a copyrighted photograph in the article; because each photo is a separate copyrighted work, reprinting one in the article requires permission.

The simple answer to the question about from whom to seek permission is the copyright owner, but that is not always easy to determine. The professor should start with the magazine publisher and ask for permission to reprint the ad. She will probably be referred to the advertising agency that produced the ad, and the agency will know whether it or the company that hired the agency owns the copyright in the advertisement.

CHAPTER 3

Library Reserves

Libraries have utilized and managed reserve collections for many years. Originally these collections housed original volumes that were removed from the circulating collection so that they could serve more patrons by using a short restricted borrowing period. Over time, faculty members began to request that books and periodical volumes be placed on course reserves.[1] These activities raised no copyright concerns because the library was not reproducing the works. With the advent of the photocopier, libraries had the ability to substitute photocopies of book chapters and articles for the original book or journal volume in the reserve collection. This raised copyright issues because now the library was reproducing materials for course reserves.

Section 108 of the Copyright Act is silent about reproducing for library reserves, perhaps because course reserves are an adjunct to the classroom. Therefore, library reserves are a section 107 fair use issue. At the request of librarians, in 1982 the American Library Association produced the *Model Policy Concerning College and University Photocopying for Classroom, Research and Library Reserve Use* (Model Policy), which offered guidelines for libraries with regard to photocopy reserve collections (Reserve Guidelines).[2]

---

1   *See* 3 Libr. J. 271, 271 (1878).

2   *See* American Library Association, *Model Policy Concerning College and University Photocopying for Classroom, Research and Library Reserve Use* (1982),

In recent years many libraries have replaced print reserves with electronic reserve (e-reserve) collections that contain scanned copies of the same material that in the past had been photocopied for reserve. Additionally, audiovisual works and sound recordings may be represented in reserve collections, and some libraries make them available to users by streaming. Photographs and other images may also be considered for e-reserves.

This chapter addresses issues such as whether libraries must own copies of the items that they reproduce for reserves or whether they may accept a faculty member's personal copy; textbooks on reserve; copying faculty-produced materials for the reserve collection; the difference between course packs and copying for reserve; and e-reserves, including linking to licensed products to which the library subscribes. Whether the TEACH Act, section 110(2), is relevant for library e-reserves is also covered.

• • •

Q56 *May a library place on reserve a copy of a journal issue that is personally owned by a faculty member? If so, may it remain on reserve for multiple semesters?*

Yes. If a copy of the journal issue is owned either by the library or by a faculty or staff member, it may be placed on reserve indefinitely. Putting an original copy on reserve does not implicate copyright in any way since the library is not reproducing the work for reserve; it is only reproductions that raise copyright concerns. If it is a photocopy that is being placed on reserve, whether personally owned by a faculty member or made by the library, it is a reproduction and permission should be sought for use after the first term it is on reserve for that faculty member.

• • •

Q57 *An academic library is trying to get copyright clearance for a 1925 article to put on reserve for students. The journal is out of*

reprinted in 43 *Coll. & Res. Libr. News* 127 (1982). Reserve Guidelines available at http://www.unc.edu/~unclng/ALA-modelpolicy.htm.

*print and the publisher has disappeared. Is it safe to put the article
on reserve without copyright clearance?*

Most libraries do not seek permission to put copies of works,
(i.e., reproductions) on reserve for use the first semester or term.
For subsequent semesters, they do seek permission based on the Reserve Guidelines from the 1982 ALA *Model Policy Concerning College and University Photocopying for Classroom, Research and Library Reserve* (*see* http://www.unc.edu/~unclng/ALA-modelpolicy.
htm). Assuming that this is use in subsequent semesters, the following applies.

The article may still be protected by copyright. The journal publisher copyright holder received 28 years of protection, so the work
was protected through 1953. In 1953, the publisher could apply for
a renewal of copyright. If it did so, the copyright would have been
renewed for an additional 28 years, or until 1981. If that renewal
occurred, the journal would be protected until 2020 because the
term was expanded to 95 years after first publication by the Copyright Act of 1976 and its subsequent amendments. If the 1953 renewal did not occur, the journal is now in the public domain and no
permission is necessary. (*See* section 304(b) of the Copyright Act.)
The Copyright Office records can answer whether the copyright was
renewed in 1953.

After the library has done all that it can to determine whether the
work is still protected and to locate a copyright owner, then the library
must do a risk assessment. What is the risk of liability for placing a
photocopy of a 1925 article on reserve when the journal is defunct and
the publisher has disappeared? While the risk in this situation surely
is very low, the best solution is to consult university counsel in order
to make this decision.

• • •

Q58 *A faculty member brought copies of music CDs that he owns
to the library and has asked to put them on reserve for his class. These
are not purchased copies of original CDs but rather are reproduced
copies. The library does not own the CDs in question. The library*

does not seek to copy or stream the CDs but only to place the copies on reserve. Is it permissible to put copies of works on reserve that the library does not own?

Under the ALA Reserve Guidelines from the *Model Policy Concerning College and University Photocopying for Classroom, Research and Library Reserve Use* (*see* http://www.unc.edu/~unclng/ALA-modelpolicy.htm), either the library or the faculty member should own a copy of the item placed on reserve. The complicating factor here is that the faculty member's copies are not legitimate copies. If they were, then placing them on reserve for use by his students would be no problem. The fact that the CDs are reproduced makes it a more difficult issue for the library. Perhaps the faculty member had permission to copy the CDs, but that is not clear. The library then is faced with a dilemma. Does it adopt a policy that all works placed on reserve must be owned by the library, or permit faculty-owned copies and occasional copies from interlibrary loan on reserve? Further, if it accepts faculty-owned copies for reserve, must these be legitimate copies?

• • •

Q59 *If an instructor owns a copy of a commercially produced video, may she make an additional copy and place that copy in the library for course reserve materials? Does it matter that the video is out of print?*

Duplicating videos is pretty clearly copyright infringement, except for preservation by the library under the narrow conditions detailed in sections 108(b) and (c) of the Copyright Act. Imagine that the work was a copy of a book that the faculty member owned. Would it be infringement if the faculty member duplicated the entire book and placed the photocopy on reserve? Yes, it would. It is no different for videos. Reproduction of the work as described in the question is infringement, and out of print does not mean out of copyright.

Q60 *A professor makes a CD with excerpts of various musical recordings, thereby creating, in essence, a "compilation" or anthology. The professor is unable to identify the sources of most of these recordings. He wants to place these "homemade" CDs on reserve indefinitely (i.e., beyond even an academic year) so that students may listen to them in the library's listening rooms in preparation for aural examinations. May he do so?*

The Guidelines for Educational Uses of Music actually permit faculty members to make a single copy of an audio recording of various musical recordings for the purposes of constructing aural exercises. The Music Guidelines are silent about placing the recording on reserve in the library, however. It likely is a fair use to place these recordings on reserve so that students can check them out to review them for the aural exercise. The Music Guidelines are silent about reuse of the compilation recording, so it should not be problematic to use the recordings also in subsequent semesters. It would be preferable if the faculty member remembered the source of these recordings, but for copyright purposes it is not essential.

• • •

Q61 *If an instructor puts on reserve a journal reprint that she purchased, is it permissible to keep it on reserve for more than one semester without copyright permission? Does the first sale doctrine apply?*

If the professor paid for the reprint or paid royalties, then the library is not further reproducing it by putting that one reprint on reserve. It is a purchased item just as if the library itself purchases a copy of a book and places it on reserve. Therefore, the one-semester limitation from the ALA *Model Policy Concerning College and University Photocopying for Classroom, Research and Library Reserve Use* Reserve Guidelines (*see* http://www.unc.edu/~unclng/ALA-modelpolicy.htm) does not apply. Under the first sale doctrine, found in section 109(a) of the Copyright Act, the owner of a lawfully acquired copy of a work may dispose of that copy however the owner wishes. This would include putting it on reserve in a library but not reproducing it.

• • •

Q62 *A faculty member says, "I don't want the students to have to pay . . ." and asks the library to put a copy of the required textbook for his course on reserve. If one cannot make copies of "consumable items," how does a library deal with the textbook on reserve?*

According to the legislative history that accompanied the Copyright Act of 1976, a textbook is not defined as a consumable item. Consumables are those works that are "used up" after purchase. Congress gave as examples standardized tests, workbooks, answer keys, and so forth. The school is supposed to purchase copies of consumable works for each student. Textbooks, on the other hand, are not used up by a single student. In fact, a thriving secondhand market exists for used textbooks, and according to the section 109(a) first sale doctrine, one can resell a copy of a lawfully acquired textbook. This first sale doctrine also permits libraries to lend materials, including textbooks.

There are some practical reasons that a single copy of an assigned textbook on reserve is unlikely to be problematic. First, there is a legitimate reason to put a copy of an assigned textbook on reserve: a student may have failed to bring a copy to class and needs to read an assignment at school. Second, as opposed to a standardized test, an entire textbook is unlikely to be photocopied by a user. It is just too labor intensive, the final copy is messy, and most people would prefer to own the book.

Perhaps the faculty member should be reminded that library reserves are not intended to substitute for a student's purchase of a textbook. Students definitely should not be directed to photocopy or scan the textbook that is on reserve. The library could put one copy on reserve as a backup copy, however.

Q63 *A campus library does not permit textbooks to be placed on reserve. But what about supplemental reading material that is not the assigned text for the course? Much of the supplemental reading material appears to be textbooks, but not the ones assigned by faculty members. If it is required reading, does that mean it is a textbook?*

Actually, even assigned textbooks can be placed on reserve as long as they are used as a backup copy for a student who may have forgotten to bring the text to class that day and not in lieu of students actually purchasing the textbook for a course. Some libraries have policies against putting textbooks on reserve, however. Typically, when the term "textbook" is used, it means the assigned text for the course that all students are supposed to buy. But the definition of the term is broader than that. It really means a book that is produced with the intention that it be adopted for use in a course. Certainly, a non-assigned textbook may be placed on reserve for supplemental reading, even if it is assigned reading. Reproducing copies for reserve from a non-assigned textbook should also follow the ALA Reserve Guidelines from the *Model Policy Concerning College and University Photocopying for Classroom, Research and Library Reserve Use* (*see* http://www.unc.edu/~unclng/ALA-modelpolicy.htm).

• • •

Q64 *Instructors ask the library to copy chapters of supplemental books to put on reserve. How much of a book may be photocopied for reserve? It seems that some instructors ask for different chapters of the same book every week, so that by the end of the semester the library has copied 90% of the book.*

Certainly the library could put the original book on reserve without reproducing chapters, but the making of copies as described above has likely moved beyond what would be considered reasonable. Whether the library uses the ALA Reserve Guidelines from the *Model Policy Concerning College and University Photocopying for Classroom, Research and Library Reserve Use* (*see* http://www.unc.edu/~unclng/

ALA-modelpolicy.htm) or general fair use to make the decision, 90%
of the work is too much. Typically the library might reproduce a single chapter, or a few of them if the book has many chapters. In other
words, if the book has 45 chapters, reproducing 5 chapters for reserve
is a small number. On the other hand, if the book has only 7 chapters,
5 is too many.

If faculty members want to provide copies of 90% of a book to
students, they need to either assign it for purchase or put it in a
course pack, request permission, and have the students purchase
the course pack and pay royalties, which usually are rolled into the
price charged to the students. It could also be an electronic course
pack, but permission and royalties would still be required. The campus-wide Copyright Clearance Center license covers reproduction
both in print and electronic format for both library reserves and
course packs.

• • •

Q65 *Engineering and science faculty members create folders
of factual, unpublished materials that include their class notes and
sample problems, along with solutions for test preparation. These
folders are placed on reserve in the library with no expiration date.
Are there any restrictions on students copying the material?*

Section 102 of the Copyright Act excludes facts from copyright protection. So, the factual material contained in the folders is not copyrightable. On the other hand, the arrangement, organization, indexing,
and selection of facts may be copyrightable as a compilation. Math-
ematical problems typically are not copyrightable but are treated as
scientific truths; however, compilations of problems might be. Problems with a great deal of written description (story problems) might
be protected as text.

Assume that the material in the folder is copyrightable. If the material is created by the faculty members themselves, then they are
the authors of these works. If the faculty authors populate the folders with this material, the only restriction on student copying would

be restrictions that the authors themselves place on materials in the folders. There would be no limitation on how many terms the folders could remain on reserve other than ones the authors dictate. The faculty authors are already giving permission by creating the folders and asking that they be put on reserve.

· · ·

Q66 *May a library make multiple copies of clinical guidelines that are published in an association publication or a professional journal and put the copies on reserve?*

Clinical guidelines may or may not have copyright protection. It is possible that the organization that creates the guidelines does not pursue its copyright rights, but assume that they are copyrighted. The guidelines are then treated just as any other article from the journal or publication with regard to reserves. The ALA Reserve Guidelines from the *Model Policy Concerning College and University Photocopying for Classroom, Research and Library Reserve Use* (*see* http://www. unc.edu/~unclng/ALA-modelpolicy.htm) would permit reproduced copies being placed on reserve for the first term, but for subsequent semesters permission should be sought.

· · ·

Q67 *A faculty member attended a workshop about grant writing in a nearby city, and he wants to put on reserve the manual they used that day. It is a large manual that says nothing on it about being copyrighted. Is there any problem with putting the manual on reserve as first time use material?*

Regardless of whether or not the manual contains a notice of copyright, it is copyrighted. If the library is placing the faculty member's original copy on reserve and not photocopying or otherwise reproducing the manual, then there is no limitation on how long it may remain on reserve. If the faculty member is asking the library to photocopy a small portion of the manual and then place that photocopy on reserve, the one-semester limitation without permission applies. The library certainly should not reproduce the entire manual for reserve.

• • •

Q68 *A faculty member would like several popular videos placed on reserve. (1) May a library purchase the videos so that a faculty member can show them in class? (2) May the library lawfully put these titles on reserve so that students can check them out for viewing either in the library or at home?*

The answer to both questions is yes. Section 110(1) of the Copyright Act permits a nonprofit educational institution to perform videos in a face-to-face classroom if showing the video to the class is a part of instruction. The school could either purchase or rent the videos that are shown in the classroom. Note, however, that performance of entire videos in distance education classes is not permitted without a license to do so according to section 110(2). (*See* chapter 6, "Performance and Display: Nonprofit Educational Institutions.")

Only public performances are reserved for the copyright holder. Placing videos on reserve so that students may check them out for viewing them either at home or in individual viewing stations in the library is not a problem. These are private as opposed to public performances. If the library should conduct a public performance of videos, then permission must be requested and royalties paid.

• • •

Q69 *In an academic library's reserve system, there is an article that several different faculty members want on reserve for a variety of different courses. Does the library need to get separate copyright permissions to use the article for each course, or just one?*

Just one permission request is needed if the request for permission is broadly worded and is granted. But sometimes the publisher will ask how many classes or how many students will access the reserve copy and will charge accordingly. If the college has a campus-wide license from the Copyright Clearance Center, reserve copies are covered, both photocopies and digital copies for electronic reserves.

• • •

Q70 *A professor has asked the campus copy services to create a reader for him. Copy services is the unit at the college that gets copyright permissions for readers or course packs and then produces them. The professor is hoping to have 70% of a book reproduced to be included in his reader. If copyright permission is granted to reproduce this material for the reader, does this cover his putting this same material in the electronic reserves system, which is password protected for students in the class?*

Although there is not much functional difference in a reader and e-reserves, permission to reproduce materials for a print reader/course pack does not generally cover e-reserves. Separate permission would have to be obtained. The Copyright Clearance Center provides permissions both for photocopying for readers/course packs and for e-reserves, but the fees are separate. The CCC offers a campus-wide license that covers both, however.

• • •

Q71 *When seeking permission to use a copyrighted work for an electronic reserves system, is e-mail permission sufficient?*

Yes, an e-mail is considered a "writing." Copies of permissions received to reproduce material for reserves should be maintained either online or in a print file so that they can be retrieved. More difficult is telephone permission. Verbal permission is worth only the paper on which it is printed, that is, none. If permission is obtained over the telephone, one should follow up with a memo sent to the copyright owner summarizing the permission received, and maintain a copy of this in the permissions file. Copies of permissions received via fax also should be retained.

• • •

Q72 *A college library has offered electronic reserves for four years. Should it now revise its e-reserves policies based on the TEACH Act?*

An amendment to the Copyright Act of 1976, the TEACH Act revised section 110(2), which deals with distance education. The TEACH Act covers performances and displays in distance education, or that are transmitted in any form in which the course is offered, including online, and online components of face-to-face courses. Nonprofit educational institutions that wish to qualify for the exceptions offered under TEACH must meet a number of requirements. Traditional reserves do not deal with performance or display—instead, they deal with either putting original copies of books, videos, sound recordings, and journal articles on reserve or the reproduction of materials to support the classroom. These works are reproduced, and because of their nature are not performed or displayed. Works that are typically performed include audiovisual works, musical works, and sound recordings; works that are generally displayed include slides, photographs, charts, and so forth. Thus, for full copies of printed works, the TEACH Act simply does not apply. Therefore, revising the e-reserves policy is not needed for printed works.

For a reserve collection that consists of sound recordings that are streamed, the TEACH Act is applicable since these works are performed. The TEACH Act allows performance of entire nondramatic musical works, but it is unclear whether it covers sound recordings that embody the musical work. It is also possible to rely on fair use for providing access to this material, and relying on fair use may be a better choice. Moreover, many musical works are dramatic, such as opera and musical comedy, and therefore cannot be performed online in their entirety without a license. Images that may be displayed via e-reserves also may be covered by either the TEACH Act or fair use.

Video that is streamed for e-reserves also could fall under the TEACH Act because videos are works that are performed. The TEACH Act does not permit the performance of entire audiovisual works without a license but only a "reasonable and limited portion" of a work. Placing an entire, lawfully acquired DVD on reserve does not implicate TEACH. Copying the entire copyrighted video, however, would constitute an unlawful reproduction. Reproducing a reasonable and limited portion of a performance for e-reserves would be permitted by TEACH if all of the requirements are met. Thus, for streaming music and video and for displaying images, a library may wish to update its e-reserves policy.

• • •

Q73 *A new faculty member at a state college (A) wants to place several articles on reserve in the library for his class. He accessed these articles through full-text databases at the library of the major state university (B) where he is enrolled as a graduate student. The faculty member has asked if he can send a PDF from (B)'s databases to the library staff at (A) to be placed on electronic reserve. In the alternative, may he make paper copies that could then be scanned for e-reserve as long as he signs (A)'s agreement to seek copyright permission?*

This database of full-text articles is licensed to (B), and the use is probably restricted to (B)'s own faculty, staff, and students. Although (A)'s new faculty member is a also a student at (B), and therefore has access as a student for his own research and study, duplicating the articles in any format and putting them on either print or e-reserve at (A) is infringement because it is not a lawfully acquired copy for (A).

There is some possibility that (A), as an institution in the state system, is covered under the same license agreement, but it is not definitely so. This is a matter of contract law rather than of copyright. Whether the faculty member makes paper copies from the database or sends a PDF file to (A), the issue is the same. Copying to put articles on reserve in another institution likely violates (B)'s database license agreement and the library at (A) should refuse to accept the copies for reserve unless it has proof that the faculty member actually sought and received permission from the database owner to do so.

· · ·

Q74 *An instructor at the college makes extensive use of electronic reserves for her course. This term she accessed an online magazine (for which she has a personal subscription) and found the particular articles she wanted to put on e-reserves as readings. She saved them as PDF files and then asked the library to make them available on e-reserves. If the library does so, is there a copyright problem?*

Yes, there is a problem. If the library had a subscription to the print journal and then scanned the article, it would need to follow the usual ALA Reserve Guidelines from the *Model Policy Concerning College and University Photocopying for Classroom, Research and Library Reserve Use* (*see* http://www.unc.edu/~unclng/ALA-modelpolicy. htm). If the articles came from the faculty member's personal subscription to a printed journal, then scanning them for reserve for a one-semester use without permission would be allowed under the Guidelines. If the articles came from a subscription to an online journal that the library maintains, then the library's license agreement for the journal would control whether copying articles in PDF format and putting them on e-reserves is permissible.

Here, however, the subscription to the online journal is a personal subscription, and online journals are almost always licensed products. It is highly unlikely that the click-on license that the faculty member must have executed in order to get access to the magazine would permit such copying and wide availability from a personal subscription. The faculty member should be asked to print out the license from the online journal for the library in order to prove that copying and putting the articles on e-reserves from a personal subscription is permitted. If it is not, then the only alternative is for the faculty member or the library to seek permission from the publisher to include the PDF of the article in the e-reserves system.

• • •

Q75 *For electronic reserves, is it permissible for the library to link to an article in an online database?*

Usually yes, but not always. It is the license agreement for the on-line database that controls whether linking from an e-reserves system is covered under the terms of the license agreement. If it allows link-ing, then the link should lead to a dialog box where the user has to be authenticated to ensure that access is covered under the license. If the license does not permit such linking, the library may want to renego-tiate the license to ensure its ability to link to online sources to which it has access under the terms of the license for e-reserves.

• • •

Q76 *The library has a collection of unpublished letters from the nineteenth century that were written by community members in the town in which the library is located. For a local history course, may the library photocopy the letters and put them on reserve? What about scanning them for electronic reserves?*

In all likelihood the letters are in the public domain, but not defi-nitely so. For example, if the author of an 1885 letter lived until 1945, that unpublished letter is still under copyright. Unpublished works that existed as of January 1, 1978, that remained unpublished through the end of 2002 entered the public domain at that point, or life of the author plus 70 years. If the author has been dead for more than 70 years, the letter is in the public domain and the library can do what-ever it wants, including putting photocopies on reserve, or scanning and putting the letter in the e-reserve system.

In the example of an author who died in 1945, the letters would be under copyright until 2015. Duplicating the unpublished letters in any format could be done only if the library determines that such reproduction and distribution satisfies the four fair use factors (purpose and character of the use, nature of the copyrighted work, amount and substantiality used, and market effect).

• • •

Q77 *The library has been asked to scan a number of copyrighted images and to put the copies into the electronic reserve system. Is it infringement to duplicate photographs and images for reserve collections?*

If the images are copyrighted, then it is important to remember that reproducing a single image is the equivalent of copying an entire book. It may be fair use to reproduce a single image and put it into a reserve system, but reproducing many images from a single work may not be fair use. Limiting access to a single class for a limited time may also be fair use; further, the TEACH Act display portion would apply (i.e., the number of images that would typically be displayed in a face-to-face class). Most libraries that use a significant number of images acquire a license. Many images are not on the web, and it may be possible for the library to create a list of links to the images for the faculty member interested in copies of the images for reserve.

• • •

Q78 *What is the responsibility of a faculty member who learns that her students are reproducing full copies of materials placed on reserve for a course?*

Faculty members have a responsibility to not suggest or recommend that their students reproduce full copies of the material that faculty members request be put on reserve for their courses, but there is no policing function that faculty members must perform. Faculty may wish to talk to their classes about copyright and copying, however.

CHAPTER 4
Permissions and Licensing

Despite fair use and the Copyright Act section 108 exceptions, libraries and archives sometimes must ask permission to reproduce a work. Increasingly, libraries are dealing with permissions and are operating under license agreements that are required when a library acquires access to a particular work.

Locating copyright holders in order to seek permission to reproduce and/or distribute copyrighted works continues to be problematic for librarians, publishers, authors, and faculty members. Related questions in this chapter focus on requesting permission in good faith and pay royalties, including permission to reuse works prepared by student authors in their course work, and obtaining releases from speakers to record and distribute their presentations.

Libraries have been signing license agreements for many years in order to acquire access to certain works for their users. Section 108(f) (4) of the Copyright Act states that nothing affects license agreements that libraries sign to acquire a work in their collections. In other words, license agreements trump section 108's exceptions for libraries. Related questions focus on license terms, the difference between license fees and royalties, and a library's desire to use licensed content to answer e-mail reference questions and to provide interlibrary loan copies, especially when the library subscribes to both the print and the electronic versions of the journal. Librarians in all types of libraries ask about licenses from the Copyright Clearance Center, as well as performance licenses from the American Society of Composers, Authors and Publishers (ASCAP), Broadcast Music Inc. (BMI), and SESAC Inc. Other questions pertain to providing contract library services to other libraries under license agreements, covering satellite corporations and campuses under license agreements, conflicting license terms, and e-book licensing and lending.

• • •

Q79 *What constitutes a good faith effort in trying to contact copyright owners? Does it differ if the work is an orphan work?*

There may be a difference in what constitutes good faith when the owner of the copyright is known as opposed to when the owner is not. In the case of known owners, the problems usually arise when a library has contacted the owner to seek permission for a particular use but the owner fails to respond. The lack of a response may not be treated as an affirmative response, so the library must try various ways to contact the owner, such as e-mail, snail mail, fax, and/or telephone calls. The library should document all of the steps it has taken to contact the owner. It is possible, however, that the use the library seeks to make of the copyrighted work is so important that the library is willing to assume the risk after it has tried to contact the author by various methods and still received no response. In this instance, the library staff should recognize that there is still some risk, and that if it proceeds to use the work without permission, and the owner later sues for infringement, the repeated attempts made by the library to contact the copyright holder will not be a defense to infringement. Copyright infringement requires no element of intent; it is a strict liability cause of action. The documented efforts to obtain permission could help to mitigate the damages at trial, however.

In the case of an orphan work, the copyright owner is either unknown or cannot be located. The element of good faith here is not in repeatedly contacting an owner, but in trying to identify the owner so that owner may be contacted in order to seek permission. The 2006 U.S. Copyright Office Orphan Works study, available at http://www.copyright.gov/

orphan/orphan-report.pdf, recommended that once a library had used best efforts to identify and locate the copyright holder and failed, should the library proceed with the use of the work without permission, it would not be liable for damages if the owner later comes forward and sues for infringement. "Best efforts" likely would include a thorough search of the registration records at the Copyright Office, searching the web for information, and perhaps other steps to be specified by the Copyright Office. Unfortunately, this recommendation was not enacted.

• • •

Q80 *How does one prove that that he or she has permission to copy (generic for reproduce, perform, display, and so forth) a copyrighted work? Must one have a signed document to that effect?*

Any written document can serve to prove that permission to copy was received. A letter that is signed is great, but other writings can also establish proof. If one obtains permission over the telephone, sending a confirming follow-up memo to the copyright owner restating the permission that was granted over the telephone is useful. If permission to copy a work is received via e-mail, the e-mail should be printed and retained, or saved electronically.

• • •

Q81 *The library wants to send out some long overdue reminders to let borrowers know that the maximum fine is only $2 per item, and encourage them to return the books. In order to attract their attention and set the tone, the library wants to use Shel Silverstein's "Overdues" poem (with its cartoon illustration) from A Light in the Attic. Shel Silverstein is deceased, so the 1981 copyright must have transferred to someone else. Does the library write the publisher? Can it give permission? Or will the publisher just provide the name and address of the copyright holder?*

The estate of Silverstein will own the copyright if he still owned it at the time of his death; thus, the copyright may be owned by his spouse, children, other heirs, or someone else entirely to whom he bequeathed the copyright. It will last for 70 years after his death.

Or, prior to his death and even at the time of publication, Silverstein may have transferred the copyright to the publisher. In either event, it is much easier to contact the publisher for permission rather than trying to locate heirs. Publishers know if they hold the rights while heirs often do not know. And if the publisher does not own the copyright, it may be able to help locate the heirs.

• • •

Q82 *A liberal arts college is being asked to put digital copies of student theses on a server. If the theses contain copyrighted images, standardized tests, and the like, is permission needed? Or should access be by password only? Is there any disclaimer that the college should use if the theses are posted on the web?*

Whether the theses are available on the open web or on a password-protected site makes considerable difference in this situation. In the print world, for published theses and dissertations, clearly student authors were required by the publisher to get permission to include copyrighted photographs and other materials. When the thesis or dissertation was held only in the degree granting institution's library collection, seldom did the student seek permission for incorporating copyrighted material since the thesis was not going to be published. Posting on the web, however, is a type of publication with one major difference—the college is the publisher, and a copyright holder is more likely to blame the college than the individual student for any infringement. Making theses available on a password-protected website is more akin to having the typewritten copies available only in the library. However, students and others who have the password can access the images and can download them, so the college should make some effort to discourage downloading.

While a disclaimer on the web might make college officials feel better, it is unlikely to have any legal effect. On the other hand, a notice on a password-protected site that users may not download images from the theses would be useful to alert them that downloading

may be problematic and would show efforts to discourage infringement by users.

If the college decides that it does want to put theses on the web,
then student authors should be charged with the responsibility of seeking permission for their use of copyrighted images and other materials.

$$\bullet\ \bullet\ \bullet$$

Q83   *A librarian in a public high school is often asked for help
by students who are completing class research papers and projects.
When a student uses an image from the Internet in a research paper,
how can he seek permission if it cannot be determined who produced
the image? Would use of an image from the Internet most likely be
permitted under fair use if the use was only for a research paper for
one course? To cite to the origin of the image, is the URL sufficient?*

Actually, to include the image in a research paper that will be submitted only to the teacher likely is a fair use and the student would not
be required to seek permission. If the paper is to be posted on a website or widely distributed, permission is necessary. Attribution is not
a copyright issue, but crediting the photographer or copyright owner
is a good thing to do. Including the URL tells someone where to find
the photograph online, which is helpful to readers, but the attribution
should be to the photographer (author).

$$\bullet\ \bullet\ \bullet$$

Q84   *A community college regularly films the lectures of speakers invited to speak on campus. In order to place a video copy of the
lecture online, must the institution seek permission? Is a webinar
the same thing?*

In order to record the lecture of the guest speaker, the institution
should obtain prior written permission from the speaker. The release
should also specify what the institution intends to do with the recording, such as podcasting it, and how long it will remain posted. The
institution also needs to have the permission of the speakers and to

specify how the webinar will be used, whether it will be repeated, and so forth. Speakers' releases are both copyright and privacy issues, but typically speakers have waived privacy by agreeing to participate in the program. Releases protect the institution from liability.

• • •

Q85 *If an educational institution sponsors a conference with speakers, educational materials, and handouts, should the institution ask presenters and speakers to confirm that they are the sole authors of any conference materials or, if not, that they have obtained copyright permission from the owners to distribute their works at the conference? Should speakers be asked for permission to copy their presentations and materials onto a CD for distribution to conference participants or for posting on a website?*

It certainly is a good idea to ask speakers to sign a speakers' agreement certifying that the material included in handouts and slides is their own work, or if someone else's copyrighted works are used, that the speaker has permission to distribute those works at the conference. This is especially important if distribution will be beyond the attendees at the conference, such as publishing the proceedings or posting them online with the handout material included. Some institutions ask for a list of materials that speakers want to use and actually seek permission themselves rather than rely on the speaker to have obtained appropriate permissions.

Any planned distribution of speakers' original conference materials should be detailed in the speakers' agreement. Some speakers will give permission for distribution in handouts but not for any electronic distribution, whether on CD or on a website.

• • •

Q86 *A faculty member is writing a book about the history of a corporation that was founded in the 1930s. He retained the Writers Research Group to negotiate permission for the use of photographs, copies of newspaper articles, and excerpts from books, magazine ar-*

ticles, and monographs. In at least two instances, Writers Research Group identified and sent permission requests to the presumptive copyright owners for things that were published prior to 1941—a book that was published by a leading New York publishing company and photographs that were published in a magazine around the same time. The magazine still exists but has changed ownership twice during the interim. The Writers Research Group has received no response from either despite repeated follow-ups. What should the faculty member do?

Unfortunately, receiving no answer from the publisher happens all too commonly, and it creates negative feelings about copyright holders. The faculty author has some choices at this point: (1) He could find other excerpts, photographs, and so forth, for which he can clear copyright. (2) He could decide to go ahead and publish the materials without permission and assume the risk, which likely is pretty low due to the age of the book. In fact, assuming a 1941 publication date, the copyright existed until 1969 at which point it either entered the public domain or was renewed for an additional 28 years, now expanded to an additional 67 years. So, if the copyright was renewed, it will not expire until 2036. The magazine photos may be a bit more problematic, but in all likelihood, the copyright was not renewed on these items. The degree of risk one is willing to assume is dependent on how important that particular item is to include in the faculty author's book. The publisher of the faculty author's book may or may not agree to this assumption of the risk, of course.

• • •

Q87 *A librarian recently sent someone an e-mail message; the recipient responded asking permission to quote a sentence out of the message in an article he might write. The librarian was surprised by this request, but the requester said he is obligated to ask permission for such things. Is this correct? If so, the librarian's copyrights have been abused left, right, and center over the last few years!*

Assuming that the length of the e-mail message was more than a couple of sentences or so, and that there was enough originality in the message to meet the very low originality/creativity standard, the e-mail message is protected by copyright just as other literary works are protected. When one wants to use all or a portion of an e-mail message in a publication, one would use the usual fair use factors to determine whether the use is a fair use. A good rule of thumb for both publications and web pages is to think of these as scholarly works, and whether messages from such a work can be quoted, and how much can be quoted with attribution but without permission from the author. Most publishers do not require permission for short quotes, maybe even for quotes of a paragraph or two. But beyond that, publishers generally require their authors to get permission.

Although this question dealt specifically with private e-mail messages, a similar application exists for listservs. The copyright law does not say so, but many people seem to believe that there is an implied license to use listserv submissions without seeking permission from the author of the message. No court has so held, so it is safer to follow the rule of thumb about quotes.

• • •

Q88 *A librarian with curatorial responsibilities for a university library music collection is making an educational/promotional film about one of the collection's donors, a classical musician of note. The film is part of the fundraising efforts to support the collection. As a member of a performance group, the donor made many classical music recordings on the Philips label, and the librarian wants to obtain permission from Philips Records to use part of one track from one of these recordings in the film.*

Assuming that the music on the recording is under copyright, the right the librarian is seeking is called the synchronization or "sync" right, which involves the use of a recording of a musical work in audiovisual form, such as in a film. It is called the synchronization right because the music is "synchronized" or recorded in timed relation with the visual images. Sync rights are licensed by the music publisher (the publisher of the sheet music) and not the recording company, and typically the Harry Fox agency is the source for acquiring sync rights.

The reason that the sync rights belong to the owner of the copyright in the musical composition is that the sync right is a part of the right of public performance right, and sound recordings do not have public performance rights.

• • •

Q89 *Is it necessary for scholars who are writing historical works about a particular region of the country to obtain permission to quote three stanzas from relevant old songs?*

This question is somewhat complicated and the answer is based the age of the song. First, consult my chart, "When U.S. Works Pass into the Public Domain" (*see* Appendix; also available at http://www. unc.edu/~unclng/public-d.htm). Assuming that the work is still protected by copyright, one would do a fair use analysis. Three stanzas sound like a fairly significant portion of a copyrighted song, and seeking permission likely is required. Contact the music publisher and not the recording company. Sometimes recording companies will direct users to the proper publisher or other owner of the copyright in the musical composition, which most often includes the lyrics. If the songs are in the public domain, however, no permission is needed.

• • •

Q90 *Are there any guides, fact sheets, or other resources to help librarians determine whether to sign an Annual Copyright License from the Copyright Clearance Center? Since the corporate library subscribes to so few journals compared with the overall number of print journals, the cost of the license seems out of line. Are there any rules of thumb that dictate what a library should reasonably be charged?*

Many corporate libraries have decided that the ability to make digital copies rather than photocopies is extremely important to them and have taken an Annual Copyright License. The CCC has a number of explanatory materials on its website at http://www.copyright.com.

Another good source is other librarians in similar companies. Whether they can reveal pricing information depends on the company's negotiations with the CCC. A CCC representative can also discuss costs in similar companies without revealing what any one particular company pays.

The Annual Copyright License uses an algorithm to determine the annual fee for an organization. The license covers internal photocopying, digital copying, posting of covered works on corporate intranets, copies required for regulatory filings, and many other uses. These are all detailed on the CCC website.

• • •

Q91   *What are the pros and cons of a blanket license from the Copyright Clearance Center for a noneducational but nonprofit organization?*

The main benefit of a CCC blanket license is that all in-house copying from library materials covered under the license is protected. It eliminates the necessity of keeping records for pay-per-use copying on which royalties are due. The organization no longer has to seek permission from individual copyright holders to distribute articles to employees. Moreover, now electronic publications are also covered by the CCC Annual Copyright License. Under the license, organizations can post digital content on their intranets; republish content in newsletters, books, and journals; and e-mail copies of online articles and PDFs. Required federal agency filings are also covered.

• • •

Q92   *A library recently signed an Annual Copyright License with the Copyright Clearance Center. In so doing, the library would be permitted to make unlimited photocopies of materials of publishers that are registered with the CCC. Are there are other organizations similar to the CCC that operate in the United States? What is its international counterpart? Is having a "middleman" operation like this an effective way of protecting copyright interests?*

The CCC is the only royalty collection agency representing publishers for the reproduction of works in the United States. There is also the Authors Registry (http://www.authorsregistry.org/) for individual authors who own the copyright in their works. So, someone reproducing a work can pay royalties directly to the author through the Registry. Additionally, there are performance rights organizations in the United States—the American Society of Composers, Authors and Publishers (http://www.ascap.com); Broadcast Music Inc. (http://www.bmi.com), and SESAC Inc. (http://www.sesac.com)—that collect royalties for public performances of music. There are foreign equivalents of both the reproduction rights organizations and the music royalty agencies, and they typically have agreements with the U.S. organizations, so they collect the royalties for foreign materials and then account to the foreign agency for the funds.

• • •

Q93 *Why do so many journal publishers include in their license agreements restriction on divulging the terms of the license, including price of the subscription?*

Nondisclosure clauses in licensing agreements are fairly standard legal practice for all types of licenses. For library subscriptions, the matter has been in the press recently, and a number of large academic libraries are refusing to sign such agreements as they come up for renewal. Cornell University is one such institution, and a document detailing the reasons for its stance can be found at http://www.library.cornell.edu/aboutus/nondisclosure. Many suspect that the reason publishers require nondisclosure clauses in their licenses is that they make various price deals with different libraries, even libraries of the same type. In addition to price, there could be other terms that differ for various sizes of institutions, geographical locations, subject emphasis, and so forth.

The problem, of course, is that if a publisher has a nondisclosure clause, one simply cannot know whether there are differences from institution to institution or consortium to consortium. Further, libraries want to be treated fairly in comparison to other libraries. Thus, librarians have increasingly refused to sign license renewals that have nondisclosure clauses.

• • •

Q94 *Sometimes a publisher's terms and conditions posted online contain contradictory terms even regarding use of the company's digital materials for interlibrary loan. May a library simply follow the copyright law and the ALA Interlibrary Loan Guidelines and still be legal?*

In negotiating such a license, the library is responsible for getting terms clarified if staff believes them to be contradictory. If an authorized representative of a library signs a publisher's license agreement, then according to section 108(f)(4) of the Copyright Act, the library is bound by the terms of the license. According to the library section of the Copyright Act, the license agreement takes precedence over the copyright law and guidelines for libraries.

The question about online licenses is a bit more complicated; assume that a publisher has a click-through license and some of the terms are contradictory. Under section 108(f)(4), a library is still bound by the terms of that license, even though it was not able to negotiate the terms. Contradictory terms typically are enforced by courts in favor of the party that did not draft the contract since the drafter of the license (the publisher) had every opportunity to correct terms.

If a library goes forward and relies on the law and Interlibrary Loan Guidelines in lieu of the license agreement, a court may find that this is not infringement due to the conflicting terms. On the other hand, it may support the publisher's view.

• • •

Q95 *May a university library provide temporary access to the university's online databases to individuals who are not enrolled students?*

Only if the library's licenses to those databases permit such access. The question does not indicate who these individuals might be. Are they faculty and staff of the university, or are they totally unaffiliated with the institution? Most licenses provide access to faculty and staff of that university, along with enrolled students. The issue is more complicated if the individuals seeking access are unaffiliated users. Many libraries attempt to include in all of their licenses access for "walk ins." However, if the license says that access is available only to the university's faculty, staff, and enrolled students, then walk-in access is not allowed. Section 108(f)(4) indicates that license agreements trump copyright for libraries.

• • •

Q96 *A small college library serves as the library support for some contract schools that are both online and for-profit. The commercial institutions pay an annual fee for services to the library. What does the library need to know in terms of copyright as well as using the database to provide materials to students from these schools?*

In the days before licensing was prevalent, contracting with a library to provide services was pretty straightforward. The library would provide reference services, permit students from other fee-paid schools to come and use the collections, and provide other in-person services. It would borrow materials through interlibrary loan for students at these schools and generally serve as the college library for them. Licensing of access to materials has changed this dynamic somewhat.

Typically, a license provides access to databases and other electronic materials only to students, faculty, and staff of the institution signing the license. Under such a license, providing access to non-enrolled students would violate the terms of the license agreement. It may be possible to negotiate some of the database licenses in order to provide access to students who are enrolled at these other institutions. However, absent such provisions in the license agreement, access to non-enrolled students violates the terms of the contract.

• • •

Q97 *If the library gets full-text articles through Ovid or Dialog on the web, are copyright royalties included in the price? Or, must* *articles be tracked like interlibrary loan copies and the library pay royalties through the Copyright Clearance Center or directly to the publisher when the suggestion of five is reached?*

When a library subscribes to an online service, the license fee is in lieu of royalties. Whether the library may provide copies of articles obtained through Ovid or Dialog to outside users depends on the terms of the license agreement executed by the library. Many licenses restrict use to students, faculty, and staff of the institution. Should providing articles to outside users not be permitted, and if delivery of those articles is important to the library, it should contact the copyright holder to see if the contract can be renegotiated to include the desired activity, or if it can pay royalties for providing copies to outsiders.

• • •

Q98 *May public libraries use tutorials created under a Creative Commons license on their library websites without worry about infringement? What would happen if the owner decided to sue for infringement?*

Creative Commons (CC) offers a variety of voluntary licenses that a copyright owner may adopt that work along with copyright. So, the answer to the question depends on the type of CC license and the rights that it grants to users. For example, if the CC license for the tutorial is an attribution license, then the library may post the tutorial on its website, but it must give credit to the author of the tutorial. The CC licenses are detailed on its website at http://creativecommons.org/licenses/.

Should a copyright author wish to sue someone who violates the terms of a CC license, the suit would be filed in state rather than federal court since it is a contract matter rather than a copyright matter. The author still has a U.S. copyright and could offer the work under different license terms, but the person who began to use the work under the CC license is protected.

Q99   *What are the copyright rules for downloadable books?*

It is more likely that the downloading of e-books is governed by a license agreement (contract) rather than just by copyright law. Copyright certainly applies, but a license agreement most likely covers such e-book issues as access, reproduction, distribution, display, and so forth.

• • •

Q100   *Many libraries are lending e-books on a Kindle. Is this infringement to lend a Kindle loaded with copyrighted books acquired from Amazon?*

The Amazon license has changed and now public libraries are permitted to lend Kindle devices and books. There is even an Amazon FAQ (frequently asked questions) section that answers questions about borrowing Kindle eBooks from public libraries (*see* http://www. amazon.com/gp/help/customer/display.html/ref=hp_200527380_ library?&nodeId=200747550). The FAQ includes instructions on how to download eBooks to one's own Kindle from the public library. Amazon is to be commended for responding to library demand for this option.

• • •

Q101   *A college dance teacher has a personal use license for music recordings from iTunes. She has loaded songs on her laptop for her personal use but also wants to play the songs in her dance classes. Is this permitted?*

The question is answered by the Apple iTunes license agreement. Typically, a "personal use license" does not allow use even within nonprofit educational institutions because that is not a personal use. Apple does offer educational licenses, however, as well as licenses for a number of other organizations (*see* http://developer.apple.com/ softwarelicensing/agreements/itunes.html). Thus, the individual teacher, as well as the school, could be liable for using the recordings from her personal use license for a dance class. She should encourage the institution to provide licensed music for her dance classes.

• • •

Q102   *In order to save space, each year a corporate library that has a CCC Annual Copyright License has its journals microfilmed by a library microfilming house, which either uses the hard copy the library provides or provides film from the microfilming company's own collection. It does not seem to be a problem when the microfilm is received and the hard copies are destroyed. The library considers the microfilm version to be a different format of information that has already been purchased, and the microfilm is used in place of hard copy by document delivery staff and scientists.*

Actually, it is a problem. The library is reproducing the journals cover-to- cover which is not permitted under the Copyright Act. Such reproduction requires permission of the copyright holder. The publisher may not want its journal reproduced on microfilm. Or, if the publisher offers its own microfilm edition of the journal, it is unlikely that it will grant permission for a particular library to make its own microfilm version, but the library certainly may ask. It is possible that the "library microfilming house" has a license for such reproduction and is paying royalties, but the corporate library should inquire before such an undertaking. The Annual Copyright License from the Copyright Clearance Center typically does not include cover-to-cover microfilming.

• • •

Q103   *For an e-mail reference question, may a reference librarian copy and paste something from an online database into the response to the user?*

The answer to this question is found in the license agreement that the library signed with the database vendor. If the reference question comes from an affiliated user who is covered under the license agreement, then providing that patron with material from that database is permitted by cutting and pasting the material into the e-mail answer to the reference question. If the inquiry comes from an outside patron who is not covered under the library's license agreement with the database vendor, then cutting and pasting would violate the terms of the license. The license agreement could contain a provision that permits use of material from the database for responding to reference questions. Thus, under this condition, it would not be a violation of the license agreement to include material in any response to an e-mail reference question. The answer to all of these questions is found in the license agreement itself, however.

• • •

Q104 *An academic medical library is often asked to provide access to full-text journals to other libraries located in federal buildings on its campus. The full-text journals are free to the library with print subscriptions. Is it a copyright violation to provide such access?*

This is not a copyright violation, but whether there is some type of liability for the library depends on the license. License agreements are contracts governed by state contract law instead of federal copyright. If a license for the online journals says that access is restricted to the school's students, faculty, and staff, then it violates the contract to allow the federal employees to access the electronic version of the materials. If not, then it is permissible, but each license agreement should be consulted for that title or group of titles. Providing these users with copies made from the print journals would be permitted under sections 108 (d) and (e) of the Copyright Act if the requirements of those sections are met.

• • •

Q105 *A library has subscriptions to periodicals databases (e.g., Wilson and ProQuest), and all of the university's satellite locations also have access to them. The university is now opening a new satel-*

lite location in a foreign country. Will the university be in compliance with the database licensing agreement if students in the new satellite location overseas are given access to the databases?

The answer depends on the license agreement itself. Does the library have separate license agreements for each satellite location, or is there one license that covers the university's main campus and all satellite campuses? The language of the contract controls. The contract could state that access is limited to students of the university and be silent about the location of those students. This would mean that any enrolled student, regardless of the branch or satellite the student attends, is covered under the agreement. Or the license might state that it covers only the main campus or the main campus and its satellites in a particular state or country. As a rule of thumb, if the license agreement does not contain any geographical restriction, one should assume that it is worldwide in geography but limited to enrolled students, faculty, and staff of the university.

•••

Q106 *A U.S. academic institution sponsors a study abroad program taught by its faculty and staff. The students are U.S. students who are studying in foreign countries, and some courses are offered online from the home institution. Students access databases from the home institution. Does operating in a foreign country make any difference? What if there are a few foreign nationals enrolled in the U.S. study abroad program?*

The good news is that U.S. law applies to students enrolled in the U.S. institution's study abroad program. Typically, enrolled students who access licensed databases from the U.S. institution are covered under the license agreement for that college or university. This is true whether the students are U.S. nationals or not. In future license negotiations, however, it would be a good idea to clarify that study abroad students enrolled in the U.S. institution's foreign study programs are included in the license.

Q107 *A hospital parent company has acquired electronic access to full-text medical journals from Ovid, MD Consult, and others for employees and physicians on the medical staff of the hospitals. The library has purchased print copies of many of the same journals from the publishers. If often receives a request from a physician for copies of articles, sometimes two to three per issue, from these journal titles. (1) Does the license agreement for electronic access to the journal trump the statute that restricts the library to providing only one article per journal issue to that physician? (2) If the physician (or a member of the physician's staff) infringes copyright, who is liable?*

(1) Yes. An employee covered by the license agreement who prints the articles from the electronic version is bound by the terms of the license agreement, and most such licenses do not contain a restriction about the number of articles per issue. The Copyright Act section 108(d) exception has the "one article per issue to a user" restriction on a library for reproduction and distribution because it covers instances when there is neither permission nor a license from the publisher.

(2) The hospital is liable because of agency law since the physician is an employee. However, if the license does not restrict the number of articles per issue that can be printed, then there is no problem. A publisher could sue an individual physician, but is unlikely to do so. In most instances, publishers opt instead to sue the larger institution. If it does, then the licensee institution is liable and not the individual physician. The institution could then take disciplinary action against the individual infringer, of course.

• • •

Q108 *The principal in a small private school wants to photocopy a musical play that is permanently out of print. The school would also like to perform the play. Would the school have to pay royalties, too?*

Just because the play is out of print does not mean it is out of copyright. The school needs to contact the copyright holder for permission to reproduce copies of the play if the work is still under copyright. Additionally, if the school wants to perform the play, it also must have the public performance rights.

• • •

Q109 *A university professor has purchased five CDs from the iTunes store, and the originals are hosted on her personal computer. Two of these purchased from iTunes are available commercially as CDs, but the other three are apparently not. The professor has burned CD copies of all five, and wants to place them on reserve for her class. If the burned CDs do not meet fair use guidelines, is there an alternative way to provide access to the students and meet copyright fair use guidelines?*

This is not a fair use matter but instead is a licensing issue. The faculty member's purchase through iTunes was accompanied with a personal license agreement. That license does not permit putting on reserve copies of works burned from her personal computer downloaded under a personal license from iTunes. The only way for the library to place the CDs on reserve without infringing is for the school to purchase the CDs from iTunes, or another source, and put the originals on reserve. For the three CDs that are not available for purchase, the faculty member should contact iTunes to seek permission to make the copy for the library.

• • •

Q110 *A University professor wants to use his own personal Netflix streaming account to show an entire documentary in a face-to-face class. Can he do this, or show part of the documentary in class? The Netflix website (http://www.netflix.com) contains the following language:*

> *Unless otherwise specified, our DVD rental service and the content on the Netflix website, including content viewed through our instant watching functionality, are for your personal and non-commercial use only and we grant you a limited license to access the Netflix website for that purpose. You*

may not download (other than through page caching neces-
sary for personal use, or as otherwise expressly permitted
by these Terms of Use), modify, copy, distribute, transmit,
display, perform, reproduce, duplicate, publish, license, cre-
ate derivative works from, or offer for sale any information
contained on, or obtained from, the Netflix website, includ-
ing but not limited to information contained within a mem-
ber or members' Queue, without our express written consent.

According to this agreement, the answer is no. This is the license agreement for personal use with Netflix. Even if the school owned a copy of the documentary, it would need permission from the copyright owner to stream the entire film to a class.

Under section 110(2) of the Copyright Act (the TEACH Act), non-profit educational institutions may stream reasonable and limited portions of films without permission, but only by following the stringent provisions of the TEACH Act. For example, only students enrolled in a particular course may view the transmission of the film, the school must take reasonable efforts to prevent downloading, and so forth. To transmit (stream) the entire documentary, the institution must have permission and pay permission fees if requested. This applies whether it is truly for distance learning or is just a transmitted portion of a face-to-face course. If the professor wants to use the documentary from Netflix in his courses, either he or the school should contact Netflix and seek permission.

CHAPTER 5

Performance and Display: Libraries and Other Organizations

Two of the exclusive rights of the copyright holder are public performance and public display. To "perform" is defined in section 101 of the Copyright Act and means "to recite, render, play, dance or act it, either directly or by the means of any device or process, or in the case of a motion picture or other audiovisual work, to show its images in any sequence to make the sounds accompanying it audible." The same section defines display as "to show a copy of it, either directly or by means of a film, slide, television image, or any other device or process, or in the case of a motion picture or other audiovisual work, to show individual images nonsequentially." A public performance or display is any performance or display outside the normal circle of family and friends, any performance in a public place, or a performance or display that is transmitted. Private performances do not require permission of the copyright owner but public ones do. Transmitted performances or displays are still public, even though they are experienced at different times by people who are geographically dispersed.

There are statutory exceptions for some types of public performances that would otherwise require permission. There is an exception for nonprofit performances outside of the nonprofit educational setting. Section 110(4) of the Copyright Act provides that public performances of nondramatic literary and musical works (other than by transmission to the public) are excused if the following conditions are met. First, either there is no admission charge, or if there is one, proceeds go to charitable, religious, or educational purposes. Second, there is no payment of fees to promoters, organizers, or performers. Another exception, section 110(5), permits small establishments (including libraries) to play radio and television broadcasts on the equivalent of a "home receiving set." There must be no charge to see or hear the performance, however.

This chapter covers performances in public libraries, corporations, and nonprofit organizations. Nonprofit educational performances and displays are covered in chapter 6. Section 109(c) permits the display of lawfully made copies of works (projecting no more than one image at a time), but no transmission beyond the place where the copy is located. Libraries lend and play videos, music recordings, and mixed media works. Some lend playback equipment also. Questions in this chapter address displays of record album covers, book dust jackets, cartoons, and other images. Performance-related questions cover story hours for children where books are read aloud, playing background music to enliven the physical environment, and for-profit dance schools performing copyrighted music.

• • •

Q111 *May a library book club show a commercial motion picture to its members and still comply with copyright?*

Certainly it is possible for a library book club to view a movie together, but the viewing is a public performance. Therefore, the library must seek permission and pay performance royalties, if required. If the library acquired the public performance rights when it purchased the copy of the movie, however, then no further permission is required. But simply purchasing the movie on DVD does not typically provide the public performance rights.

• • •

Q112 *A consortium of health facilities pools its money to purchase videos selected by members of the consortium. Each member contrib-*

utes a fee depending on bed size. The videos are actually purchased by the library and added to its collection. These videos are then loaned to the members for viewing at their facility at no charge. Is there a copyright problem with this consortial activity?

There are several issues here. First, when the library purchases the videos are they licensed to one institution only? If so, then the videos can be used only within that one facility. If not, then lending the videos to other facilities is no problem. Of course, the videos cannot be duplicated, but the question does not appear to involve reproduction.

There are also performance rights issues involved, however. If the videos are used only for individual patient viewing in patients' rooms, there is no problem. If, however, the videos are shown to groups or in public areas, it is a public performance, and the library must obtain the public performance rights for the consortium.

• • •

Q113 *May a library show a DVD series in its lobby on a plasma television set in order to promote interest in the series? The library has purchased a copy of the DVD series for the collection.*

One of the rights of copyright owners is the right of public performance. Showing a video series in a public place is a public performance, and the lobby of a library clearly is a public space. The library should acquire a license if it wants to perform the video series in the lobby. It is possible that showing very small clips of the DVD series would qualify as a fair use, but it is not certain that this would be the case.

• • •

Q114 *What is a public library's affirmative obligation when a patron charges out a movie on DVD and tells the circulation librarian of his intention to use it for a public performance?*

Actually, the library has no obligation. Librarians do not inquire about what a user is going to do with books they check out, nor should they about videos. Section 108 of the Copyright Act applies to reproduction and distribution of copyrighted works, and there is an obligation found in subsections (d) and (e) for the library not to reproduce articles, chapters, and so forth for a patron if the library has notice that the patron is planning to use it for other than fair use purposes. On the other hand, librarians are not required to ask about the use the patron plans to make of the reproduced material.

Checking out a motion picture on VHS or DVD is permitted under the first sale doctrine found in section 109(a) of the Copyright Act. There is no affirmative duty not to check out the work to the user even if there is notice that he plans to use it for commercial purposes. Many libraries label their videos to indicate whether the library has the public performance rights for the video, however. If the patron publicly performs the motion picture he is liable, but not the library.

• • •

Q115 *DVDs in a library collection are not purchased with public performance rights. Does it infringe copyright if patrons view a DVD in the library after they check it out? Does it make a difference whether they use their own laptop or the library's computers to view the DVD?*

If the patron is using an individual viewing station in the library or viewing the DVD at home, it is not a public performance at all and therefore not a problem. Who owns the equipment is irrelevant. If the library's DVD viewing equipment is "an individual viewing station" then it is also not a public performance. However, if the patron is in a public area, and the volume is turned up so that anyone may hear, and anyone can join the patron in viewing the DVD, it likely is a public performance regardless of whether the performance is on an individual's laptop or on library equipment.

• • •

Q116 *Recently a hospital library received a gift of CD players and CDs for patient use. The library wants to lend CDs and CD players* *to patients in their rooms so that they may enjoy listening to them. This is a not-for-profit hospital and the library offers the service free of charge. Even though almost all of the rooms in the hospital are private rooms, the administration is concerned that this activity will not comply with copyright law. Is there any way to design this service to ensure that it is copyright compliant?*

Assuming that the donor purchased the CDs and that they are not downloaded via the Internet without permission of the copyright holder, there is no problem at all with lending these copyrighted works to patients, along with the necessary equipment. The first sale doctrine permits libraries to lend copies of legitimately acquired materials from their collections. The service as described does not entail reproducing the CDs but merely lending the original CDs the library received as gifts, and it creates no copyright problems. Placing the CDs in an individual patient room is a private performance.

• • •

Q117 *An art museum is trying to put together an online gallery consisting of images of the paintings in its collection. Is artwork automatically copyrighted because it is considered to be unpublished? Does the chart "When U.S. Works Pass into the Public Domain" (http://www.unc.edu/~unclng/public-d.htm) apply to artwork? The collection mainly consists of pre-1950 artwork.*

Works created before 1978 are covered by the 1909 Copyright Act, and federal copyright applied only to published works. When the work in question is a painting, what does "publication" mean? Publication certainly has a more consistent meaning for books, journals, and the like. The central question is whether display in a gallery or museum constituted publication. Unfortunately, the 1976 Copyright Act was not consistently applied in cases from various federal circuits. The majority view was that public display was equivalent to publication, however. Prior to 1978, the majority of courts held that sale of the original work transferred the copyright in that work unless the parties otherwise agreed. So, the museum may actually own the copyright in many of the works in its collection. Moreover, when no claim of copyright was made on the original painting, and there was no effort made by the artist, museum, or gallery to prevent copying, courts in some circuits have held that the work has become public domain.

Generally the "When U.S. Works Pass into the Public Domain" chart does apply to paintings, but it is not 100 percent accurate for pre-1978 paintings, depending on the federal circuit and whether the museum actually acquired the copyright when the original work was purchased either by the museum or by a donor who then gave the painting to the museum.

Since January 1, 1978, publication of a painting has not been an issue because copyright attaches automatically, and the copyright belongs to the artist. Sale of the painting does not transfer the copyright to the buyer. Instead, transfer of the copyright requires a written agreement to transfer it. The artist may want to hold onto the copyright or may be willing to sell the copyright along with the painting.

• • •

Q118 *If a library wants to play a live television broadcast within a nonprofit library, is there a copyright problem?*

Not if the library simply uses the equivalent of a "home receiving set." In other words, if it uses a regular television set and there is no charge for seeing the performance, then there is no problem with playing the television set. Section 110(5) of the Copyright Act provides this exception. It does not apply to the recording of the broadcast, or to any further transmission of it—simply the performance of a broadcast television program that can be viewed by patrons who come into the library.

• • •

Q119 *May a children's library show videos in is leisure section to pacify children while the parent looks for a book? What if the library instead permits an individual child to come in and select a video, and* *then the librarian inserts and runs it just for that one child at an individual viewing station?*

While it would very useful to find a way to occupy children to permit their parents to search for books in peace, the first situation described is a public performance of that video. The library can legitimately show videos for groups of children or in a public space only if it has the public performance right, which often requires paying a fee for the performance.

If the library has individual viewing stations, a child could watch a video at such a station without it becoming a public performance. An individual viewing station envisions a single user and earphones, and it is a private performance for which no permission is needed. If the video viewing equipment is in a public area where other children may join in, then the performance is still a public one, even if only one child is present. The Copyright Act defines a public performance as one outside the normal circle of family and friends, or one that occurs in a public place, such as a public library.

· · ·

Q120 *Is a home school class in a public library the same as a traditional classroom for fair use purposes?*

Typically a nonprofit educational institution is a school that is organized as a school under the tax codes of the country. In the copyright sense, the problem with home schooling is that the exceptions that apply to nonprofit educational institutions apply to schools themselves. Home schooling is not a school in the traditional sense. The exceptions recognize the public good of nonprofit educational institutions, and there is no institution in a home schooling situation.

On the other hand, a public library is also a nonprofit institution, and a good argument can be made that it has become an educational institution for home schooled students. If public libraries so claim, then only their activities for home schooled students count, and they will have to satisfy the same restrictions as do nonprofit educational institutions when taking advantage of the exceptions. For example, section 110(1) of the Copyright Act permits these institutions to display or perform copyrighted works, such as motion pictures, in a classroom to students and teachers as a part of instruction. But the exception requires that no one else may be present for the performance. Most public libraries would be conflicted about excluding other members of the public from such performances, but in order to qualify for the nonprofit educational institution exception for home schooled students, the library would have to do so. And a librarian or "teacher" would have to be present for viewing the video.

• • •

Q121   *Is it infringement for a children's librarian to read a book to children during story hour at a public or school library?*

No, it does not infringe copyright. While common sense does not always provide the answer to a copyright query, in this instance common sense and the law actually converge. Reading aloud to children is a time honored tradition that increases young people's interest in books and reading. Section 110(4) of the Copyright Act permits nonprofit performances of nondramatic literary works (such as books) and nondramatic musical works when there is no payment of fees to performers, promoters, or organizers and if either there is no direct or indirect admission charge, or if there is one, proceeds go to charitable, religious, or educational purposes. Story hours typically meet these criteria.

• • •

Q122   *The library in a nonprofit garden and sculpture park has a children's garden. During certain exhibits the library arranges story times for children that relate to the exhibits. Story times may take place in the library or elsewhere in the gardens. The books used are either owned by the library or borrowed from nearby public libraries, and the stories are read by volunteers on the weekends of the exhibitions. Sometimes the stories are "retold" rather than directly read. There is an admission fee to enter the* *gardens but no fee just for the story time. Do story times create a copyright problem?*

Good news! Assuming that the storytellers are not paid and there is no admission charge to see or hear the performance (which is what a reading or story telling is under copyright), then the reading of that nondramatic literary work is exempted under section 110(4) of the Copyright Act as a nonprofit performance. But if performers or promoters are paid, the exemption is lost. An admission charge to the garden is no problem, but if there is an admission charge to participate in story time, the proceeds would have to go to charitable, religious, or educational purposes in order to take advantage of the exemption.

• • •

Q123   *A medium-sized public library wants to record the story times for children and then replay them on the local community access channel. Will the library need to get permission for each book? Are there problems with filming the children who are listening to the story time reading?*

If a librarian were simply reading a book aloud to children present in the public library, there would be no problem because of section 110(4) of the Copyright Act, which exempts some public performances, such as reading the book aloud, under certain conditions (*see* responses to Q121 and Q122). The problem raised by this question is the recording of the reading and then the replaying of it on television. There is no exception in the copyright law either for the recording or for replaying on television, even on community access channels.

On the other hand, would the copyright owner object? It is hard to predict. The safest course would be to seek permission from the publisher and to ask to record the reading and play the video on the community access channel. In fact, the library could ask the publisher for permission for several titles at once and see what the response might be.

Filming children participating in story time creates serious legal (but no copyright) issues. For example, the filming will require parental permission for each child who appears in the film. The public library should consult with the city or county attorney about all legal issues and what releases may be needed to permit the filming.

$$\cdots$$

Q124   *A librarian runs a community library in the virtual Meta-verse of Second Life, located on a charity simulation, the West of Ireland, and the charity it supports is Project Children, a 501(c)(3) organization. A free client program called the Second Life Viewer enables its users, called "residents," to interact with each other through avatars. Residents can explore, meet other residents, socialize, participate in individual and group activities, and en-gage in activities from the purely social to diverse role play, ad-vocacy, continuing education, as well as in the creation of music, art, and literature. Volunteer storytellers read stories in West of Ireland and sometimes at other locations. They receive no cur-rency or gain, and no admission is charged to the simulation in which stories are read. Readings are done live in voice rather than streamed. Must the librarian obtain permission for these readings?*

To some extent, these storytellers do what is being done in every library, school, and daycare center on a daily basis. It is important that the readings are performed live to a small group of people (usu-ally about 20) and are not recorded or streamed for later playback. Section 110(4) of the Copyright Act, the so called nonprofit perfor-mance section, permits public performances of nondramatic literary and musical works without permission of the copyright holder if those performances are not transmitted and if certain conditions are met. For example, there may be no payment to performers or promoters, and there may be no admission charge, or if there is one, the proceeds must go to charitable, educational, or religious purposes.

The real question is whether Second Life counts as a transmission. Arguments exist that support both views. Typically, anything done over a computer network is transmitted. But one could argue that a live reading in Second Life is more like a live performance than it is a transmission. The law likely supports the fact that it is a transmission, however. If so, then permission would be required for the reading of the stories.

The librarian could approach a few publishers and make the argument that the readings are equivalent to a live performance. If the librarian can get them to agree, then this agreement could be used as evidence to convince other publishers to agree.

• • •

Q125 *May a touchscreen smart board be used for story time in a public library?*

As phrased, this is a technology question and not a copyright one. Use of the technology itself presents no problems on the copyright front. If one reproduces works to be displayed on the smart board, however, then the same issues are present as with photocopying or with displaying images. If the question contemplates displaying all of the words of the story on the screen to help with reading, including all of the text plus the illustrations, this is reproducing an entire work and probably is infringement. On the other hand, if permission is sought from the publisher, it is likely that permission would be granted.

• • •

Q126 *A church's Sunday school teachers and youth director routinely rent videos for various programs, including childcare. What liability might a church or other nonprofit entity need to consider with regard to showing home videos? Is it similar to the liabilities for public schools, private schools, and daycare situations?*

The exemption to the public performance right for the showing of videos is limited to face-to-face teaching in nonprofit educational institutions. Churches are not schools (even though it is called "Sunday school"). For-profit schools and daycare facilities are also not eligible for the exemptions. This is a public performance under the Copyright

Act and permission should be sought. It might well be granted with no royalties required.

• • •

Q127 *Playing music recordings at dance schools is a very common practice. Should the school pay royalties for this? What about dance classes at a college? How does copyright apply to dance clubs with a disc jockey?*

Sound recordings do not have public performance rights except for digital transmission of the recordings, but the musical compositions embodied on the recording do have performance rights. Educational institutions have an exception for the performance of musical works in the course of instruction under section 110(1) of the Copyright Act, so dance classes at a college are permitted to use recorded music as a part of instruction. Private dance schools that use music are not eligible for the exception, however, and must pay royalties to the American Society of Composers, Authors and Publishers (ASCAP), Broadcast Music Inc. (BMI) and SESAC Inc. for musical compositions registered with them. These royalties go to the composer. Dance clubs (nightclubs) also pay similar royalties for music performances.

• • •

Q128 *What happens concerning performance licenses when a private nonprofit dance school holds its performances on a university or high school stage? Does it make a difference if the music for the performance is a sound recording rather than live music?*

If the dance school has its own public performance license, then there is no problem. If the dance school does not have a license, it is likely that the performance license that the university or high school has covers all performances in its facilities, and the dance school performance thus is a licensed performance. While sound recordings have no public performance rights, the musical composition embodied in the recording does. So, a performance license provides coverage for the composer even for use of a sound recording.

• • •

Q129 *A nonprofit organization purchased the performance rights for a play. During the performance, the play was video recorded. Who owns the copyright in the recording—the playwright, the director, or the actors?*

Whoever directed the recording to be made owns the copyright, and that might be the director or the videographer as director. The real issue though is whether a license to perform the play also grants the right to reproduce the performance. If the organization knows that it wants to video record performances, then it should request permission to do so at the time it negotiates a public performance license. It might be a fair use to make a single copy of the video that is used to critique the performance, but multiple copies should not be made and distributed without permission, regardless of whether that distribution is free or is done as a fundraiser for the organization.

• • •

Q130 *The public library staff puts on an annual show for the community that consists of music with lyrics written by staff members. Is it infringement to include popular songs to which the staff writes its own lyrics?*

Lyrics are protected along with the musical composition, and changing lyrics is an adaptation of the original work. Under section 110(4) of the Copyright Act, nonprofit performances for which no performers or promoters are paid and for which the admission charge goes to charitable, religious, or educational purposes are exempted. But this is really performance of the music as it was written. On the other hand, many singing groups do exactly what the public library staff does—rewrite lyrics—and copyright holders do not seem to complain.

Q131 *Is it permissible to play ambient music in the background at a library?*

Typically, the public performance of music is licensed. In fact, entities subscribe to digital music services so that they can play background music (including when someone is put "on hold" on the telephone). Although there are no public performance rights for sound recordings except for digital transmission, the composer of the music (or the assignee) does have performance rights. Another way to provide background music is under section 110(5) of the Copyright Act, which permits even commercial establishments to play radio and television when there is no charge to hear or see the performance, and the radio or television set is the equivalent of a home receiving set.

• • •

Q132 *The Mississippi Department of Archives and History produced a series of sound recordings in the 1970s that feature live performances of blues musicians, some of whom are now famous. Are there any restrictions on how these recordings may be used? May the recordings be streamed in the media room?*

It sounds as if the Department actually owns the copyright in these sound recordings. It is possible, however, that other ownership arrangements were made at the time, but it is unlikely. Thus, the Department may do with the sound recordings whatever it wants, including streaming in the media room.

• • •

Q133 *A community group shows a feature film to an audience in the public library free of charge in order to raise awareness about an important social issue. Is this infringement?*

Yes. Even a very good cause does not convert a public performance to one that does not require a license. Motion pictures are not included under section 110(4), the nonprofit performance exception of the Copyright Act, and either the library or the community group should acquire the public performance rights. Many videos can be purchased with a public performance license, and sometimes there is no charge for that license.

• • •

Q134   *In a nonprofit library, if library staff members are making a presentation to the staff and spontaneously come across a cartoon or other graphic that fits, may the graphic be used just for the presentation without seeking permission as long as the source is attributed? What about if the staff makes a routine monthly presentation and wants to use that same graphic repeatedly?*

There certainly is a strong argument that displaying a work once for in-house use is fair use. A display is different than copying the work and distributing it to everyone who attends the presentation. When one looks at the fair use factors, a one-time display to an in-house audience has little market effect, as contrasted with multiple copying, which may have considerable market effect. Repeated use of the cartoon or image changes the dynamic, however. Now it is not a one-time use but rather is used with different audiences over time. If that display is to be repeated, permission should be sought.

• • •

Q135   *Children's librarians want to scan photographs and illustrations from books that the library owns in order to create PowerPoint slides. The slides are then used by teachers and librarians, typically along with the book. Is this permissible? Is there a limit on the number of slides that may be scanned? Is there a limit on the number of years that the slides may be used without permissions?*

If this were a nonprofit educational institution, most likely it would be a fair use for an individual teacher to use such PowerPoint slides repeatedly in teaching, but this is a public library. One would apply the four fair use factors (purpose and character of the use, nature of the copyrighted work, amount and substantiality used, and market effect) to determine whether the reproduction of the illustrations onto slides and their subsequent use is fair use. Certainly, the slides should not be posted on the web or otherwise distributed. The library could seek permission to reproduce and use the illustrations as described.

• • •

Q136 *Is it infringement to scan scientific slides or images to use in a presentation at a professional meeting?*

While there is certainly an educational aspect to using scientific images for a presentation at a professional meeting, the images may be copyrighted. The content of the image is important. Does the image contain only facts presented in a straightforward manner? Is there creativity in the way the information is displayed on the image, such that it may qualify for copyright protection? If it is purely factual, then there is no copyright and it may be freely scanned and displayed. If it is a copyrighted image, then it may be fair use to display the image at the professional meeting. If the slides are later put on a website for participants, it would be a good idea to either remove that image from the slide or seek permission for reproducing the image on the website. If the image is to be used in a classroom setting in a nonprofit educational institution, see the questions and answers in chapter 6.

• • •

Q137 *A library is planning a party around the Oscars. How far can it go in using the Oscar theme and the image of Oscar?*

The question does not specify whether the party is for the public or is for a small group of staff, family, and friends. If the latter, then it is a private party and there is little restriction on what can be displayed or used. If the party is for the public, however, the library staff should contact the Academy of Television Arts and Sciences to request permission to use the image on invitations, displays, and so forth.

• • •

Q138 *A museum is mounting an exhibition of LP record album cover art. These album covers are part of a few personal collections that are being loaned to the museum for the exhibition. The album covers will be exhibited strictly as examples of art produced for this medium. Does the museum need permission from the recording company in order to display the album covers? May the museum reproduce the covers on promotional materials, or must it create its own designs for use in promotional materials?*

In recent years there has been considerable interest in the cover art on record albums—CDs just do not inspire the same art, probably due to the smaller size. This exhibit should attract a great deal of interest. As with other works of art, the artwork on album covers is copyrighted, if the requirements for copyright protection were met at the time. Assuming that the cover art is copyrighted, whether the recording company owns the copyright in the artwork, or the artist who created it owns the copyright, is an important issue, but it need not be answered for the first part of this question.

The owner of a copy of the record album has the right to display that copy publicly under the portion of the first sale doctrine that is embodied in section 109(c) of the Copyright Act. The owner of that copy has chosen to lend it to the museum for display, so the first sale doctrine that permitted the owner to display the work is transferred to the museum to display the loaned copy publicly.

Reproduction of the artwork on the cover presents another issue entirely. Using the art for promotional materials requires permission from the copyright holder, likely either the recording company or the artist, but either could have transferred the copyright to someone else. The first step would be to contact the recording company for permission to reproduce the album cover art. The company will know if it owns the rights, or it should be able to help the museum identify the copyright owner.

This question is similar to the following one concerning the use of dust jackets.

• • •

Q139   *A library recently had a visit from a contemporary children's author and wants to create a web page with information about her and her works as represented in one of the library's collections. The dust jacket images from her book are eye-catching and would greatly enhance the web page. Is it permissible to use these images, or must the library seek permission?*

The artwork on the dust jacket is copyrighted and may not be reproduced without permission. The publisher should be contacted for permission; if the publishing company does not own the copyright on the dust jacket art, it will know who does. Often, there is no charge for such use as the library contemplates because it promotes the author and her work and can stimulate book sales.

CHAPTER **6**

Performance and Display:
Nonprofit Educational Institutions

S ome of the best exceptions in the Copyright Act are for performances and displays in nonprofit educational institutions. For face-to-face teaching in a nonprofit educational institution—in a classroom, with simultaneous presence of students and teachers in the same physical space—any copyrighted work may be performed or displayed as long as the purpose is for instruction. This section 110(1) exception is referred to as the "classroom exemption."[1] Under this exception, students and teachers may act out a copyrighted play, sing a copyrighted song, listen to copyrighted sound recordings, or view a motion picture in its entirety if the conditions previously mentioned are met. Inviting or allowing members of the public to see or hear the performance causes loss of the exception. While the word "classroom" is broadly defined, "nonprofit educational institution" is not. Whether public or private, the school must be organized under the tax code as a nonprofit educational institution. Corporations that have a nonprofit educational division do not qualify, nor do proprietary or for-profit schools.

Nonprofit educational transmissions of copyrighted works encompass both distance education and online portions of face-to-face courses. Section 110(2) is a 2002 amendment that covers performances

---

1   The language of the statute is "exemption," although it is more in the nature of an exception.

and displays that are transmitted by nonprofit educational institutions as a part of instruction. Referred to as the TEACH Act, it allows entire nondramatic literary and musical works to be performed without a license, but only "reasonable and limited" portions of other works, such as motion pictures and other audiovisual works, operas, and plays, may be performed. For display, the same number of pages, graphs, images, and so forth that would have been displayed in the face-to-face classroom are permitted. In order to qualify for the section 110(2) exception, a number of conditions must be met: (1) the nonprofit educational institution must be accredited, (2) the performance or display must be made by or at the direction of the instructor as an integral part of a class session, (3) the performance or display must be technologically restricted to students enrolled in the course, and (4) the institution must institute copyright policies and educate the campus community about copyright.

Questions in this chapter cover reproducing sheet music for performance, the use of specialized equipment to create copies of performances for the visually impaired, the use of images on PowerPoint slides for the classroom, and recording student performances of musical and dramatic works. Of importance to both faculty and librarians is the use of course management software for performance and display and the adoption of streaming and other technologies, which are also discussed.

• • •

Q140 *Art students in a nonprofit educational institution create collages using graphics, photographs, found objects, and the like. Is it fair use to display these collages in the school?*

Even better, it is not only likely to be fair use, but such displays also fall under section 110(1) of the Copyright Act when the work is to be presented in a class. Referred to as the "classroom exemption," it permits students and teachers to display or perform any copyrighted work in the classroom when it is part of instruction. While the statute is limited to the classroom, it is difficult to envision a copyright holder complaining about the display of a collage done by an art student in other areas in the school. These displays likely would be found to be fair use. If, however, the student then does something else with the project, such as to display it in a traditional gallery, permission may be needed.

• • •

Q141   *A library wants to digitize analog slide collections, such as art history, architecture, and history of graphic design, that are not otherwise available digitally so that they can be displayed to classes and made available to students for study. What are the copyright implications?*

Digitizing slides is basically reproduction and may be infringement. To some extent, it may depend on the quality of the digitized slide. For example, if the digital version is a thumbnail of low resolution, it may be less of a problem than if the digitized version is high resolution. Low resolution might be used in an index or a catalog so that the user then retrieves the original slide. The problem with high-resolution slides and wide availability is that they can then be used for further reproduction. If the slides are commercially produced, and there is no digital version available for purchase, the library may want to seek permission for the digitization.

If a library digitizes the slides that a faculty member needs to use in a class for a semester, and the digitized slides are used simply to display for a class, this may be fair use and/or it may qualify under section 110(1) of the Copyright Act, ignoring the fact that the copy was made in the first place. Clearly, a good argument can be made that this is the modern way to display slides in a classroom.

When the instructor then wants the digitized slides placed on a website for the duration of a semester, section 110(2) permits this if there is no digital version available for purchase. All of the requirements of 110(2) must be met, however, such as password protecting the site so that the slides are not generally available on the web but only to students enrolled in the class. Further, the slides should cease being available on the website or in course management software at the end of the class term.

Q142 *An elementary school music teacher acquired the rights to perform* Fiddler on the Roof *publicly. She adapted the work by simplifying it so that young children could easily perform it. Is this mutilation of the work?*

It certainly would constitute an unauthorized adaptation of the work absent permission to do so. It is possible, however, that in obtaining the rights to perform the musical she also acquired the rights to adapt the work by simplifying it for young performers. She did not publish the changes she made but simply used them. In order to answer the question fully, the terms of the license she obtained would have to be examined.

• • •

Q143 *An elementary school is performing* How the Grinch Stole Christmas *as a play tied to a family literacy night with music and other activities at the school. Parents are invited, but there is no charge for the performance. Is there a copyright problem?*

Under section 110(4) of the Copyright Act, a performance of a nondramatic literary or musical work by a nonprofit organization is exempted when (1) there is no payment of fees to promoters, organizers, or performers and (2) either there is no admission charge, or if there is one, proceeds go to charitable, religious, or educational purposes. The book is a nondramatic literary work. Under these conditions, there is no problem.

Somewhat more information is needed concerning whether "performing the work as a play" also means creating a derivative work, or whether the literary work is simply read with the characters speaking their lines. If it is a derivative work, permission would be needed. The performance should be from the book and not from the motion picture, as movies are not covered by the section 110(4) exception.

• • •

Q144 *The school purchases all of the music performed by each section of the band and provides copies of all music to each band* *member (i.e., everyone gets a copy of the sheet music for first trumpet, oboe, and so forth). Because students lose and/or mutilate their music, the band director began to file the original purchased music and then make copies for each student. This way, if the tuba player loses his music, the entire band does not suffer. Is this infringement?*

The Guidelines for Educational Uses of Music are voluntary guidelines that were negotiated in 1976. They are published in the House Report that accompanied the Copyright Act (House Report 94-1476). According to the Guidelines, emergency copying for performance is permitted as long as the school purchases the copies of the music afterward. Copying as preservation is not actually mentioned in the Guidelines. Under section 108 of the Copyright Act, a library is not permitted to do preservation copying in advance of either actual loss or deterioration. So, by analogy, this may be problematic.

On the other hand, however, it is very common practice for performers to photocopy their sheet music for ease of performance, and few would think this is infringement since they have purchased the sheet music and are just putting it in a format to facilitate performance. While there is no direct statutory authority to permit the copying described, it is unlikely that a court would find it other than a fair use. Some of the fair use factors lead to this opinion—the character of the use (nonprofit educational use and nonprofit performances) and the market effect. One could argue that there is no market effect since the music was purchased.

• • •

Q145 *At a public school, the concern is about making multiple copies of school music performances, such as students singing, graduation ceremonies, and orchestra performances. And the teachers want copies of the Christmas music program for each student to keep. Is this permissible? What section of the TEACH Act governs this?*

It is not the TEACH Act, but section 110(4) of the Copyright Act, that permits the performance itself (so long as there is no admission charge and no payment of fees to performers or promoters). If there is an admission charge, then proceeds should go to educational, religious, or charitable purposes. The Guidelines for Educational Use of Music governs copying the music performance. These are negotiated guidelines that were published in House Report 94-1476, which accompanied the Copyright Act of 1976. They are available at http://www.unc.edu/~unclng/music-guidelines.htm. The Music Guidelines state at A.4., "A single copy of a student's performance may be made for evaluation and rehearsal purposes. This copy may be retained by the educational institution or the individual teacher." Thus, the Music Guidelines do not permit multiple copying of the performance or copies to be provided to students.

• • •

Q146   *Many radio stations use sound bites of recorded music of less than 30 seconds. What is the station's obligation to the copyright owner? Does this apply to education?*

Radio stations, both commercial and noncommercial, pay blanket annual license fees to the American Society of Composers, Authors and Publishers (ASCAP), Broadcast Music Inc. (BMI), and SESAC Inc. to cover the public performance of music. These royalties go to the composer. In recent years webcasting royalties were added to radio broadcasts that are transmitted over the web; these royalties are paid to the recording companies and performers through another royalty collecting organization, Sound Exchange. So, sound clips played on the radio are covered under these licenses, as is the playing of entire songs.

Whether this applies to education depends on what is meant by this part of the question. If "education" means college and high school radio stations, the answer is yes. They also have an annual blanket license, but the royalty is considerably less than for commercial radio stations. If the question is focused on general educational uses of music, the answer is no. There may be exceptions in the Copyright Act that cover those specific nonprofit educational uses, but there is no blanket license for education.

Q147 *A school district is considering the purchase of a system to deliver videos to the classroom that would involve transferring all of its videotapes to a digital file that could then be accessed through a server by multiple users. Is this a problem?*

Yes, this is a fairly significant problem. It is unlikely that a school could get approval from a single film copyright owner to digitize its films. There is no right to reproduce films except under very narrow circumstances, such as under section 108(c) of the Copyright Act, when the library copy is missing or damaged and the staff first tries to purchase an unused copy at a fair price, or to replace a video that requires equipment that is now obsolete, such as laser disc or Betamax. VHS is not yet an obsolete format since unused playback equipment is still available on the market. The district could try approaching one film company and requesting permission as a test. Otherwise, it will have to purchase digital copies (DVDs).

• • •

Q148 *Two faculty members at the university teach film courses. They run evening showings of the films, followed by discussions, which are widely advertised to the public. Although this provides an opportunity for students in their classes to see the films, many people from the general public also attend. No public performance rights are obtained because the faculty members claim that the performances are a fair use. They use copies of the DVDs from the library's collection for the performances, and many are recently released films. Should the university be concerned about liability for copyright infringement?*

Absolutely! Faculty certainly may show films in class because of section 110(1) of the Copyright Act. To qualify for this exception to the copyright holder's exclusive right of public performance, certain requirements must be met. For example, the performance must be in a classroom (broadly defined), teachers and students must be simultaneously present in the same place, and the purpose must be instruction as opposed to entertainment.

If members of the public are allowed to view the performance, then the performance loses the exemption, which the House Report that accompanied the Copyright Act (House Report 94-1476) states is for students enrolled in the class. Thus, to have the films open to the public, or even to other students on campus who are not enrolled in the class, converts the performance from an exempted classroom performance to a public one, for which the institution must have a performance license.

• • •

Q149   *A professor teaches a film course and the students are required to make class presentations about the films they watch for class. The library owns copies of the films used in the course. These student presentations are considered part of the teaching activities of the class. When the students make their presentations, they must show brief clips or excerpts to explain the scenes to which they are referring. Is it permissible for students to copy these clips onto a DVD in order to avoid having to cue up and fast forward through the originals?*

Under section 110(1) of the Copyright Act, students and teachers are permitted to perform a film or video in the course of instruction. Section 110(1) does not cover reproduction. However, putting the clips on a DVD in order to show them to the class is more than likely a fair use. The institution should actually own copies of the films in question, though.

Another problem that faculty members and students encounter in this area is circumventing technological controls on DVDs in order to use film clips for teaching purposes. Under section 1201(a) of the Copyright Act, the Librarian of Congress has the authority to conduct a rulemaking proceeding every three years to determine whether any classes of work should be exempted from the anti-circumvention provisions. In 2010 the Librarian of Congress determined that decrypting DVDs in order to incorporate film clips into new works for the purpose of criticism or comment for "educational uses by college and university professors and by college and university film and media studies students" was permitted. However, the person making the clips must believe that circumvention is necessary in order to criticize or comment on the work.

• • •

Q150 *If it is part of the course content, may a video be streamed online for a specific group of students in a specific class, for a specific duration, through the course learning management system? The Information Technology department of the community college has been telling faculty members that they can stream no more than 10 percent of a video.*

The simple answer to the first question is yes, but the "specifics" make a significant difference. Section 110(2) of the Copyright Act, the TEACH Act, details all of the specifics about performing and displaying copyrighted works in a transmitted portion of a course. Streaming is the preferred technology for showing video in a transmitted course or portion of a course since it does not permit students to download the copyrighted work. However, there is a limit as to how much of a copyrighted work may be performed without permission of the copyright owner. If the work is a nondramatic literary or musical work, the entire work may be performed. But if the work is an audiovisual work, such as a video, then only a limited and reasonable portion of the work may be streamed (performed) without a license.

It appears that the IT department at the community college has interpreted a reasonable and limited portion to be 10 percent or less of a video. While this might be a reasonable and limited portion, it may also be far too restrictive. A reasonable and limited portion could be 20 or 25 percent, but it is certainly less than the entire work. The 1999 *Report on Copyright and Distance Digital Education* (a report of the Register of Copyrights, available at http://www.copyright.gov/reports/de_rprt.pdf) said that one judges what constitutes a reasonable and limited portion by looking not only at the copyrighted work itself, but also at the level of the course, the teacher's purpose in using the clip, and so forth. There is no absolute percentage in the statute.

As a matter of policy, however, an institution is free to define what constitutes a reasonable and limited portion as any specific percentage, but that percentage may be more or less than the statute actually allows in a given situation. A better alternative would be to determine on a case-by-case basis what constitutes a reasonable and limited portion of a particular film for a class session.

• • •

Q151 *A faculty member who teaches a number of music courses in which the students are required to listen to a wide range of music selections has asked about making CDs of the selections for the students to use. He has created a CD for his classroom presentations, which contains selections from a large number of sources. Last year he wanted to copy that CD for each student in his class and have the bookstore sell copies to the students at cost. The library convinced him that this was problematic, but he still wants to make three to four copies of the presentation CD and put them on reserve in the library. Is there a problem if the library permits him to do this?*

Under the Guidelines for Educational Uses of Music, it is permissible to make a musical anthology CD for aural exercises, and the faculty member's in-class use appears to be such. The Guidelines permit only one copy to be made, however, but one could argue that three to four copies is fair use. One copy per student without permission would not comply with the Guidelines, and it is unlikely to be fair use.

• • •

Q152 *A university professor teaches an online course and wants to provide a link to a song that she personally purchased from iTunes. Access would be restricted to students enrolled in the course, and the intent is for them to listen to the song, not download it. Will this require permission from the copyright owner to provide the link?*

The professor purchased a copy for her own use under a personal use license. She will need permission to make it available more widely.

The link was just for one person—now she wants to make it available for an entire class. Thus, an institutional license is needed. The good news is that many colleges and universities already have such licenses through iTunesU, so the professor should determine whether her school has a license for musical works.

• • •

Q153 *A librarian has questions about the meaning of specific language in the TEACH Act. What do the following mean? (1) "The following are not an infringement of copyright except with respect to a work produced or marketed for performance or display as a part of mediated instructional activities transmitted via digital networks." (2) "Does not engage in conduct that could reasonably be expected to interfere with technological measures used by copyright owners to prevent such retention or unauthorized further dissemination."*

(1) The first quote refers to modules developed for digital distance education that were created specifically for such online courses. It is a very small category of materials to date but may increase in size and importance over time. The sole market for these works is online distance education. So, no performance or display of these modules is allowed without a license.

(2) The second quotation means that even to use DVDs online, the institution is not permitted to decrypt them or to circumvent any technological protections that the copyright owner places on the work.

• • •

Q154 *If a library is connected by CAT5 to classrooms in other buildings on campus and sends audiovisual content purchased by the library to the classrooms, is that a violation of law? This is the same content that the library currently offers to faculty members for check out to show to classes as a part of instruction, using audiovisual equipment in the classroom.*

This is one place where the technology quickly got ahead of the copyright law. In 1976 when the Copyright Act was passed, it was thought that if a nonprofit educational institution transmitted a film within the same building, it still qualified for the section 110(1) exception that permits showing films face-to-face in the course of instruction. Then schools quickly moved to systems for transmitting films from a central location to other buildings within the school. In the early 1980s, this was thought to be infringement. But so many schools have adopted this technology today that it has almost become a standard.

There seems to be little complaint from the Motion Picture Association of America about use of this technology, as opposed to placing films on a website or transmitting them without a license in an online course. Perhaps this is because there is no way to download or upload the film when sending the content to another building, unlike with some of the other technologies.

· · ·

Q155 *How does an educational institution get permission to use film snippets on a class Blackboard site? Is there a difference if the institution wants to use the same snippets for executive education rather than in a regular university course?*

Assuming that the institution is a nonprofit educational institution, the good news is that using snippets of films in course management software for a class does not require permission. Under the TEACH Act, section 110(2) of the Copyright Act, transmitted performances of "reasonable and limited portions" of an audiovisual work are permitted for the online portion of classes. There are a number of requirements that have to be met additionally, such as making the performance available only to students enrolled in the course, having the performance available only during the class session, and so forth. If the instructor wants to use more than a reasonable and limited portion of a film, however, a license is required.

The question about executive education is less clear since "executive education" could mean a number of types of instruction. Assuming that it is either for continuing education or some professional certificate that is offered by a nonprofit educational institution, and students are actually enrolled in the executive education course, then the answer is the same. If, however, anyone may attend the session without enrollment, then use of the snippets likely would require permission.

• • •

Q156   *High school students put on a show each year for the public that is a parody or satire. Is there any problem with this or is it excused as a fair use?*

Traditionally, parody is excused as a fair use because it is a type of criticism or comment about a copyrighted work, while satire is not and typically is not found to be fair use. But not all parody qualifies as fair use. A parody is defined as a work that makes fun of a particular copyrighted work by highlighting its pretensions, poor quality, or lowbrow popularity. Even if the parody does this, the amount of the copyrighted work that may be used for the parody is somewhat limited. Case law dictates that a parody is not a remake of an entire work (such as a musical comedy version of *Gone with the Wind*). Instead, a noninfringing parody uses only a fair use portion of the copyrighted work and not more than is necessary to accomplish the parodic purpose.

By contrast, a satire does not poke fun at a particular copyrighted work. Instead, it may use copyrighted works to criticize society, current events, politicians, political issues, and the like. Thus, using copyrighted melodies with new words to make fun of political figures or events is classified as satire and is not excused as a fair use. So permission is required to use a work for satire. Courts have held that copyright holders are more likely to grant permission to use their works for satire than for parody since satire is not making fun of the copyrighted work itself.

• • •

Q157   *Some faculty members have developed a multimedia PowerPoint presentation as a workshop for high school students who have been suspended from school for aggressive behavior. It was*

very well received by students and by colleagues when it was pre-
sented at a conference, and a number of requests were received to
purchase the presentation for use elsewhere. It uses a Star Wars
theme, and the photographs, music, and sound effects were found
on the web at http://www.starwars.com. Is there any problem with
selling the presentation?

Certainly either the faculty or the institution may sell the presentation (depending on the agreement between the school and the faculty members). However, if one looks at the starwars.com website
and reads the terms of use, commercial use of the images and sound
is prohibited. So, while use for the workshop presentation may have
been fair use, selling the presentation makes it commercial. If there
is broad distribution, even if the sales price is only cost recovery, the
best course is to contact Lucasfilm and seek permission.

• • •

Q158 *A special education teacher at a school asks whether she*
can audiotape a book being studied in class for a child with learning
disabilities. The library wants to purchase the tape, but a thorough
search failed to reveal any source from which it is available. Since
it is unavailable for purchase, may the library and school make its
own audiotape for this child?

Under section 108 (the library section) of the Copyright Act, the
answer is no, but under the Americans with Disabilities Act, the answer is yes. The Copyright Act contains a section that deals with reproduction for the blind and other people with disabilities, section 121.
It states that it is not infringement for an authorized entity (such as
a nonprofit organization or government agency, the primary mission
of which is to provide specialized services relating to training, education, adaptive reading, and information access to a person with disabilities) to reproduce a work. There are some other requirements,
too. The reproduction must (1) be in a specialized format for the use
of someone with disabilities, (2) bear a notice that further reproduction or distribution in a format other than a specialized format is an

infringement, and (3) contain a notice of copyright. So, if a school offers special education classes, it is an entity that serves disabled individuals, and the teacher may audiotape the book for use with learning-disabled students.

• • •

Q159 *A professor requires his students to purchase a certain textbook for a class. Because students are required to have the book, is it fair use for the professor to use figures or charts from that text in course materials to supplement teaching? For example, students are required to read a chapter, and the instructor uses a chart or table from the chapter in some PowerPoint slides for further class discussion or explanation purposes. If this slide material were made available electronically in a password-protected electronic reserves system, would it be fair use since the students have purchased the text, or is permission still needed?*

The display of the materials to the class is permitted, even if the class has not purchased the textbook. Section 110(1) of the Copyright Act allows teachers to display works to students in face-to-face teaching, regardless of whether that material is from the assigned textbook.

It likely that it would also be fair use to put the same charts and graphs on a password-protected electronic reserves system for the students in that class. The fact that the students have purchased the text is important. That means no permission is needed, even after the first semester or term it is used.

• • •

Q160 *A teacher wants to use an audio recording from 1899 of an evangelist reading a portion of the Bible. Has the copyright expired? The U.S. Copyright Office says it does not deal with anything prior to 1972. A Copyright Office staff member wrote the following: "There is no federal copyright protection for a U.S. sound recording fixed prior to 1972. It is possible that material recorded (such as music and spoken words) may be protected. However, if the material*

in question consists of Bible verses, then no federal copyright pro-
tection exists." This work was put on a record in the 1950s by Word
Records with Paul Harvey, but the company does not know anything
about recordings that far back. The original recording was appar-
ently made in the state of Illinois, but the state government says that
state laws do not apply.

Sometimes it is simply worth assuming the risk when one wants
to use a work such as this 1899 recording. The great likelihood is that
if there ever was a copyright, it has expired. As the Copyright Office
indicated, sound recordings were not protected in this country before
1972. Therefore, even the 1950 placement of the recorded reading on
a record was not eligible for copyright protection. The State of Illinois
has already indicated that state law does not apply to the 1950 recording. Thus, there is no copyright protection for the sound recording.

If the words were simply being read from the Bible, then there is
no copyright in the text. Fixing the reading of the text in the sound recording in 1950 does not change the fact that the underlying work is
from the Bible, which is in the public domain, although various translations may still be protected.

• • •

Q161 *Is a college dormitory common area considered to be a*
"public place," which therefore would need public performance li-
censes to perform videos?

Yes, the lounge, living room, and other common spaces in a dormitory are considered public areas since members of the public may
be invited into those dormitory areas to watch videos. Thus, public
performance rights are needed. It is possible that that the college already has a license that covers music and video performances and displays in residence halls. To the contrary, individual dormitory rooms
are not public areas and instead are considered more like a private
home, so no public performance rights are needed for private performances in a dorm room.

CHAPTER 7

Audiovisual Works, Sound Recordings, and Software

Audiovisual works are defined in section 101 of the Copyright Act as "works that consist of a series of related images which are intrinsically intended to be shown by the use of machines or devices such as projectors, viewers, or electronic equipment, together with accompanying sounds, if any, regardless of the nature of the material objects, such as films or tapes, in which the work is embodied."[1] Sound recordings consist of recorded sounds of music, spoken words, and the like, regardless of whether they are stored on phonorecords, CDs, or tapes.

Libraries have long collected audiovisual works and made them available to users, much as they have done with other copyrighted works. While audiovisual works were often kept in separate parts of the collection merely due to their format, they were cataloged and listed in the library's catalog. Audiovisual works have many of the attributes of other works; for example, they can be lent to patrons to take home, checked out to a teacher for use in the classroom, or be used within the library itself. These works also have some unique differences. Audiovisual works require specialized equipment to enable the work to be viewed or heard, such as film projectors, phonographs, and slide projectors (although today the computer has replaced much of this

---

1 Other nonprint works, such as photographs, are also important components of library collections. They are addressed in chapter 8.

specialized equipment). Further, audiovisual works, by their very nature, are meant to be performed or displayed.

Many of the copyright issues that libraries face when dealing with audiovisual works are the same as those with printed works. For example, library users may ask the library to make a copy of a work for them. And, like books, these works suffer deterioration and loss. In fact, these works likely are more fragile than most books, and therefore librarians often want to convert the format—for example, from VHS to DVD—to preserve them.

But again, there are unique differences. Unlike with text, library patrons seldom request a copy of a portion of an audiovisual work but instead request a copy of the entire work. And perhaps the most important difference is that performance and display are crucial copyright issues for audiovisual works, and they are two of the exclusive rights of the copyright owner. Chapters 5 and 6 cover performance and display. Moreover, section 108(i) excludes audiovisual works and sound recordings from the exceptions for libraries and archives, which means that reproduction and distribution of these works by libraries is not permissible outside of fair use, except for preservation of unpublished works under section 108(b) and replacement under section 108(c).

Libraries also acquire software for their collections, often as "stand-alone" software, but software also accompanies some books that libraries acquire. Section 117 of the Copyright Act provides the only statutory support for making backup copies of works, but that is limited to computer programs.

As libraries increasingly acquire audiovisual works and computer software to serve the needs of their users, copyright questions abound. Questions in this section address using film clips, music, software, sound recordings, and other audiovisual works in libraries, in corporate settings, and in educational institutions.

• • •

Q162   *May a library make backup copies of audiovisual works and CD-ROMs in order to preserve them? They are quickly out of print, and replacing them often is impossible.*

While the practice of making backup copies makes absolute sense to a librarian, the Copyright Act does not permit it except in very narrow circumstances. For CD-ROMs one must look at the underlying work that is on the CD. If the CD-ROM contains a computer program, section 117 allows the owner of a copy of a computer program to make a backup copy. Unfortunately, this permission does not exist for audiovisual works, music recordings, and the like, which might also be on CD.

The other instance when a library may make a copy of a work is under section 108(c) to replace a lost, damaged, deteriorating, stolen, or obsolete copy. This is after the work has become damaged or lost, not before. Even then, the library must first try to purchase an unused replacement copy at a fair price before it can duplicate the work.

• • •

Q163 *How can a library stop a patron from burning CDs? The library asks no questions and places no limits on the number of CDs a patron reproduces.*

It is important not to assume that CD burning by a library user is copyright infringement, because it may not be. For example, if a patron owns a copy of a CD and makes a duplicate for use in his car, it is not infringement under the Audio Home Recording Act, which is sections 1001–1010 of the Copyright Act—even the Recording Industry Association of America agrees (*see* http://www.minidisc.org/ahra.html). Or the patron may have a subscription to Audible.com, which permits subscribers to download audiobooks to CD and other devices. In other words, the copying may be permitted by law, or by a license agreement, or as a fair use.

The only duty of the library is to post the notices on or near reproduction equipment as required under section 108(f)(1) of the Copyright Act and for the library itself to follow the law. Just as the library does not inquire about the use a patron will make of a photocopy, it should not inquire about how patrons will use copies of other media.

Q164   *May a library make a copy of an item it owns that is in an obsolete medium (for example converting VHS tapes to DVD)? If so, may the reproduced copies be used outside of the library?*

Section 108(c) of the Copyright Act permits libraries to reproduce copyrighted media in two instances: (1) to replace a lost, damaged, stolen, or deteriorating item and (2) to replace obsolete media. In order to reproduce the work, the library must first try to find an unused copy at a fair price. If one is not available, then the work may be reproduced. Obsolete media, defined by section 108(c), means that the equipment necessary to render the work perceptible is no longer manufactured or is not available in the commercial marketplace. One is not required to purchase used equipment, however. VHS is not an obsolete format since VHS equipment is still available for purchase.

Section 108(c) was amended in 1998 to allow libraries to make digital copies of analog works under the circumstances described above. These digital copies cannot be used outside the physical premises of the library, however. It is highly likely that Congress meant networked digital copies and not tangible digital copies such as DVDs. Thus, libraries do not make online replacement copies available outside the premises, but in replacing a damaged DVD, when the original could be loaned outside the library, it makes little sense to restrict to the library's premises the copy made under the section 108(c) requirements. Unfortunately, the statute treats all digital works the same and the restriction to in-library use of replaced works in digital format applies.

• • •

Q165   *A faculty member has transferred an 8mm film that he owns to videotape for his own personal use. He now wants to donate this video to the library for its collection. The tape contains two Disney short films, the first of which the library already owns on DVD. The second is not available for purchase in any form, although it is still under copyright. Since it is not available for purchase, and the library does not have the technology to show an 8mm film, may the library accept this donation and add it to the collection?*

If the library receives a copy of a work by gift, it is just the same as if it purchased the work. Should the faculty member have donated the 8mm film itself, the library could convert it to VHS because, under section 108(c) of the Copyright Act, the 8mm format is considered obsolete. First, the library would have to make a reasonable effort to purchase the work at a fair price. If it is not available, then the library may then convert the format since 8 mm equipment is no longer reasonably available in the commercial marketplace. In this situation, the faculty member has already done the conversion from an obsolete format that the library would have been able to do for itself. There should be no difficulty in accepting the already converted VHS copy.

This answer would not apply had the original work been in VHS format, and the faculty member converted it to DVD for his personal use and then sought to donate the DVD to the library. VHS is not yet an obsolete format so the library should not accept the hypothetically proffered DVD.

• • •

Q166   *As VHS tapes and playing equipment are being phased out of a library, some faculty want to convert commercial VHS tapes to DVD format so they can continue to use them in the classroom. Many of these VHS tapes are not currently available for purchase in DVD format. Would permission from the copyright holder be required to convert to DVD format if the VHS tapes were (1) "personal" copies, (2) department-owned copies, or (3) library-owned copies?*

The answer to all three is, unfortunately, yes. Under section 108(c) of the Copyright Act, there is no permission for libraries to convert format as long as the equipment for using VHS is either still being manufactured or is still reasonably available in the commercial marketplace. VHS equipment is still available, although at some future time, this will cease to be the case.

This answer applies to library, personal, and departmental copies. If, however, the library copies are "lost, damaged, stolen, or deteriorating," and the library tries to buy another VHS copy and a DVD copy and neither is available, then the library could convert the VHS to DVD format. There is no statutory permission for departmental or personal copies. If someone owns a personal VHS copy for home viewing only and not for showing at school, there is a stronger argument for permitting the conversion for use at home under section 107 fair use. This would not apply if the video is to be used at school, however.

• • •

Q167   *If a media producer installs copy protection on a film, does that remove someone's fair use rights? For example, if the library or a faculty member wants to "rip" a two-minute segment from a two-hour film, is that infringement, even though using the two minutes would likely be a fair use if it were not copy protected?*

Yes, removing copy controls is infringement. The anti-circumvention provision of the Copyright Act pretty much eliminates fair use when technological controls on access and copying are present. This provision was added by the 1998 Digital Millennium Copyright Act that amended the Copyright Act of 1976. If a copyright owner includes technological copy protection on a work, removing that copy protection, even to make a fair use, violates the statute. Despite the fact that the anti-circumvention provision, section 1201(c), says that it does not affect fair use, clearly it does so.

• • •

Q168   *A community college library has several iPods loaded with music, audiobooks, and other content for circulation to students. In collaboration with a music professor the library created a themed iPod called the "BachPod" that contains classical music and other materials purchased from iTunes. Currently, there are multiple copies of the BachPod available for checkout. The library asked Apple about purchasing something from iTunes and then putting it on multiple iPods, and Apple said this was permissible as long as students could not transfer material from one of the school's iPods to another device. Now the music professor has a set of Leonard Bernstein DVDs that he wants to transfer to the BachPod. The library is concerned that* *ripping content from a DVD would infringe copyright, but he says that it would be okay as long as the original DVDs are then warehoused and not used. Would this mean that each original DVD the library owns may be copied to only one iPod? Does the TEACH Act apply to this situation?*

The TEACH Act has no applicability to this situation. TEACH applies only when performances and displays are transmitted to students, and an iPod is a standalone playback device and not transmission. Copying DVDs onto iPods would require permission both of the composer, if the work is not in the public domain, and of the recording company. Also, the musical arrangement may be separately copyrighted, so a third permission might even be required. The fact that the DVDs are warehoused and not used is irrelevant. Converting the format is the problem since it is an unauthorized reproduction and may infringe this right for three separate copyright owners as described.

• • •

Q169 *An academic library was contacted by a person not affiliated with the university requesting the loan of a copy of a PBS video that is no longer in production and that he was unable to obtain from PBS. A faculty member at the university does not want to risk losing the video by lending it. May the library copy the video to preserve the faculty member's original and lend the copy to the community member?*

Unfortunately, this is not what is meant by preservation in the copyright law. It is infringement to duplicate videos just to lend them. In fact, only under the preservation sections can libraries copy videos at all. Section 108(b) of the Copyright Act applies only if the video is unpublished, and section 108(c) applies only when the library's copy has been lost, damaged, or stolen, has deteriorated, or is obsolete.

• • •

Q170 *The library recently received a donation of several videotapes that a user bought at a garage sale. They are all labeled "Demo* *tape," "Not for sale or rental," "Screener for video retailers," "Please return to sales rep," and the like. May these be used in the library collection? Or may the Friends group sell them in their book sale?*

These tapes should not be added to the collection as they were not intended for this purpose and were clearly marked review or demo copies only. Typically, the Copyright Act section 108 exceptions apply only to lawfully acquired copies. Sale by the Friends group raises other issues, but many libraries claim that those sale items were never part of the collection anyway. So, it may be permissible to sell the copies if the library is willing to assume the risk, but these are not legitimate copies. The library should be careful to make sure that the tapes do not contain any information to identify them with that library.

• • •

Q171 *Several faculty members at a state university have asked the library to make copies of videos borrowed from the library to send to the distance education students. Copies would be made on DVDs and then mailed to the students. Students would be required to return these copies or their grades would be withheld. May the library reproduce these videos to service distance education students? If so, would any preventative measures be required, such as encrypting the copies to block the students from duplicating them? When students return the copies, should the copies then be destroyed, or may they be reused many times?*

The problem with the described activity is not the mailing of DVD copies to distance education students for return to the library, but is the reproducing of videos without seeking permission from each copyright owner and paying royalties if requested. There may be other alternatives that the school or library should explore. For example, purchasing multiple copies of a video for lending, streaming a portion (not the entire video) to distance education students enrolled in a course, or assigning the video for students to view and then suggesting where it may be found, such as video rental stores, public libraries, or legitimate online download sites. Under section 110(2) of the Copyright

Act, a reasonable and limited portion of an audiovisual work may be transmitted (streamed) to distance education students without seeking permission of the copyright owner if the other requirements of the statute are met. To transmit the entire work, however, permission from the copyright owner is required.

The questions concerning return and destruction of the copies make no difference since it is the reproduction itself that causes the copyright difficulties. Whether downloading technologies would be required or whether reproduced copies could be lent many times does not matter if the reproduction of the videos onto DVD was infringement in the first place.

· · ·

Q172   *The library's copy of a certain video is on faculty reserve and it is required viewing. Because the tape has been used so much, it is now in bad shape. The producer of the tape is no longer in business, and the information technology staff is willing to digitize the tape so it can be streamed for viewing. Meanwhile, some enterprising member of the staff checked on the web and found that another university library had already done this. If a video can be digitized, rather than load it onto a server, could the library instead burn it onto a DVD so that it can be checked out by students and faculty?*

The good news is that there now is a way to reproduce the video, but the bad news is that the reproduced copy, if it is digital, has restrictions on where it may be used. Section 108(c) of the Copyright Act permits duplicating deteriorating works after first trying to purchase a new copy. It even allows a library to convert the format and create a digital copy if no unused copy is available for acquisition. There are restrictions, however. The digital copy may not be used outside the premises of the library. Unfortunately, a DVD copy is also a digital copy and thus would be restricted to in-library use only. So, it could not be checked out to patrons to take home to view. It could, however, be checked out for viewing within the library. Many librarians believe that Congress did not intend that tangible digital copies replaced under section 108(c) not be loaned, and they go ahead and circulate those copies if the original deteriorating copy could be circulated.

Streaming technology does not permit students or other users to copy the work but only to see the work being performed. Under section 110(2), a faculty member may transmit (stream) a "reasonable and limited" portion of a film without permission. To stream the entire film, however, requires permission.

• • •

Q173 *The school has an old filmstrip that it wants to convert to DVD. May it do so?*

Under section 108(c) of the Copyright Act, the library must first try to buy the filmstrip on DVD. If it does not exist, then because the format is obsolete, the library may copy it into the new format. The statute states that "a format shall be considered obsolete if the machine or device necessary to render perceptible a work stored in that format is no longer manufactured or is no longer reasonably available in the commercial marketplace." Moreover, a library does not have to acquire used equipment, only new. Filmstrip projectors likely qualify as obsolete today.

• • •

Q174 *A faculty member has a DVD of a Disney movie that was originally produced in 1957. She wants to take a freeze frame from the movie and make a poster from the image and is concerned about whether the work is still under copyright.*

It is still under copyright. Disney Studios has always been very careful about renewing its copyrights. The copyright in the original movie would have been 28 years, so it was protected without renewal until 1985. In 1991 the Copyright Act was amended to eliminate copyright renewals for pre-1978 works and to give works published between 1964 and 1978 an automatic 75 years of protection. In 1998 the term of copyright was extended by an additional 20 years, so the work produced in 1957 will remain under copyright until 2052.

If the poster is to be used in the classroom as a part of instruction, then it may qualify under section 110(1) of the Copyright Act, or as a fair use. The poster format makes it seem as if the use is outside of education, however. Further, Disney Studios is very vigorous in enforcing its copyrights.

• • •

Q175   *There was a video produced by the BBC in 1988 called Race for the Double Helix. It is out of print but available used through several vendors. The BBC will not respond to the library's request for permission to make a copy. Various offices have stated that they are not responsible for the film and cannot help. If the library makes every effort to get permission and fails, must it purchase a used copy, or could it make a copy from a loaner?*

The question omits some critical information. Did the library once own the video that has now been destroyed or damaged? Or is this an acquisitions question? If it is the former, section 108(c) of the Copyright Act applies. The library may duplicate the tape from a loaner after it makes a reasonable effort to find an "unused" copy at a fair price. In other words, it may replace the lost or damaged copy but only if new copies are no longer available. The fact that the BBC has not responded may be evidence that the video is not available for purchase, but not necessarily so. The library may decide to assume the risk and go forward with reproducing the work under section 108(c). Or the library could decide that a used copy would meet its needs and purchase one for the collection.

On the other hand, if the library is trying to acquire something it has never had in the collection, the Copyright Act provides no permission to reproduce the tape at all. Thus, purchasing a used copy may be the only way to add the video to the collection.

• • •

Q176   *The library has some 16mm films from the Federal Aviation Authority (FAA) that are used by the Aviation Department. If* *federal government materials are in the public domain, is it possible to convert the format of the films to video? If the library does change the format, does the film still remain in the public domain?*

If the films were actually produced by the FAA, a government agency, then they are public domain. This means that the library or anyone else may reproduce them or convert the format. It might be a good idea to examine the films carefully to make sure there is no copyright notice. It is possible that they were actually produced for the FAA by a government contractor, which actually may hold the copyright. Changing the format of a public domain work is permissible, and it does not create any new copyright in the underlying work, unless new content is added. The original content still remains in the public domain because a change in format does not create a new copyright absent new content.

• • •

Q177   *A librarian has created a children's promotional video that uses a song by the Jacksons from 1978, "Blame It on the Boogie." The video will be used only for nonprofit purposes. Is there any problem with playing the video on the local government channel?*

Many people would respond that this should be fair use and it should be! Unfortunately, it likely is not. If the librarian simply played the video for classes in a nonprofit educational institution in a face-to-face classroom under section 110(1) of the Copyright Act as part of instruction, there would be little problem. To perform the video even on cable television, the library needs a license in order to use the Jacksons's recording. In fact, the library needs both a performance license and a synchronization license (for synchronizing the video with the music). Both the underlying musical composition and the sound recording are still under copyright.

• • •

Q178   *A college has videos of faculty giving presentations, conducting review lectures, and demonstrating different techniques.*

Who owns the copyright in these videos? What happens when the faculty member leaves the institution? May the library duplicate them for other institutions?

The ownership of the videos depends on whether the institution has a copyright ownership policy. Normally, the video (the physical object) would belong to the institution, but, the faculty member may own the rights in the presentation that is captured on the video. The tradition in higher education in the United States is that faculty members own the copyrights in their works. When the taping was done, if it was done correctly, the faculty member was asked to sign a release form to permit the video recording in the first place. That form may also have assigned all or some of the rights to the institution. Most of these forms also specify the uses that the college may make of the video.

In the absence of a signed agreement, what can then be done with the video depends entirely on the ownership policy. If the institution owns the copyright in the video of the faculty presentation, it is the copyright holder and may therefore duplicate the videos if it so desires and share copies with other institutions. If the faculty member owns the copyright, then any duplication and distribution requires his or her permission.

Many copyright ownership policies spell out the rights of both the faculty member and the institution when the faculty member leaves the institution. In the absence of a policy, if the faculty member holds the copyright, then the video could continue to be used locally within the institution, but it could not be duplicated without permission.

• • •

Q179 *A faculty member at the college has videotaped a performance of all of the plays performed at the school over the past few years. He uses these videotapes in his classes and has recently offered to donate them to the library.*

Assume that the college does obtain the rights to perform these plays publicly. The performance rights normally do not include the right to video record the performance, although the school may be able to obtain a license for this. The copyright holder likely would be concerned about how the video was going to be used. For example, if the purpose of the video is to permit the drama faculty to critique the performance, then making the video may be permitted. Using the videos for showing to classes raises other issues, and copyright holders may be far less likely to grant permission for this.

The Guidelines for Educational Uses of Music grant permission for faculty to make a single recording of student music performances for purposes of critique, but there is nothing similar for dramatic works.

• • •

Q180   *PowerPoint Viewer is a free download. A librarian wants to put the program on a CD and distribute it at no charge. Does it require permission to do so?*

Yes, permission is required. Only the copyright holder has the right to distribute a work, whether in analog copies or by permitting downloads, and regardless of whether or not there is a charge for the work. Others may not distribute the work absent permission from the owner. The fact that the PowerPoint Viewer is a free download does not change its status as a copyrighted work. As an alternative, the librarian could provide the link so that others could download their own copies.

• • •

Q181   *Do publishers have the right to grant or deny permission to libraries to circulate CD products? Publishers in the legal arena seem to assume that they have the right to specify how the products are used after library purchase. Has the law addressed this issue?*

Publishers generally do not have the right to specify how libraries use CD products that they purchase. With a purchased CD, the first sale doctrine permits the library to lend the item in its collection. However, if the CD is licensed to the library rather than sold, then the publisher can control the use.

The law does address this issue. Section 108(f)(4) of the Copyright Act states that libraries are bound by the license agreements they sign when they obtain copies of a work for their collections. So, license agreements trump copyright for libraries by statute. The use of licensed products may be restricted in a variety of ways by publishers, such as no use for interlibrary lending, no circulation of the work, and so forth.

• • •

Q182 *A teacher has asked the librarian to record a television program from CNN about the future of U.S. education to be shown only within the school. The question is to what extent is CNN covered under fair use for educators. With the change to digital reception of all programs, has the law changed to reflect the change in television reception?*

The law has not changed to reflect digital television reception, since the underlying copyright issues remain the same. In fact, throughout the Copyright Act, the language concerning technology is "now known or later developed." Recording the program to show it within a class with only students and teachers present is likely fair use. The performance of the video in the classroom is permitted under section 110(1) for face-to-face teaching. The recording should not be posted on the web, however.

Another alternative is to contact the network and seek permission. Should the librarian select this alternative, then the performance rights can be requested at the same time to permit in-school, including online instruction, use, rather than just face-to-face classroom use. If the video of the program is to be shown outside of a classroom, then a public performance license is needed.

• • •

Q183 *Section 108(f)(3) of the Copyright Act appears to be a very unusual section that allows libraries to record television news programs. What is the reason for this provision?*

When television news programs began, their value was not fully appreciated by the networks. In fact, for years CBS did not videotape

The CBS Evening News with Walter Cronkite. Vanderbilt University Library started the Television News Archive and recorded network news daily. A library could borrow a copy of a specific news tape from the Archive. At some point, CBS began to videotape Walter Cronkite and sued Vanderbilt University for infringing its reproduction and distribution rights. During the debates on the Copyright Act of 1976, Congress recognized that there was something unique about televised news, and it gave libraries the right to record it. According to House Report 94-1476, this exception was aimed at daily newscasts of the national news networks that report on the major events of the day. After passage of the Copyright Act, CBS dropped the suit against Vanderbilt, which still maintains the Television News Archive (*see* http://tvnews.vanderbilt.edu/).

• • •

Q184 *May a library circulate software (e.g., Microsoft Office products), as long as they contain the copyright warning?*

Yes, nonprofit libraries may do so. Section 109(b) of the Copyright Act permits nonprofit libraries to lend copies of software for nonprofit purposes. In order to do this, however, the library must include a copyright warning on the software package specified by the Register of Copyrights and published in the Code of Federal Regulations (*see* http://www.law.cornell.edu/copyright/regulations/201.24.html). If the library signs a license agreement to the contrary, however, the license agreement controls.

• • •

Q185 *When shareware or freeware has been downloaded from the Internet, is it copyright infringement to "beam it" to a colleague's handheld device?*

There is a difference between shareware and freeware that is pretty important in this instance. Freeware generally means that it is free of charge and free of restrictions on the use of the software. Therefore, duplicating it by copying it to someone's handheld device would not be infringement. There is a possibility, however, that there are restrictions included in some click-on license agreement that accompanied the software on the web. Further, the terms "freeware" and "software" are often used interchangeably, even though there is a difference.

Traditionally, shareware means that the software is protected by copyright but that the copyright owner makes it available for one to examine. Anyone who decides to use the software is then expected to pay for the copy. Sending a copy of this software to someone violates the copyright holder's reproduction right. The most important thing, however, is to pay attention to any online license when downloading the software.

• • •

Q186 *The Copyright Act appears particularly outdated as it pertains to audiovisual works. Why does Congress not update it?*

There are many reasons that Congress hesitates to amend the copyright law. Moreover, it is not just the provisions dealing with audiovisual works that sorely need to be modernized. First, technology changes so rapidly that lawmakers have difficulty deciding how to amend laws so that they do not impede technological developments. Second, there have been some changes in the law (pretty minor as applied to audiovisual works), but not since the Digital Millennium Copyright Act of 1998. Third, copyright owners and users of copyrighted works are pretty polarized right now, and any changes that one side wants likely will be fought by the other side. The spirit of legislative compromise seems to be dead on many fronts—not just copyright.

CHAPTER 8

Photographs and Graphics

P hotographs and graphics are included in the category of pictorial, sculptural, and graphic works in the U.S. Copyright Act.[1] The
term "photograph" is not defined in the Copyright Act, but a common definition is "an image, especially a positive print, recorded by
a camera and reproduced on a photosensitive surface."[2] Images may
be embodied in actual photographs, glass plates, or negatives, or as
digital copies. The format of an image is irrelevant; it is the underlying photograph that is the copyrighted work. Libraries and archives
have collected photographs since the earliest days of photography, and
have been the recipients of photographs and even whole photographic
collections. Often the photographer of these works is unknown; it is
unclear whether the works were ever published; and the date of the
image can be ascertained only by guesswork based on the subject's
clothing, automobiles in the picture, and so forth.

Librarians are often asked to duplicate images for users, and libraries seek to make some of these photographic collections available
on the web. Images of public domain works of art are crucial to faculty
members from a range of disciplines—from art history to law, from
medicine to anthropology. Establishing whether an image was ever
published is crucial in determining whether the work is protected by

---

1   17 U.S.C. § 102(2)(5) (2006).
2   *The Free Dictionary*, at http://www.thefreedictionary.com/photograph.

copyright. Photographers are often unknown, and libraries are repeatedly asked to reproduce copies of images for scholars and researchers. Photographers seldom put copyright notice on their works, and they do not often register them. Moreover, the copyright information may have been removed by the owner of the copy of a photograph later donated to a library, leaving the library without any way to identify the photographer and copyright information. As a result, there are more orphans in photographic works than in other types of works.

Although there are exceptions to lack of notice on photographs and registration, lack of information about the photographer creates problems for libraries. Section 108(i) of the Copyright Act details the exclusions from the library exceptions, which include pictorial works. When a library may reproduce and distribute images includes: (1) to preserve an unpublished work under section 108(b); (2) to replace a lost, stolen, damaged, or deteriorating image under section 108(c); (3) for scholarship, research, or preservation under section 108(h); or (4) when images are included in materials, such as journal articles that are reproduced for a user under sections 108(d) and (e).

Two other issues relating to photographs are important: the right of privacy and the right of publicity. Individuals may object to having their photographs displayed in libraries, and if they are private citizens, it is possible that they may be able to complain about a library's use of their likeness for such display. Because of this, many libraries try to use a disclaimer and then seek permission of the individuals depicted, even though the copyright belongs to the photographer and not to the subject of the photograph. By contrast, the right of publicity typically belongs to famous individuals, who can control the use of their images for commercial purposes. However, the Internet has had a tremendous effect on these rights, with fan sites proliferating daily.

Questions in this chapter pertain to copyright ownership, disclaimers for posting photographs on the web, granting access to photographic collections to scholars, the display of images in the academic classroom, the use of images in scholarly conferences and in public presentation, and reproduction and distribution of photographic images. Although outside the purview of copyright law, questions of privacy and permission are raised as they pertain to the use of a person's likeness in library promotional materials and on the web.

Chapter 7, "Digitization," and chapter 11, "Preservation and Archiving," also discuss images.

• • •

Q187 *Are photographs published or unpublished for copyright purposes?*

Photographs are just like other copyrighted material and may be either published or unpublished. Even unpublished photos may be protected, however. If published in a book or journal article, the photograph is published for copyright purposes. Today, posting photos on a website is considered to be publication.

Publication was a much more important issue prior to 1978 because only published works were eligible for federal copyright protection. Unpublished works remained in "limbo"—they did not enter the public domain, nor did they receive any protection. If published without notice before 1978, the work passed into the public domain. Works that existed as of January 1, 1978, but which remained unpublished through the end of 2002, entered the public domain at the end of 2002, or life of the author (photographer) plus 70 years, whichever is greater. Photographs that existed as of January 1, 1978, that were published before the end of 2002 pass into the public domain at the end of 2047, or 70 years after the author's death, whichever is greater. Works created on or after January 1, 1978, are protected for 70 years after the death of the author, regardless of whether or not they are published.

• • •

Q188 *A faculty member wants to post on the course web page photographs taken by students in the class and papers written by them. Does this present a copyright problem?*

One could argue that students give permission to post photographs they take and their papers simply by enrolling in the course if the course syllabus indicates that permission for such posting is a requirement of the course. In order to protect the institution, however, having the students sign an agreement at the first of the semester stating that they give permission for inclusion of their copyrighted works on the course web page is useful. If the students give their permission, there is no need to password protect the web page since the students own the copyrights in their photographs and papers, unless their permission is conditioned on restricting access to the web page.

• • •

Q189   *A university library received the photography archive from a famous woman photographer upon her death in 1990. One of her more famous photographs is a portrait of an author that was used on the book jacket of his most popular book. When the author died, the library was asked repeatedly for permission to use this portrait in news stories to announce the author's death. Is it a copyrighted photograph? Does the university own the copyright?*

The copyright status of the photographer's body of work is likely unclear. If the photos are pre-1978 and were published with notice, then they were protected by copyright from the date of publication. If the photos were published without a copyright notice, they entered the public domain. The term of copyright depends on when they were published with notice. Consult my chart, "When U.S. Works Pass into the Public Domain" (*see* Appendix; also available at http://www.unc.edu/~unclng/public-d.htm) to determine the term. Moreover, 28 years later the copyright in the photographs would have had to be renewed or they would have entered the public domain. Not many photographers actually renewed their copyrights. If the photographs were taken after 1978, the term is 70 years after the photographer's death, and those photos clearly would still be under copyright.

Another important question is whether the photographer transferred the copyright to the publisher of the book or to the author, or whether she retained the copyright in this particular photograph when it appeared on the dust jacket. It will require some research to determine the publication arrangement between the publisher and the author. Also, outside of copyright, the right of publicity may apply, and some authors claim that all rights belong to them.

Purely on the copyright question, while the university is the legal owner of these photographs, it likely does not own the copyrights unless the deed of transfer actually transferred the copyrights to the institution. So, the library owns the physical copies but probably not the copyrights. The library can display the copies locally, but not post them on the web, reproduce them, and so forth, without permission unless the library owns the copyrights. On the other hand, if the photographer has no heirs or if the heirs agree to reproduction and display more broadly, then the library can do that. The library can grant access to the author's photograph but, unless the library owns the copyright, it cannot grant permission to use the photo.

• • •

Q190 *How does one deal with copyright on a photograph taken prior to 1900 where the photographer is unknown and not identified on the image?*

In order to solve these problems, there are several issues that need to be addressed. Has the photograph ever been published? If so, the copyright is dated from that publication date rather than the date when the photograph was taken. Publication started the running of the copyright term if the work was published with notice. The great likelihood is that even if the work was published, it probably was not renewed for copyright so it would have entered the public domain 28 years after publication with notice. If it was never published, the photograph was still under copyright until the end of 2002, or life of the photographer plus 70 years, whichever is greater. But the photographer's name is not included on the photograph, so this is, in effect, an orphan work and the library cannot determine a death date.

Is the photograph well known? If so, then one of the stock photography companies may hold the rights. In any event, due to the date of the photograph, it is likely to be in the public domain, and the library may decide that the risk is small and go ahead and use the photograph.

Q191   *The library is having a bookstore-like "staff picks" competition. It has been suggested that the library reproduce the cover art from the book (or CD or video case) to highlight the staff picks in a special section of the library's web page. Is there any problem with using the Amazon.com images of the covers to promote the items without asking permission from either Amazon or the individual publishers? If the library scans the covers, using its purchased copies of the items, can it forego asking permission from the publishers?*

The bad news is that it is infringement to scan the covers and use them on a web page without permission. Section 109(c) permits a library to display a book or even an image of the cover art, but not to project the image beyond the place where the copy is located. Scanning the book jackets and putting the images on a web page constitutes a reproduction of the graphic work (the book cover art), and the copy is transmitted beyond the place where the copy is located. Moreover, often the publisher does not even own the copyright in the cover art, so it cannot give permission to use the book jacket.

Either online bookstores get permission from the copyright holder since they are promoting sales of their works, or it is viewed as increasing the publishers' income, so bookstores are not sued over this activity. It should not be difficult for a library to obtain permission to include cover art on a web page. Start by contacting the publisher of each work and ask.

• • •

Q192   *Is free clip art considered to be public domain? What is expected of writers when they use clip art from Microsoft programs?*

Free clip art is copyrighted just as are other graphic works, if they meet the originality/creativity and fixation requirements. "Free" means that there is no charge for using the clip art, not that it is free from claims of copyright. By contrast, "public domain" means that there is no copyright at all, either because the work itself does not qualify for protection (for example, because it is not original with the artist) or the term of copyright has expired. Clip art is too new to have expired copyrights at this time.

The question about the use of clip art from Microsoft is governed by its license agreement. Typically, clip art acquired via a Microsoft license is intended to be used on web pages, in documents, and so forth, but the library should review the Microsoft license to determine whether a particular use is permitted under the terms of the license.

• • •

Q193 *A new faculty member is publishing a book with a university press. She wants to include three photographs in the book, and the status of the copyright of each is unclear. (1) The first photograph was published in 1921. (2) The second photograph was taken in the 1930s, and the photographer is unknown; it was provided to the author by a family member who had a copy of the photograph. Is there a copyright owner for this photo? Does it matter that the photograph had no notice of copyright indicating when the photo was taken? (3) The third photograph is from a local college yearbook, was taken in 1946, and the identity of the photographer is unknown. Is the photographer the copyright holder? Or is the college the owner of the photograph that was published in its yearbook? Is the work is in the public domain if the copyright was never registered?*

Each of these three photographs presents different issues.

(1) The photograph first published before 1923 in the United States clearly is now in the public domain. So that is the easy question to answer and the faculty author may use the photo without permission.

(2) For the second photograph, as with most photos, the problem is that it is an unpublished work. No notice of copyright was required unless the work was published. Notice was essential on published works or the copyright holder lost rights in the work. More than likely, this photo has never been published. Unpublished works that existed as of January 1, 1978, entered the public domain at the end of 2002, or life of the photographer plus 70 years, whichever is

greater. Assume that the photo was taken in 1930. If the photographer died soon after, then it entered the public domain at the end of 2002. But, if the photographer lived until 1960, the copyright will not terminate until 2030. So, it is likely that this photograph is still under copyright, but it is unclear without knowing the name of the photographer and the date of death. On the other hand, if the photograph is a family photo that has never been published, then the chance of anyone complaining is very slight, especially if it is a snapshot and not a studio photograph. Often it is worth taking the risk to go ahead and publish such a photograph because the likelihood of any complaint is so slight. However, the university press publisher may dictate otherwise.

(3) The third photograph presents yet another issue because it was published in a college yearbook in 1946. It is not certain who owns the copyright in the photograph since it may or may not have been a work made for hire. In all likelihood, the college owned the copyright in the photo because the photographer was hired by the college and the photograph was published in its yearbook. If published, not only would the yearbook have had to contain a notice of copyright in 1946, but registration was also required. Even if both notice and registration were present, unless the copyright was renewed in 1974, it would have entered the public domain that year. If renewed, the copyright will not expire until 2041. Renewal of a 1946 college yearbook copyright is unlikely, so the photograph is probably public domain. Again, there is some risk to the faculty member, but only a slight one.

• • •

Q194 *A library in a botanical garden has a large archival collection of photographs, many of which are quite old. Unfortunately the photographer is not always identified or apparent, but some were clearly created by a studio/professional photographer and are marked with attribution. For others the provenance is unclear. In some cases the library has the negatives, but in other instances the photographs appear to be copies of copies. (1) Does the library own the copyright in the photographs in its collection? (2) If not, how can the library sort out the copyright issues for photographic images* *acquired over many years? (3) How can the library create a digital archive of these photographs that is available to the public without infringing copyright?*

(1) Ownership of the tangible item, the photograph or negative, is ownership of a copy of the work, which may be the only copy of the work in existence. This is absolutely separate from ownership of the copyright. The only way an institution owns the copyright in a photograph is if the photographer or other copyright owner transferred the copyright to the library in writing, or if the photographer was on the staff and the work was a work made for hire. Most likely, the library owns the copy but not the copyright.

(2) If the photographs were published before 1923, however, they are in the public domain. So publication is the important question. If a photograph was never published, it entered the public domain at the end of 2002, or life of the photographer plus 70 years, whichever is greater. So, the library should make this determination and seek permission from photographers identified on the photographs. Those with no provenance are more difficult.

Clearly, creating a digital archive of these photographs would be very useful both to the library and to the public.

(3) While creating a digital copy of some of these photographs may be infringement, in all likelihood, there is little risk. Many digital collections of photographs include a disclaimer to the effect that the copyright status of these works is presumed to be public domain due to the age of the work. If someone has other knowledge, that individual is invited to contact the library with that information.

• • •

Q195 *A photographer has donated his negatives to the library. Does the library now own the copyright in the photographs?*

No, the library owns the physical objects, the negatives. The copyright is separate from any physical object in which the work may be stored, such as a print or a negative. The library may even own the only existing copy of a photograph, but it does not own the copyright unless the copyright owner (in this case, the photographer) specifically transferred the copyright in writing.

•••

Q196   *For bulletin boards in a public library's children's area, is there any restriction on posting graphics found on the Internet or copying them from books?*

Yes, there are restrictions. One of the rights of copyright owners is the right of public display. So, copyrighted graphics and illustrations from books and those found on the web should not be reproduced for public display without permission of the copyright holder. There is an exception for displaying books and book jackets, but not for reproducing them for display. Section 109(c) of the Copyright Act states that "the owner of a particular copy lawfully made under this titles, or any person authorized by such owner, is entitled, without the authority of the copyright owner, to display that copy publicly, either directly or by the projection of no more than one image at a time to viewers present at the place where the copy is located." So, enlarging graphics or illustrations from a book or reproducing them from the Internet for a bulletin board in a public library requires permission, but placing the original book jacket or original pages from the book on display is not a problem.

•••

Q197   *A faculty member wants to use one graph from an article available in electronic format in the* New England Journal of Medicine *in a PowerPoint presentation at a national conference. Does he need to get permission, especially since there is the possibility that the PowerPoint presentation might be put on the national organization conference website, or that a CD might be made of all presentations? Do the Fair Use Guidelines for Educational Multimedia help?*

These guidelines did not enjoy wide adoption and certainly do not have the same stamp of Congress as do some of the other guidelines.

One certainly could argue that displaying a graph to a live audience at a national conference of educators is fair use, but it certainly would be prudent to seek permission if the chart is likely to be reproduced on the conference website or in multiple copies on CDs distributed to participants. Another alternative would be for the faculty member to display the chart in the live presentation but simply to include a link to the chart on the slide that is reproduced on the website and on the CDs, rather than including the chart.

• • •

Q198   *A teacher wishes to use photographs and other material in a professional presentation for which she is not being paid. Is this the same as an "educational" presentation since it is an employment-enhancing activity?*

The Copyright Act does not automatically exempt even educational presentations. The fair use exception sometimes permits use in a nonprofit educational institution for instruction, but not always. Section 110(1) of the Copyright Act covers classroom performances and displays in a nonprofit educational institution, which is a limitation on the exclusive rights of the copyright holder. Professional presentations may or may not be fair use, but they are not the same as use in a nonprofit educational institution and do not qualify according to section 110(1). If the presentation is live and no copies of the images are distributed, it may be fair use, but not definitely. Often speakers use images without permission for such presentations and assume that their use is fair use. If the presentation is to be placed on a website, then the presenter should remove the copyrighted photographs, or seek permission to post or otherwise reproduce and distribute them.

• • •

Q199   *The institution recently sponsored a film festival at which a staff member took photographs that are to be posted on the library's website. Some of the photos depict members of the library staff, all* *of whom have agreed to have their likenesses posted on the website. For other festival goers who can be identified, does the library need to get their permission for posting the photos? Do they have to be identified by name?*

This is not really a copyright question but is a right to privacy or, if the person is famous, a right of publicity question. Typically, schools and organizations do not worry about it when photos are taken at a public event. If a person complains about his or her photo being on the website, the library can then remove that photo. If the festival goers are students, however, the library may want to seek permission because of the Federal Educational Rights and Privacy Act (FERPA) concerns. This is a situation in which university counsel should be consulted.

• • •

Q200   *In 1969, the student photography editor for the university newspaper photographed a student sit-in that appeared in the student paper with "Photo by XXX" under the picture. The original photograph eventually was donated to the library by the publications department. It was not marked by the student with a copyright notice or any attribution. The photograph has been presumed to be university property and was reprinted in a book celebrating the institution's sesquicentennial a few years ago. Since then, the student has become a professional photographer and sought money from the school for reprinting the image, which it thought it owned. In order to make the threat go away, the publicity department wants to promise the photographer that it or any similar photo will be marked on the back with the line "Copyright 1969 XXX XXXX Photography, contact 555-555-5555 CLASS OF 1970)." Were student newspaper contents and photos owned by individual students or the college in 1969?*

Under the law, the student photographer (the author) would own the copyright unless there is some agreement with the student newspaper that the newspaper itself or the university owns the copyright. If the photography editor position was a paid position (student newspaper positions usually do have a stipend), then the photograph is a work made for hire and the university owns the copyright. Note that some student newspapers are separate incorporated entities, and these newspapers, rather than the university, may own the copyright.

• • •

Q201 *The e-learning division of a for-profit educational institution wants to use images of some standard workplace notifications such as one would see in a company cafeteria (e.g., dealing with workplace safety, mandatory lunch breaks, and so forth). The images would be used as part of an instructional program. Is there a problem with using them if they came from an Equal Employment Opportunity Commission (EEOC) website?*

While materials produced by the federal government are not eligible for copyright protection according to section 105 of the Copyright Act, government websites also include copyrighted studies and such that were commissioned by the agency with outside contractors. If the images were created by government employees within the scope of their employment, then they are copyright free. Although copyright notice is not required on works, often those commissioned studies and other works that appear on a government website do contain a copyright notice, so this would be the first thing to check. If in doubt about the copyright status, the educational institution should contact the EEOC webmaster and seek information about the copyright status of the images. If the webmaster answers that they are copyrighted, then ask permission to use them.

• • •

Q202 *The library is sponsoring a book talk by a famous author. May it post a photograph of the author and a photocopy of his work* *on the library's website? What about the book jacket from his latest book?*

Only with permission are such reproductions and displays allowed. The library should contact the author or the author's agent about the photograph. Sometimes the agent will even supply the latest photograph, in digital format, and there is seldom a charge for use of the publicity photo. The publisher should be contacted about photocopying the work and about scanning the book jacket. The publisher can answer directly about the photocopy of the work but may not actually own the art work on the jacket. Often publishers contract with an artist to use his or her work on the jacket but the copyright remains with the artist. The publisher will know this, however, and can either further license the library (depending on its license from the artist) or put the library in contact with the artist.

• • •

Q203   *An academic author wants to use a digital image of a painting owned by a museum. The painting appears to be in the public domain since the painter died in the sixteenth century. Is the author required to get permission from the museum to use the image on the dust jacket for his book?*

For many years, museums claimed copyright in the photographs of public domain works of art since photographs are protected by copyright. After *Bridgeman Art Library v. Corel Corp.*, 36 F. Supp. 2d 191 (S.D.N.Y. 1999), this matter was clarified. The court held that although some photographs are copyrightable, exact photographic reproductions of public domain paintings lack originality and therefore do not quality for copyright. A photograph of a three-dimensional sculpture may have sufficient originality to qualify for copyright, however. So, the author should be able to reproduce the public domain image on his book jacket. However, attribution is a benefit to readers to identify the painting and the artist, and to specify where the original is housed; it also acknowledges the museum as the owner of the painting.

Q204   *What is permitted in reproducing images of works of art, not only for library slide collections, but also on the web. Clearly there are many works of art, such as the* Mona Lisa, *Sistine Chapel,* Van Gogh's Self Portrait, *and* Toulouse-Lautrec's At the Moulin Rouge *that are in the public domain. Photographs of three-dimensional works may be the "creative" work of the photographer and therefore copyrightable by the photographer. What about photographs or two-dimensional images of works of art? May they be reproduced at will in slide form for the library or by faculty on their web pages? What about copying images from more recently published books and periodicals, or does the publisher or photographer now own the copyright?*

Photographs generally are protected by copyright. In fact, for years it was assumed that photographs of two-dimensional works of art were protected by copyright. The *Bridgeman Art Library* case (cited in Q202) changed this when the underlying work is in the public domain and the photo is an exact duplication of the painting. The reason for this change was the court's recognition that photographs of two-dimensional works of art that are in the public domain lack sufficient originality to qualify for copyright protection. The same is not true of photographs of three-dimensional works, which do contain enough originality with lighting, angle, and so forth, to attain copyright protection. Therefore, photographs of two-dimensional public domain works of art may be posted on the Internet.

Who owns the copyright in photographs published in books and journals depends on the agreement between the photographer and the author of the book. The photographer initially owned the copyright but may have transferred it to the book author or publisher. Most likely, however, the photographer simply licensed the use of the photo in that publication.

• • •

Q205   *A public library has created a digital archive of local photographs that were donated to the library over the years and has posted them on the web. The librarian has been contacted by a member of* *the community asking for a photograph to be removed from the on-line display because he is the photographer and owns the copyright. What should the library do?*

A purely legalistic answer would focus solely on whether the individual actually owns the copyright, the date of the photo, whether it had been published, registered for copyright, and so forth. The library certainly could take such a stand, research the ownership issue, and work with the city or county attorney for a legal solution to the problem.

There are other serious concerns in addition to copyright ownership, however. For example, how important is that particular work to the overall collection of photographs? Is it worth causing hard feelings with a member of the community? Is it possible to work with the individual to ensure that he receives credit as the photographer but get him to grant permission for the photograph to remain online? The library also may want to make sure that its website asks for copyright holders to come forward so that they may be credited, and the website should contain a statement that the library will remove any copyrighted photograph from the posted digital archive should the owner object to its inclusion.

• • •

Q206 *A librarian has been hired to create a web page for a business that provides costumes, and she is interested in using images from 1930s through 1950s Montgomery Ward catalogs on the web page. May these images be used on the Internet, or are they protected by copyright law? The complicating factor is that Montgomery Ward is no longer in business.*

The photographs may or may not still be protected by copyright. They were published and likely were registered for copyright as a part of the catalog. Assume that they originally were protected. Now, the question is whether the copyright was renewed. Consult my chart, "When U.S. Works Pass into the Public Domain" (*see* Appendix; also available at http://www.unc.edu/~unclng/public-d.htm) to determine when works enter the public domain.

If the photographs were registered and the copyright was renewed at the end of the first 28-year period, the photographs may still be under copyright. When Montgomery Ward went out of business, it would have transferred assets to another company, and copyrights are considered assets. A search of the U.S. Copyright Office registration records will help to determine if the copyright was renewed and/or transferred. The records are online only since 1978, however, and not all transfers are recorded. For these earlier works, one would either have to hire the Copyright Office itself to do the search or engage a private search firm.

Another possibility is simply to assume the risk of going ahead and using the photographs. The risk is probably slight that anyone would complain because: (1) the photos are old, (2) they were used in widely distributed sales catalogs, (3) it is unlikely that the copyright was renewed after the first 28 years, and (4) the company is no longer in business. This does not mean that using the photos is risk free, but just low risk. One can always remove the images if the copyright owner complains. A complicating factor, however, is the fact the photographs will be put to commercial use rather than nonprofit use, which reduces the potential that the use would be found to be a fair use.

• • •

Q207   *A faculty author wants to use some wedding photos from the 1940s and 1950s that he found in the state archives. They seem to have been originally published in the local newspaper's society section, and later they were given to the archives. It would be very difficult to trace these people 40 or 50 years later, but the author wants to use the photos in a book. Is this a problem?*

This is a fairly complicated issue that may just boil down to whether the faculty author is willing to assume the risk. Interestingly, in U.S. copyright law it is not the subject of the photos who owns the copyright but rather it is the photographer. Since these were published in the newspaper, the first step would be to determine whether the photos were taken by a newspaper staff photographer, in which case the newspaper would own the copyright, or by regular photography studios. If the latter, then the photographer owns the copyright.

The copyright would have expired 28 years after publication unless the copyright holder renewed the copyright for an additional 28 years (this has now been expanded to 67 years). To trace this by date, consult my chart, "When U.S. Works Pass into the Public Domain" (*see* Appendix; also available at http://www.unc.edu/~unclng/public-d.htm).

After all of this, however, it is highly unlikely that any photographer from that long ago, or his or her heirs, would be around to complain. So, the faculty member may well decide to assume the risk.

• • •

Q208   *If a patron asks to scan an entire collection of postcards or photographs for personal use, should the library permit her to do so?*

What a user can do for herself is very different from what a library can do for the user. It may well be fair use for the patron to make personal copies of the works, even in digital format. The library may want to alert the patron to the fact that there could be copyright problems should she put the works on a website or use them in a publication, but the library is not required to do so. If the patron is using a library scanner rather than her own, that equipment must contain the same notice required by section 108(f)(1) of the Copyright Act for photocopiers and reproduction equipment.

CHAPTER 9

The Internet and the Web

The digital environment has affected the users of copyrighted works as well as the producers. Not only are librarians and teachers increasingly familiar with locating information on the web, so are library users, who often request digital copies. The wide availability of much free material on the Internet has caused many librarians to question whether the same copyright rules that exist for print and analog works apply when the work is found on the Internet.

For many schools and libraries, digital works are licensed (*see* chapter 4, "Permissions and Licensing"), and what a library may do with materials is governed by the license agreement. But what about materials found on the open web? Copyright still applies just as always. There is no requirement that authors put notice of copyright on their works, so lack of notice does not mean lack of copyright.

On the other hand, many works are posted on the Internet by their authors with an invitation for others to use them freely. There are user-generated content sites, such as blogs and *Wikipedia*, that are made available under a Creative Commons license (*see* http://creativecommons. org/). Materials found on the Internet are subject to fair use and the other exceptions to the exclusive rights of the copyright owner.

Two sections of the Copyright Act apply only to the Internet. Enacted in 1998, the Digital Millennium Copyright Act (DMCA)[1] amended

---

1   Pub. L. No. 105-304, 112 Stat. 2860 (Oct. 28, 1998).

the Copyright Act and added two new sections to the Act. Section 512, online service provider (OSP) liability, is designed to excuse from liability e-mail service providers as well as providers that host Internet content if the service provider meets certain requirements. This is important to libraries, educational institutions, and corporations that provide e-mail service to their employees and/or host Internet content. While the user of the online service is still liable for copyright infringement, the service provider can escape liability. These "passive conduits" that provide only e-mail services are not liable for a user's infringing activity if they neither direct the content, nor select the recipients, nor receive any financial benefit from transmitting the copyrighted content in an e-mail message. For both types of OSPs, the provider must terminate the access of any user who is found to be infringing.

For OSPs that host content, the requirements are more stringent. The OSP must remove any material that it knows or has reason to believe is infringing. Further, if it receives notice from the copyright holder that protected works are posted, it must take down the material and may not return it to the web until it determines that it is a fair use and so notifies the copyright holder.

The second provision added by the DMCA is section 1201, the anti-circumvention provision, which has a small exception for libraries. It violates the statute to remove any anti-circumvention devices that copyright owners use on a digital work to control access to it. Moreover, trafficking in devices that circumvent these technological protection measures is infringement, and there are even criminal penalties for such activity. Libraries, however, may circumvent such technological protection if the purpose of the circumvention is to examine a protected work to determine whether or not to purchase it.

Questions in this chapter pertain to reproduction of works from and for the Internet, audio podcasts, website password protection, faculty-created works on the web, sharing Internet searches within a corporation, and posting versus linking.

• • •

Q209 *Is three paragraphs of a copyrighted work too much to put on a web page?*

To answer this question requires a fair use analysis.
(1) What is the purpose of the use? If the text on a password-protected website is restricted to enrolled students in a particular course in a nonprofit educational institution, the purpose of the use is different than if the text is on an open website.

(2) What is the nature of the copyrighted work? Is the work a novel, a poem, a scientific article? How old is the work? Is it still in print?

(3) What percent of the copyrighted work do the three paragraphs represent? If the three paragraphs are from a full-length novel, then they are a very small portion. However, if the work is a poem printed on two pages, three paragraphs represents a fairly substantial portion. Even if the copied paragraphs are a small portion of the copyrighted work, if the copied paragraphs represent the heart of the work, then the amount is too much.

(4) What is the impact of the copying of the three paragraphs on the potential market for or value of the work? Does the use interfere with the sales of the work? Does it destroy the value?

If the three paragraphs are from a mystery novel, and they reveal the "whodunit," then not only do they represent the heart of the work, but using them could also destroy the market for the novel. It is always possible to seek permission from the copyright holder to use the three paragraphs on the web page.

• • •

Q210 *May a library use any material found on the web that does not contain a notice of copyright and incorporate that material into a library web page?*

Material that is published on the web is protected by copyright if it is original. After March 1989, there is no longer a requirement that works contain a notice of copyright, so the assumption must be that the work is protected unless it clearly is in the public domain or is a U.S. government document. The library may link to content without permission, but to incorporate that content into another web page requires permission of the copyright owner, unless it passes fair use muster.

Q211   *How much of a copyrighted video may be copied and put on a web page by a public library?*

Only a fair use portion may be posted on a web page without permission. Some companies have produced DVDs containing movie clips for which permissions have been cleared. These are licensed products and include permission to use the clips on a web page. Other royalty collectives may offer licenses in the future. Otherwise, the copyright owner must be contacted for permission to use the video clip.

• • •

Q212   *A library patron downloads an article from the library's online subscription to a journal or database and alters it. He then posts the altered article on a web page. Who is liable, the library or the patron?*

The patron normally is liable. If the library's license agreement requires the library to monitor use and certify that no infringement is occurring, the library would be liable, however. Libraries typically do not agree to such monitoring but instead agree to discourage conduct by posting warnings. If the library has agreed to warn patrons, and it does so, then the library has met its obligations.

• • •

Q213   *May a corporate library archive and put its Internet searches on the company intranet? If the library conducts a search and downloads it to a library hard drive, archives it on one company server, and then e-mails the results to a patron, there are now three copies of the material. Is this a problem?*

The term "Internet searches" indicates that the search really involves material on the open web or digital products for which the company has a license. For licensed material, the terms of the license agreement control what use may be made of search results. Material on the Internet is copyrighted just as it is in print. Reproducing the material widely and putting it even on an intranet raises copyright concerns. If putting the searches on the intranet means simply repeating the question and then including the URLs where the information was found, this is no problem. It is the reproduction of copyrighted works, such as articles, book chapters, and the like, that raises concern.

Generally, making one copy for a user is permitted under section 108(d) of the Copyright Act, but multiple copying is not. Making works accessible digitally to multiple users within the company counts as multiple copying. If the copies are "transitory" and are destroyed as soon as the patron has received the results, there is no problem. But if the library is indeed making three copies and retaining them, it should seek permission absent a license agreement. An alternative is an Annual Copyright License from the Copyright Clearance Center, which would cover such reproduction, including posting on the intranet.

• • •

Q214 *A medical library plans to post on its intranet site an article from a journal to which it subscribes. The library has obtained written permission from the publisher to do this. What is the proper verbiage to post with the article to indicate that permission has been received? Is "reprinted with permission from the publisher" sufficient?*

The suggested language is just fine. If the publisher does not specify that any special wording must be used, the library is free to indicate that permission was received in any way it chooses. Often the wording is just "reprinted by permission." It probably is a good idea to make sure that the publisher's name appears somewhere, either with the permission statement or on the article itself.

• • •

Q215 *A hospital is considering posting on its intranet four articles in PDF format. The library does not have an institutional subscription to the journals, either in print or in electronic format. Further, no copyright royalties have been paid or even contemplated for intranet* *posting. What alternatives does an institution have to be able to post the articles on the intranet without infringing copyright?*

The first step is to check to make sure that there is no institutional license through services such as EBSCOhost and or MD Consult. If there is a license, then the terms of the license control whether the articles may be posted on the intranet. PDF format is really irrelevant since the format does not change the copyright status of the underlying work. Another alternative is to seek permission directly from each publisher, stating the potential use of the article, the length of time it will be posted, the number of potential users, and so forth. The hospital library could also pay royalties directly to the Copyright Clearance Center for the posting of these articles on a per-use basis. The CCC also offers the Annual Copyright License to both for-profit and nonprofit hospitals, which permits intranet posting.

• • •

Q216 *A librarian is delivering a presentation at a professional conference and finds a cartoon on the Internet for which there is no copyright notice or other information. What are the risks and problems if she uses that cartoon in a PowerPoint presentation at the conference? What if either the presenter or the conference organizers publish the presentation on the web, including the cartoon? Suppose that the librarian used the cartoon in the past without knowing that the cartoon was copyrighted?*

The fact that the cartoon is found on the Internet does not alter the copyright status of the work in any way. It is a graphic work that in all likelihood is copyrighted. Since there is no longer any requirement of notice in the Copyright Act, the lack of a notice does not affect the status of the work. There is a slight possibility that the cartoon is public domain, but it is unlikely. So, assume that the cartoon is copyrighted.

If there is no identifying information, the first examination the librarian should make is whether the style of the cartoon is such that its authorship can be traced. For example, New Yorker cartoons all have a particular style, and "Far Side" cartoons are readily identifiable as such. Should there be no way to trace copyright ownership from the style, then the librarian should conduct a risk assessment. Using the cartoon creates some risk, but it may be slight depending on how widely the presentation is to be distributed. Including the cartoon in a PowerPoint slide for a live presentation at a conference with no other reproduction could be a fair use and is not as risky as publishing the slides containing the cartoon in print. The risk for publishing them on the web is greater, however. The librarian should evaluate how critical it is to use the work, how widely it will be reproduced and distributed, and how much risk she is willing to assume. The copyright owner is far more likely to learn of the reproduction and display of the cartoon if the presentation is posted on the web—thus, the heightened risk.

The final part of this question asks whether past use of a cartoon creates liability. Ignorance of the law is no excuse, and copyright law does not have an intent requirement, so one infringes even if she did not mean to do so. If the infringement occurred during the last three years, the answer is yes since the statute of limitations in the Copyright Act is three years. The owner of a registered copyrighted work may file suit for infringing activity going back three years.

• • •

Q217 *Faculty members often want to copy material from other websites for course web pages rather than linking to the websites. Is this copyright infringement?*

Reproducing copyrighted works on the web is no different than reproducing them by photocopying or any other method. In this situation, linking is a much better alternative. Reproduction is the problem. When this reproduction is done for the class just for display, it may be exempted under section 110(1) of the Copyright Act, the classroom exemption. If it is posted in course management software, then the faculty member should make sure that the work reproduced complies with the Guidelines on Multiple Copying for Classroom Use (Classroom Guidelines) for text, or section 110(2) for performances and displays for distance education and online instruction, or that it qualifies as a section 107 fair use. Otherwise, the faculty member should seek permission.

• • •

Q218   *A library is considering downloading audio books as a less expensive alternative to purchasing the books on CD. Would this present copyright concerns?*

Yes, there are copyright concerns if the intent is to download books onto a server so that multiple users can listen to them rather than paying a license fee. While individuals may purchase downloads from Audible.com and other companies, the license agreement assumes that the downloading is being done for one listener. The proposed activity is equivalent to buying one copy of a printed book and then making photocopies of it to lend rather than purchasing multiple copies. It may be possible to obtain a multiple listener license from these companies, which the library should do if it intends to substitute downloads for purchasing books on CD.

• • •

Q219   *A librarian teaches various levels of web page development for students and faculty. Students are very interested in downloading materials from the Internet such as photographs of works of art, incorporating sound from CDs, and the like. There is software that permits them to do this. If they cite the source, are there still copyright concerns?*

When students are creating a presentation for classroom use, it well may be fair use for them to incorporate material from Internet websites, clips of musical recordings, and the like. Further, section 110(1) of the Copyright Act permits the performance of nondramatic literary and musical works and the display of any work in face-to-face teaching by either students or faculty in a classroom in a nonprofit educational institution. One could certainly argue that reproducing the work to incorporate it into a web presentation for classroom use is a fair use. If the slides created by students for class projects are to be put into course management software or on a password-protected web page, section 110(2) for online performances and displays in non-profit educational institutions applies. There are numerous conditions that have to be met to permit the use of copyrighted works under this section, however.

• • •

Q220 *A faculty member has downloaded articles from a licensed online database and wants to mount them on his web page so that students may use them. Is this copyright infringement?*

In order to evaluate this situation, one must know what the license agreement specifies about use of material from the database. It may permit this use if the faculty member password protects his website so that only students in his class have access to the downloaded material. On the other hand, the license may be a personal license and may not permit any further electronic distribution. If this is the case, and the faculty member is using a library-licensed database, he should simply include a link to the articles on his web page. Students would have access to the same database if they are enrolled students in the academic institution. Further, there may be educational reasons to require students to follow a link rather than providing them with a digital copy.

• • •

Q221 *As faculty members create course web pages, many questions arise about whether putting certain materials on a web page constitutes copyright infringement. When faculty authors put copies of their own journal articles on a web page, is that a problem? Does it make a difference if the web page is password protected?*

If the faculty author transferred the copyright in the articles to the publisher in order to have them published, he is infringing when reproducing them for a web page that also enables others to reproduce them by printing or downloading. It is always difficult to explain to faculty authors that if they transferred the copyright to the article, then they have no greater rights to the article than would a stranger. Sometimes publishers will give faculty authors permission to put articles on a course web page if the page is password protected for the class, or the publisher's permission may be time sensitive. In other words, the publisher may allow the faculty author to put the article on the course web page but only six to twelve months after the article appears in the journal. Even if these conditions do not exist, the faculty author may still be able to put the article on a course web page or in course management software following the Guidelines on Multiple Copying for Classroom Use (Classroom Guidelines). (*See* Chapter 2, "Copies for Users"). This would require password protection as well as meeting the brevity, spontaneity, and cumulative effects tests. The faculty author could also evaluate the posting under the fair use factors.

• • •

Q222   *Some of the faculty members in a particular academic department want to post their published articles on the institution's external website in PDF format. Will publishers readily give permission for this?*

It depends. If a faculty author owns the copyright, certainly he or she may post the article. If the author has transferred the entire copyright to the journal publisher, then naturally permission must be requested to post the article in any format. If the faculty author retained the electronic rights to the article, then the article may be posted on a web page without permission. Some copyright transfer agreements even state that the author may place the work on the web six months or a year after it appears first in the journal. So, there is no across-the-board answer; instead, it depends on what rights were transferred to the publisher and the language of the actual copyright transfer. Faculty authors could seek permission from the publisher to post these PDFs.

Q223   *Is it necessary to password protect course web pages, Blackboard pages, and the like, or can they be accessed by anyone?*

It depends on the contents of the web page or the course management software site. Should the web page contain no material copy-righted by anyone other than the faculty member, no password is required under copyright law. If copies of copyrighted works, or even portions of such works, are included on a web page without permission of the copyright holder, however, access to this material should be restricted to members of the class. If the copyrighted material consists of such things as articles and book chapters, then placing them on a web page or Blackboard page (or any other course management software page) for students to use should conform to fair use under the Guidelines on Multiple Copying for Classroom Use (Classroom Guidelines). Password protection or another method of restricting access to students enrolled in the class is crucial.

If the copyrighted material consists of material that is performed or displayed to students, the TEACH Act, section 110(2) of the Copyright Act, also requires that access to the material be restricted to students enrolled in the course. Only the course web pages that contain these copyrighted works must be restricted. Should the faculty member so desire, the course web pages that do not contain copyrighted works may remain open to anyone.

• • •

Q224   *When posting materials on course management software (e.g., Blackboard) for a class, if the articles and chapters are documented and properly cited, is it necessary to seek permission to post them? Or is documenting/citing the source enough to satisfy copyright concerns?*

This question mixes two things: copyright and plagiarism. The copyright concern is reproducing the materials in the first place because reproduction is one of the exclusive rights of the copyright holder. Plagiarism is claiming original authorship of someone else's work or incorporating it without adequate acknowledgement. So copyright is not concerned with citing or attribution typically, but with reproduction, distribution, display, and so forth.

Before the development of the web and course management software, faculty members often photocopied handouts and distributed them to the members of a class. The Guidelines on Multiple Copying for Classroom Use (Classroom Guidelines), published in House Report 94-1476, were negotiated guidelines that Congress endorsed in 1976 as a good balance of the interests of publishers and those of educators. They specified which activities and within what limits would constitute fair use for producing handouts of copyrighted works for students in nonprofit educational institutions. One requirement is that the faculty member seek permission when the same item is used as a handout for a second term. In the electronic environment, this means that an article posted for a class on Blackboard (within the limits of the Guidelines) requires permission for use in subsequent class terms, and must be password protected to ensure that it is accessed only by students enrolled in the course.

An excellent alternative is to provide a link to the item on the web or to a licensed resource to which the educational institution subscribes. No permission is needed to link.

• • •

Q225 *Are web links (just the URLs) copyrightable?*

Individual links are not copyrightable. They represent a web address, which is a fact, and facts are not copyrightable according to section 102(b) of the Copyright Act. Compilations of URLs are copyrightable if the compilation is not a total universe of data and there is sufficient originality/creativity in the selection, arrangement, or value adding, such as annotating the URLs.

• • •

Q226 *The library offers e-mail reference service to its patrons. In order to answer the reference question, often it is necessary to send a hyperlink in an e-mail to the user. Is there any problem with* *sending a deep link or must one link only to the website's home page?*

There is no problem with using a deep link to respond to an e-mail reference question. A link is merely a pointer to another website, like a cross-reference. The website owner can control technologically whether someone may enter a site at any location or must register and enter only through the front page, pay a fee, and so forth. Courts have recognized that deep linking is not infringement.

• • •

Q227 *A corporate library is in the process of updating its website and wants to link to different industry resources, associations, and the like. Is permission needed to deep link? Some competitor websites have these links and use the logos from the companies as the link. Is this infringement?*

When the web was new, courts often did not understand linking and some held that a link actually reproduced the work. Over time, this has changed as courts better understood the fact that a link is simply a pointer or cross-reference. Whenever a company or association creates an open website that is neither password protected nor otherwise access controlled, the common understanding is that a link is not a problem. Some scholars call publication on the web an "implied license to link." Thus, no permission to link is required today. On the other hand, in a for-profit company, as a matter of business courtesy, seeking permission to link may be the norm. It clearly is no longer the norm in the nonprofit world.

Using other corporate logos on web pages as the link or next to the link raises trademark law questions and not copyright. The corporate logo is a trademark, and the company whose logo is pasted onto another website may be forced to complain about this activity in order to maintain its rights in that logo as a trademark. Thus, generally one should ask permission to reproduce the logo on the library's web page. There are companies that indicate on their website that anyone who wishes to link to their site should use their logos, but this is on a company-by-company basis. Typically web-based businesses are the ones that want others to use their logos for linking.

• • •

Q228   *A hobby group has a listserv with active discussions. A librarian member of the group located articles that answer some of the questions the group has been discussing. Is it infringement to supply these articles as PDF files to the listserv so that everyone in the group can see them?*

Posting PDFs of articles without permission of the copyright holder is problematic. Attaching a PDF file is a mass reproduction and distribution since anyone who opens the file is considered to have made a copy. If the article is available online from the publisher or legitimately from the author, providing a link to the members of the hobby group by e-mail or otherwise is a good alternative. If the articles come from licensed products, the license agreement determines whether it can be uploaded to a listserv without further royalties.

• • •

Q229   *If a journal wants to publish papers on a journal website that were not accepted to appear in the printed version, what are the copyright concerns it should address for the web publication?*

This can be handled quite simply by revising the copyright transfer form. On that form, the journal should indicate that some papers will appear in print while others will appear only on the journal website. Then on the copyright transfer form, require that the author transfer the reproduction and distribution rights for both printed and electronic versions.

Additional considerations might include what other uses of the article the journal is willing to permit the author. For example, (1) whether the author may post the article on his or her own website; (2) if author website posting is permitted, is there an embargo period before the work can be posted (e.g., six months); (3) whether the author may publish the paper that is published only on the website in another journal, and if yes, whether in a printed journal or in another e-journal; (4) whether the author may reuse the paper as a book chapter; (5) what rights does the author have to reproduce the article in photocopies and distribute to classes; and (6) whether the faculty author may post the article on a password-protected website or in course management software for students. Additionally, does the journal want the author to credit the journal website in any permitted uses? Publishers should be encouraged to grant these rights to their authors.

• • •

Q230   *A school takes the position that fair use does not apply to audio podcasts since they are syndicated and are not confined to the classroom. Is this correct?*

Actually no. A podcast is simply a way to disseminate a speech or a talk. So, it depends on the podcast content and the copyright owner. The owner may be delighted to have the podcast made public to everyone; on the other hand, the owner may restrict access or require anyone who obtains access to agree to the terms of a license. Fair use does apply to podcasts, but if the work is licensed, the license agreement trumps fair use.

• • •

Q231   *In a government research library, the agency routinely purchases translations of foreign language articles. These foreign articles were published in the open literature. The library now wants to digitize the English translation and put the full text version on its local area network. The translation itself is not copyrighted, but would this be an infringement of the original language copyright? Since the English translation is technically speaking a "government work" would this be considered in the public domain?*

Making these translations available on the network equals publication, and the copyright owner's right to prepare derivative works includes making or authorizing translations of their work for publication. Having one copy translated for internal use is not a problem. But this wider distribution on the LAN infringes the exclusive rights of the copyright holder by publishing the article within the agency. Under various treaty obligations, the United States gives foreign works the same protection it provides for works published in this country.

The English translation is not a public domain work because the original work was not a U.S. Government publication. Instead, it is a derivative work that can be published only if authorized by the copyright owner. Making these translations available within the agency requires permission of the copyright holder.

• • •

Q232   *In a corporate information center, most of the research conducted is reactive to staff member requests. All of the information gathered is released to the requestor once the research project has concluded. The information center maintains only a detailed list of citations. If the information located comes from a website, may the information center retain a hard copy of that research material for its files? If so, for how long? The Copyright Clearance Center does not deal with this. How do other corporate information centers handle this?*

Material located on a website is copyrighted just like anything else if it is an original work of authorship. It is automatically fixed by being stored on a website. Maintaining a copy of a work that is ephemeral to provide some evidence that it was searched and used seems very reasonable and likely a fair use. Because of the nature of the web, those pages may disappear and the information center will have nothing to document what it has done. There are no guidelines on how long the center may retain the copy; therefore, retain the copy as long as is reasonable to do so. The Internet Archives (http://archive.org/) is another excellent source for older (mostly noncommercial) web pages.

To obtain information on what other corporate information centers do, the best source is the Special Libraries Association (http://www.

sla.org/), and perhaps listservs for libraries in similar industries. For law firms, the American Association of Law Libraries (http://www. aallnet.org/) is an excellent resource.

• • •

Q233   *The library has been asked to scan the school yearbooks onto a CD-ROM to use in the library and then to publish the year-books from 1920 to the present on the web. Are there copyright problems with doing this?*

If the school owns the copyright, there is no problem at all since it holds the rights to reproduce and distribute the yearbook in any format. Nor is there any difficulty with yearbooks published between 1920 and 1922, since they are in the public domain.

Assume that the yearbook publisher owns the copyright. For year-books published from 1923 forward, several additional facts are required in order to answer the question: (1) Did the yearbooks published prior to 1978 contain a notice of copyright? (2) Did the yearbooks published between 1978 and 1988 contain a notice of copyright, and if not, was an effort made to correct this accidental omission of notice? (3) For the period 1923–1963, was the copyright renewed?

For yearbooks published between 1923 and 1963, notice of copyright on the copies was essential; if published without a notice, they entered the public domain. Assuming there was a copyright notice on the yearbooks published between 1923 and 1963, they passed into the public domain after 28 years if the copyright was not renewed. It is most likely that if they were registered for copyright, they were not renewed, so assume that these are also in the public domain.

Yearbooks published from 1964 to date are unlikely to be in the public domain. Those published between 1964 and 1977 also had to be published with notice in order to be protected by copyright. They did not have to be renewed, however, so they were automatically extended 95 years of protection after first publication since they are works of corporate authorship. Those published between 1978 and 1988 were also required to have a notice of copyright or the owner had to make an effort to correct "accidental omission of notice." Notice became optional in March 1989. If published with notice, yearbooks from 1978 to 1988, along with those to the present, receive 95 years of copyright protection from the date of first publication.

• • •

Q234　*A college library wants to make available to its users a functionality like Amazon's "Search Inside This Book." The librarian's supervisor has said the following, "I cannot imagine that Amazon is calling tens of thousands of publishers to get permission to be able to offer a "search inside" functionality. Since Amazon probably is using the fair use doctrine, could the library not claim fair use and download Amazon's scans?" How does Amazon get permission to use covers, contents, and chapters from publishers without contacting thousands and requesting permission? Would a library need something in writing from Amazon to download its scans?*

Amazon is selling books, and many publishers may not object to the "search inside" feature because it benefits the publishers and stimulates book sales. Others have objected, however. Many publishers view libraries as interfering with book sales, so clearly they are not likely to permit libraries to do this without seeking permission directly from the publisher. Amazon probably has permission for this feature, but whether it does or not, libraries are not in the same position as a bookseller.

• • •

Q235　*When a library creates a website, is the HTML code protected by copyright? There appears to be some disagreement among the experts on this matter.*

No, the code is not protected. The underlying work is what is protected—for example, the literary work, musical work, audiovisual work, and so forth—but not the HTML code. Section 102(a) of the Copyright Act details the eight categories of works that may be protected by copyright; while it is possible that other types of works might also be protected, a judgment would be made based on the originality/creativity requirement of the Copyright Act. Although HTML code is very useful, the code underlying a web page is not copyrightable, although the page itself is as an audiovisual work if it meets the requirements of originality/creativity.

• • •

Q236   *If a library has scanned various photographs, local documents, newspaper articles, and the like, and has created a searchable local history database, should the library use any disclaimer about copyright?*

Although there is no legal responsibility to do so, many libraries use disclaimers on such databases. The following are appropriate items to include on a copyright page for the database: (1) The materials included in this local history database may be protected by copyright. (2) The library has done its best to identify copyright owners and to seek permission to scan and post this material. (3) When it was not possible to locate the owner, the library decided to include the material, but it asks copyright holders to come forward so that they can be credited for the work. (4) The library will then seek their permission to continue to post the material.

The disclaimer provides a statement to indicate that the library has not ignored copyright concerns and has done its best to locate copyright owners and seek permission to scan and post their works.

CHAPTER 10

Interlibrary Loan and Document Delivery

Libraries have long participated in interlibrary loan (ILL) activities. Traditionally, lending activities consisted of a borrowing library receiving a request from a user for a volume (usually a monograph or treatise) that the borrowing library did not have in its collection. Libraries developed systems to facilitate the search of holdings records across libraries that so a borrowing library could request the loan of a title from another library that owned a copy of the work. The lending library would then agree to provide the requested volume and mailed it to the borrowing library on the condition that the borrowing library would be responsible for ensuring that the volume was returned within the loan period. These activities did not implicate copyright because there was no reproduction. Though cumbersome, the system worked well and continues to be used to supply volumes for ILL. The primary borrowers were faculty and researchers, and the huge majority of lending libraries were in academic institutions, although some public and corporate libraries also participated in ILL activities.

With the development of the photocopier, it became possible to reproduce book chapters and journal articles to satisfy ILL requests. While books continued to be sent through the mail for ILL, few libraries were willing to lend journal volumes. When a user needed only one article from a journal or one chapter from a book, lending a photocopy became standard practice. The photocopy was mailed, and in later years faxed, to the borrowing library.

Section 108(g)(2) of the Copyright Act states that nothing prevents a library or archive from participating in interlibrary arrangements that do not have as their purpose or effect receiving copies in such aggregate quantities as to substitute for a subscription to or purchase of a work. As Congress debated the Copyright Act of 1976, it became clear that section 108 needed more specificity about ILL, and so Congress appointed the National Commission on New Technological Uses of Copyrighted Works (CONTU) and asked it to develop guidelines for ILL.[1] CONTU produced and published the ILL Guidelines.[2] The Guidelines state that each year a borrowing library may request five items from a journal title going back over the most recent 60 months of the journal. For books, the borrowing library may make five requests per year, each year, for the life of the copyright. The borrowing library must retain ILL borrowing records for three calendar years. The Guidelines suggestion of five is just that, and occasionally, a library may exceed that number and still conform to the spirit of the Guidelines. The borrowing library is also responsible for staying within the section 108(d) limits on one article per journal copy per user and to provide the copyright warnings to the user.

In addition to the CONTU ILL Guidelines, libraries also follow the strictures of the Interlibrary Loan Code.[3] The Code regulates the exchange of materials between libraries in the United States; it details the responsibilities of both borrowing and lending libraries and enjoys wide acceptance in the library community.

As with many other library processes, ILL has become digital, and it uses electronic means to identify lending libraries that might supply the needed item, to forward the request, and even to provide the copy. Many lending libraries now send a digital copy to the borrowing library for the user. Borrowing libraries may post the article on a password-protected website for retrieval so that only the borrower who made the request may access it.

---

1   The other task was to decide what to do about computer programs.
2   H.R. Rep. No. 94-1733 (1976).
3   American Library Association, *The Interlibrary Loan Code for the United States*, rev'd 2008, http://www.ala.org/rusa/resources/guidelines/interlibrary.

Document delivery, as contrasted with ILL, involves providing copies to users, typically for a fee. Document delivery services may be commercial or nonprofit. If a nonprofit library charges for document delivery, the charge must be no more than cost recovery or the library must pay royalties for the copies, as do commercial document delivery services.

Questions in this chapter cover using licensed databases to fill ILL requests, putting the burden for any royalty payments due on the requesting entity, and recordkeeping for ILL, as well as the responsibilities of both borrowing and lending libraries.

• • •

Q237 *Are there different rules that apply for interlibrary loan copying?*

Yes, although these are not truly rules but are in the nature of guidelines or suggestions. In 1976 Congress appointed the National Commission on New Technological Uses of Copyrighted Works (CONTU) and asked it to prepare guidelines for library reproduction for interlibrary loan (ILL). The resulting CONTU ILL Guidelines were published as a Conference Report in House Report 94-1733. Under these Guidelines, each calendar year a library may request only five items from a journal title going back over the most recent 60 months of that journal. The borrowing library must maintain records of the number of times it borrows from each journal title, covering the most recent 60 months for each. These records must be retained for three calendar years.

When the library makes the sixth request from that title, it should then seek permission, pay royalties to the publisher, purchase the article from an authorized document delivery service, or pay royalties to the Copyright Clearance Center.

• • •

Q238 *An interlibrary loan librarian in an academic library has received requests to photocopy a chapter instead of sending the book. If it is just a chapter from a book that the library owns, does* *the library own the copyright? Must the library pay copyright fees in order to supply the requested copy?*

The library does not own the copyright just because it purchased a copy of the book; the author or publisher owns the copyright. Section 108(d) of the Copyright Act permits libraries to make single copies of articles, book chapters, and the like, at the request of a user if (1) the copy becomes the property of the user and (2) the library displays prominently a copyright warning where the orders are placed and on the order form. Even if the library must borrow copies of items requested by users from another library via ILL, it should still follow the sections 108(d) and (e) requirements.

Further, libraries may provide reproductions of the materials mentioned in sections 108(d) and (e) to borrowing libraries through ILL if the borrowing library makes the appropriate CONTU ILL Guidelines certifications. So, under these conditions, there is no problem with reproducing book chapters for ILL.

• • •

Q239   *A faculty member has requested seven articles from volume 5, number 1, of a journal published in 2010, which constitutes the entire issue. The library has a current subscription to the journal, but it does not begin until volume 5, number 2. The library has tried to purchase the issue, but it is not available. May the library request the issue from another library and reproduce it or is the library restricted to one article from the issue as permitted under the Interlibrary Loan Guidelines? Could the library request all seven articles from different lenders and pay royalties on two articles that would exceed the ILL suggestion of five?*

Unfortunately, this is not a replacement issue since the library never had volume 5, number 1, in its collection. Therefore, section 108(c) of the Copyright Act does not apply and give the library permission to copy the entire issue and add it to its collection.

The CONTU ILL Guidelines permit a library to request five items from the journal title during a calendar year, but section 108(d) still applies to the requests from an individual user. Since the library does have a current subscription to the journal it may request the items for the user, subject to the section 108(d) limitation—one copy of a single article from a periodical issue. The ILL Guidelines say that the library does not count in its suggestion of five any item for which the requesting entity has "in force or shall have entered an order for a subscription to a periodical." So, royalties would be due for all but one of the articles requested through ILL under section 108(2) due to the limitation of one article per issue for a user without payment of royalties.

Another possibility is to use section 108(e), which permits libraries to reproduce a larger portion or even an entire work for a user. The copy would go to the user and the library still could not add a copy to its collection. The library would first have to try to buy the issue at a fair price for the faculty member to use, which the library has already done. The ILL Guidelines still apply, and royalties would be due for all but five articles in the issue under section 108(e) and the ILL Guidelines.

• • •

Q240 *A patron requested an interlibrary loan of a 124-page article published in an e-journal that is on the web. The patron could not download or read the article in the 30-minute time limit that the library imposes on patrons using library computers. The library printed the first 20 pages for free and the patron paid for copying the remaining pages. Did the library violate the copyright law?*

No, it did not. In fact, the library could have printed the entire 124 pages for the patron had it chosen to do so. Under section 108(d) of the Copyright Act, libraries are permitted to reproduce a single copy of an article from a periodical issue for a patron. If that article is available on the web with no license agreement, then printing or downloading that article for the patron is the same as reproducing from a printed journal, and is no problem. Whether the library charges the patron for the cost of printing or photocopying is up the individual library and has nothing to do with copyright. This assumes, however, that the fee represents cost recovery only.

Q241   *The libraries in X Corporation want to harmonize the way they maintain interlibrary loan records. Corporate counsel has advised that only loans between the corporation and outside libraries are defined as interlibrary loans. Further, librarians have been told that it is not necessary to keep records of photocopies obtained from any of the thirteen libraries that make up the corporation as these are covered by its Copyright Clearance Center license agreement. The same instruction was provided as to not keeping any records of photocopies obtained from an outside, for-profit photocopy vendor. Complicating this issue is the fact that some of these libraries work with vendors that send itemize bills showing separate copyright payments, while other libraries work with a vendor that has sent a letter saying that it will pay the royalties to the CCC. So, is it necessary to keep interlibrary loan records?*

Corporate counsel is correct. The only records that must be maintained are those for ILL for which none of the X Corporation libraries pays royalties, that is, from libraries external to X Corporation libraries, that is, true interlibrary lending. If the copies come from a vendor that pays the royalties, no records are necessary. This activity is document delivery and not ILL, and royalties are paid. Only authorized document delivery services that pay the royalties for the copies should be used or the corporation will need to pay for those copies directly to the publisher or through the CCC.

If one of the libraries obtains a photocopy from a university library, then that is an ILL. If the corporation pays royalties for all ILL also, then no records are required, but libraries may want to do so to provide documentation of that compliance, but it is a corporate decision. As legal counsel suggests, providing reproductions to other libraries within the corporation is not ILL. In fact, these are "intra" library or "intra" corporation loans, and sections 108(d) and (e) of the Copyright Act apply, not the ILL Guidelines.

• • •

Q242   *When filling an interlibrary loan request, what information regarding copyright does the lending library need to include?*

Under section 108(a) of the Copyright Act, every copy reproduced, under any of the subsections, must include the notice of copyright contained on the work as detailed in section 108(a)(3), including ILL copies. This provision was amended by the Digital Millennium Copyright Act in 1998 to add language about what a library does when the work being reproduced does not contain the notice of copyright. Then the library may substitute a legend stating that making a copy may be subject to the copyright law. So, lending libraries must include notice on the copies they provide.

• • •

Q243   *How can the provider of full-text articles in a database restrict delivery of articles from that database via interlibrary loan? Is there a difference between electronic delivery versus printing and manual delivery?*

Most databases are not only copyrighted, but they are also governed by license agreements. Section 108(f)(4) of the Copyright Act states that libraries are bound by license agreements they sign; in other words, license agreements trump the section 108 library exceptions. So, a license agreement certainly may restrict the use of those articles to a particular organization or institution and may absolutely prohibit their use for ILL outside the organization. Librarians should read the license agreement to determine whether or not articles included in the licensed database may be used to satisfy ILL requests.

There is no difference among types of delivery of articles via interlibrary loan. The issue is whether the library complies with the CONTU Guidelines and abides by all license agreements for obtaining access to and use of articles from databases.

• • •

Q244   *A library has a current subscription to a journal but does not have the 1953 volume. The library has received four interlibrary loan requests for the same article from the 1953 volume within the* *past year. Should the library refuse the sixth request or look into purchasing the volume?*

The CONTU Interlibrary Loan Guidelines apply only to the most recent 60 months of a journal title; thus, the suggestion of five is inapplicable to requests for a 1953 volume. Actually, this volume may no longer be protected by copyright. It would have received 28 years of protection, but in 1981, the copyright would have had to be renewed. If it was so renewed, the volume is protected until 2048. If not renewed, then the volume is in the public domain and may be freely copied, and no recordkeeping is required. On the other hand, four requests within a calendar year for a particular article from this volume points to the conclusion that the library may wish to acquire the volume unless this level of requests appears to be a one-time anomaly. Another alternative is to seek permission and pay royalties for those articles.

· · ·

Q245 *A public library has an interlibrary loan request for a dissertation from the University of Wisconsin. A librarian found a PDF copy of the 26-page dissertation on WorldCat, which the library accesses through a license. May the library print the dissertation for the patron and charge him the library's standard printing charge of ten cents per page?*

Under section 108(e) of the Copyright Act, a library is permitted to make a copy of an entire work for user if it first makes a reasonable investigation to determine that a copy cannot be acquired at a fair price and (1) the copy becomes the property of the user, (2) the library has no notice that the copy will be used for other than fair use purposes, and (3) the library gives the user the prescribed copyright warning. All of this also applies even if the library has to obtain the copy of the work for the user via ILL.

In the described situation, however, there is another solution that avoids all of this, and that is to provide the link to the user and let him print it for himself.

Q246   *Is it necessary to maintain a paper record of interlibrary loan borrower requests that are submitted by patrons, or is an electronic record of the past three years' requests sufficient?*

Records in any form are sufficient. The CONTU Interlibrary Loan Guidelines simply say that the borrowing library must retain records for three calendar years. Certainly the intent of the Guidelines is that the library be able to search the records by title in order to determine when the library has reached its "suggestion of five" for that journal title for the calendar year. The Guidelines, however, are silent as to the format in which records must be retained; thus any format is permissible.

• • •

Q247   *When an academic library obtains a copy of an article for a user through interlibrary loan, may it place an electronic copy of the article on a password-protected website for the user to retrieve rather than placing a photocopy of the article in the campus mail or e-mailing it to the user? If so, how long may the library leave it on the website for retrieval?*

Many libraries have adopted this practice, even though the current section 108 of the Copyright Act does not envision such activity since the statute was adopted for a print and analog world. On the other hand, if only a single user can retrieve the article, one could argue that it is the equivalent of delivering one photocopy of the article to the user.

Articles should remain available on a website for only a limited time, such as one to three weeks. The user should be alerted that the article is available on the website with a single-user password and that it will remain available only for a limited period. After that time, the article should be deleted, even if the user has not yet retrieved it.

• • •

Q248   *When a library receives a copy of an article from a document delivery company through ARIEL in response to an interlibrary* *loan request, how long can the library keep or archive this article? Can it be reused to satisfy another request for the same article by another patron?*

This question mixes language somewhat. If the article is obtained from a document delivery company, it is not an interlibrary loan (ILL). Instead, it is document delivery, which does not have to satisfy the CONTU ILL Guidelines. If the copy of the article was obtained from such a company, that means that royalties were paid for the copy. In this instance, because royalties were paid, the library may reuse the copy. After the patron for whom the copy was purchased uses it, the patron can return it to the library, where it may be archived. The only restriction on the use of that copy is that it can be reproduced only if that reproduction is a fair use. Having determined that it should obtain the copy of the article from a document delivery company as opposed to a library under ILL, the requesting library may have made the decision that the use is not a fair use. If additional copies of the article are made, additional royalties are due since the library has paid only for one copy.

If the article is obtained from another library as an ILL, then royalties may not be due if the request is within the suggestion of five. The ILL Guidelines, however, place more restrictions on what may be done with a copy of an article so obtained. For example, the copy must become the property of the user. Thus, the library may not archive the article at all.

• • •

Q249 *In a nonprofit research institute, can a researcher send a PDF of an article that the institute purchased to multiple collaborators on a project? It is to support the work on a project.*

This question seems to indicate that the copy of the article was obtained from a document delivery service and that royalties were paid. But, royalties were paid for only one copy. If multiple collaborators share a printed copy of an article by passing it around, there is no problem because the article is not reproduced. If a PDF file is sent to multiple users, the law treats it as if a copy was made for each researcher. Royalties should be paid for each of those copies.

• • •

Q250 *An academic library maintains the following information for each interlibrary loan: publication title, citation, date ordered, name of the librarian who ordered it, and name of the patron who wanted the material. Is it permissible to strip the identifying patron name from the records to be more compliant with patron privacy and still conform to the law?*

It is true that borrowing libraries are required to retain interlibrary loan (ILL) records for three calendar years in order to comply with the CONTU ILL Guidelines. The Guidelines do not speak to the format in which the records must be maintained. Clearly, to determine whether a library has reached the suggestion of five, records must be searchable by journal title.

The issue of patron privacy is not contrary to the requirements of ILL recordkeeping requirements. There is no reason for the patron's name to be included in the records, and most libraries do not retain patron identification data in the ILL records.

• • •

Q251 *A librarian in a for-profit educational institution asks about interlibrary loan and making copies for "the customer." The lending library sent an electronic copy, which the borrowing library then printed for its patron. (1) How does section 108(d) of the Copyright Act, which allows libraries to make single copies of articles for users, affect license agreements? (2) Could the article be forwarded to the patron in electronic format and still comply with the copyright law? (3) Does it matter if the article requested through ILL was published more than five years ago?*

Assume that the library satisfies the section 108(a) requirements.

(1) When a patron requests an article that the library does not own, the first question is whether the for-profit library qualifies for the section 108 exceptions. This matter has never been litigated, but most librarians believe that even for-profit college libraries may take advantage of the CONTU Interlibrary Loan (ILL) Guidelines.

(2) The Copyright Act is silent on providing electronic copies via ILL, but many libraries certainly offer this. Whether the lending library itself scanned the article or whether the electronic copy came from a licensed product is important, however. If the latter, then the terms of the lending library's license agreement applies as to whether sending an electronic copy to satisfy an ILL request is permitted. Assume that the lending library's license agreement allowed use of the database to satisfy ILL requests and also permitted the library to send electronic copies to borrowing libraries for ILL. Then the borrowing library should be able to provide the electronic copy directly to the patron. If the lending library scanned the article itself, it may or may not be fair use. The ILL Guidelines do not deal with digital copying. Again, many libraries do it anyway. But the issue is less clear than under a license agreement.

(3) If the request is for an older article, then the ILL Guidelines do not apply because only the last five years of a journal title are governed by the Guidelines. Thus, there is no five-copy restriction per journal title each year and no recordkeeping requirement

Borrowing libraries that receive electronic copies from lending libraries typically deliver those to the user either as an e-mail attachment or by placing them on a password-protected website, and only that user has the password to retrieve that particular item. The library then should delete the item from the website within a limited time.

• • •

Q252 *Should a public library include a copyright notice on all copies of articles it provides to satisfy interlibrary loan requests?*

Yes. Section 108(a) of the Copyright Act says that, in order to qualify for the exceptions provided in all of section 108, one of the requirements is to include a notice of copyright on copies made. If the library has licensed journal databases, then the license dictates (1) whether the library may use an article from the database to satisfy an ILL request and (2) whether the library must include a notice of copyright on copies it provides for ILL. Typically, the copyright notice appears automatically on copies from licensed databases, however.

• • •

Q253 *A university library has provided interlibrary loan (ILL) services to a small nonprofit institution and has done so since 2002 through a contract. The smaller school has its own library staffed by a librarian and one other staff member. The contract requires that the university library provide ILL services directly to students at the smaller institution, presumably based on an annual payment. How does this contract affect the ILL Guidelines and the suggestion of five? Must either the university library or the smaller college library pay royalties on copies provided?*

The contract to provide ILL services does not change any responsibilities under the Copyright Act or under the CONTU ILL Guidelines. The Guidelines apply, and either the university, as the lending library, or the smaller institution, as the borrowing library, must maintain the ILL records and follow the suggestion of five. Typically, the borrowing library would do this. Under the contract, however, the university library may have assumed the recordkeeping function for the smaller school. The university library may have contracted to charge a higher fee for services, keep the records of these transactions for the borrowing library, and pay the royalties for copies beyond those that are fair use. Or, it may put the responsibility on the borrowing library. One or the other must do it, though.

• • •

Q254 *In keeping with the copyright law, an academic library gets an interlibrary loan request to copy more than one article from the same journal issue. It copies only one article and sends the other requests back unfilled, explaining the copyright law to the borrow-*

ing library. A borrowing library insists this is incorrect and that if it (the requesting library) is paying copyright royalties, then the lending library should copy for them whatever they ask. Which library is correct?

The borrowing library is correct in this instance. Section 108 of the Copyright Act is written so that a library does not have to pay royalties. If interlibrary loan (ILL) copying goes beyond the CONTU ILL Guidelines, then the library should seek permission and pay royalties, if requested. Here, the borrowing library is paying royalties, so the library is not limited to the section 108(d) one article per user per issue restriction. Moreover, the one article restriction applies to an individual user, not a library borrowing for users. In fact, the library may have multiple requests from the same journal title from different users, which results in the request for more than one article from a periodical issue. It is the borrowing library that is responsible for enforcing the one article per issue for a user, or for paying royalties in order to provide more than one article per issue to a single user. The suggestion of five from the CONTU ILL Guidelines applies only to the borrowing library.

• • •

Q255   *One of the library's requests for an interlibrary loan photocopy of a 1999 article was referred on to an association library. That library refused to copy the article, saying that it would violate copyright. A librarian at the association explained that it refused to copy more than one article from the same journal title if the requesting library has made previous requests from that journal in the past five years. Is this not a misinterpretation of the CONTU Interlibrary Loan Guidelines?*

The association has it wrong, and it appears to be confusing section 108(d) of the Copyright Act with the CONTU ILL Guidelines. Section 108(d) deals with the borrowing library in the ILL situation; it states that the local library cannot copy for a user (meaning an individual, not a library) more than one article from a journal issue without paying royalties.

For ILL, a library may borrow five articles a year from the journal title. The requests can even be for the same article five times, for five separate users, but section 108(d) still applies to the ILL request from a particular user. The lender does not need to maintain records; however, the borrowing library does. It is the responsibility of the borrowing library to conform to the Guidelines. All the lender need do is to require that the borrower certify that it is conforming to the ILL Guidelines or that the request is a fair use, a replacement copy, or the like.

In fact, the borrowing library may even borrow more than the five articles from a journal title within the calendar year as long as it seeks permission or pays royalties. As described earlier, the borrowing library may not even be in this situation since the lending library apparently is misapplying the ILL Guidelines concerning five requests from a title within a calendar year over the most recent five years of the journal.

• • •

Q256 *A library does not subscribe to a particular journal in either paper or electronic format. It used its "suggestion of five" from the CONTU Guidelines for calendar year 2011. The serial title is listed in the Copyright Clearance Center (CCC) with a royalty of $25 per article plus $2.25 per page. The library has recently discovered that the journal is freely available on the web back to 2003. Does it need to pay copyright royalties for interlibrary loan copies under the CONTU Guidelines or may it use the article from the web to satisfy patron requests?*

There is no reason to request the article through interlibrary loan if the free web copy was placed online by the copyright owner or with the owner's permission. If the issues were put on the web by someone else, then these are infringing copies should not be used.

• • •

Q257 *The library recently acquired some additional volumes of a journal to which it no longer subscribes. These volumes cover years missing from the library's holdings of this title and were obtained from a* *library that has merged with another library, meaning that at the time that they were acquired, a valid subscription was maintained. May the acquiring library use the donated volumes for interlibrary loan?*

Yes. The first sale doctrine found in section 109(a) of the Copyright Act permits libraries to use gift volumes that were originally acquired by a library at the institutional subscription rate (if that rate is different than the subscription rate for an individual). The library may add the gifts to its collection and use them as if they were purchased volumes. This would include using them to fill interlibrary loan requests.

• • •

Q258   *If a library is the only one in the region that has a license for a full-text journal, what is the library's responsibility to fill interlibrary loan requests from that journal by making a copy for requesting libraries?*

Under copyright, a library has no responsibility to fill an interlibrary loan (ILL) request at all. There may be other interlibrary agreements that require libraries to respond to ILL requests generally, but online journals are governed by license agreements that may restrict a library's ability to lend copies of articles from that journal to other libraries. Section 108(f)(4) of the Copyright Act states that nothing affects license agreements to which the library agreed when it acquired access to a work in its collection. Thus, license agreements trump copyrights. Some vendors will permit ILL from their online journals while some exclude it. Other vendors allow limited ILL but may require the lending library to maintain records of how often it lends from the title rather than the borrowing library as the ILL guidelines dictate. The license agreement controls and supersedes any ILL agreements among libraries.

• • •

Q259   *An institution has an online subscription to a journal but not to the print version, and there is a 12-month embargo before is-*

sues appear in the online product. For interlibrary loan purposes, does the library "own" those issues that have not yet appeared online, or must it pay royalties for articles acquired via interlibrary loan from that journal during the embargo period?

The CONTU Interlibrary Loan (ILL) Guidelines were written in 1976 and naturally did not envision this situation. ILL assumes that the borrowing library is obtaining materials that will be lent (they are original volumes) or given to the patron if the copies are photocopies or other reproductions of the copyrighted works. The Guidelines indicate that if the library has the title on order or owns the work but it is missing from the collection, an ILL request need not be counted in the suggestion of five and would not generate the need to pay royalties. In this situation, however, the library neither owns the work nor has a subscription to it; instead, the subscription is for 12 months hence and not for the current material. Therefore, the library must count ILL requests for articles in the embargoed issues within its suggestion of five and pay royalties when it exceeds the suggestion of five.

• • •

Q260 *In a law firm, the medical malpractice group relies upon medical articles from experts and asks the library to provide copies. The library orders articles from a document supplier that pays copyright royalties and charges them to the firm as a part of its fee. Sometimes, an article ordered for one case might also be useful in another pending case. The lawyers and nurses who work with the articles would like to keep the original in the first case file, and make another copy for the second case file. May a second copy be made for a new specific case? Or does the library need to request a new copy each time one is needed?*

When a library obtains a copy of an article from a document delivery service and pays the royalties for that copy, the library may use that copy for multiple purposes such as for multiple pending cases. Use and reproduction are not the same thing, however. Reproducing that article for another case file means that additional royalties should be paid for the second copy since the firm lawfully acquired only one copy of the article and paid royalties for that copy. Multiple reading and multiple copying are two different things.

• • •

Q261   *More and more frequently the library is being asked to reproduce a whole journal for document delivery. Is there any reason not to do this?*

There certainly are reasons not to reproduce entire journal issues for document delivery. The first question is what is meant by "document delivery." Does this mean delivery of copies to primary patrons who are part of the same organization? If the journal issue is a printed journal, and the library does not have a Copyright Clearance Center Annual Copyright License, then the library may reproduce only one article from the journal issue to deliver to a patron under section 108(d) of the Copyright Act, unless it pays royalties for all articles except one in the issue. If the journal subscription is electronic, the license agreement prevails and controls whether copying entire issues for persons covered under the agreement is permitted under the license.

If, on the other hand, document delivery means supplying copies to an outside entity that pays royalties for the reproductions, then there is no problem. If document delivery means interlibrary loan, then the CONTU Interlibrary Loan Guidelines apply.

• • •

Q262   *The staff in a health sciences library regularly supplies copies of articles from journals in its collection to unaffiliated customers for a fee. These customers include lawyers, researchers, and community health professionals. The library also fills requests from members of the general public for copies of library documents that are listed in a locally produced health bibliographic database. The library is considering charging a fee for copies of these documents that are not available online. (1) Do these activities make the library a commercial document delivery service? (2) Does it have to pay roy-*

alties anyway? (3) Is there a standard cost recovery formula? (4) If so, does it make any difference that publishers can now provide the same service to users for a fee?

(1) The real question is whether the fee that the library charges is cost recovery only or whether the library makes a profit by providing these copies. If the fee is cost recovery only for the service (e.g., personnel costs, mailing, and copy costs, but not cost of the collections), then the library is not a commercial service.

(2) If that fee is greater than the cost to provide the service, then it is for profit. In that situation, the library is a for-profit center and must pay royalties for providing all of these copies. If the library's document delivery is not for profit, and the library is not paying royalties, it may want to stamp the copies it provides to indicate that if royalties are due, the recipient of the copies is responsible for them. Often users assume that the service fee covers the royalties, so it is good to clarify that the service fee does not include the royalties.

(3) There is no known standard cost recovery formula. The library may charge whatever fee it wants for the service. For example, if the library wants to discourage the request for copies, it may charge a fairly high fee, which may result in the library having to pay royalties.

(4) The fact that publishers can provide the same service and copies is irrelevant. Publishers are concerned that commercial document delivery services (ones that make a profit) actually pay royalties, of course.

CHAPTER 11

Preservation and Archiving

L ibraries and archives have long been involved in preserving materials in their collections. Historically, this involved preserving the artifact, that is, the book volume, the periodical issue, the newspaper, or handwritten letters and manuscripts. Institutions conserved books by treating the bindings and pages of books. They created climate-controlled facilities aimed at stopping deterioration. They also microfilmed back runs of journals and newspapers, both to facilitate use and, primarily, to preserve them. Then, in the 1980s and 1990s, as computer technology was developing, it became clear that many nineteenth century works had been printed on acidic paper and these "brittle books" threatened to decimate library collections because of rapid deterioration. Not only were library collections threatened but also the country's literary history.

While preservation of original artifacts continues, it is now possible to digitize these works in order to preserve the content. Further, digitization presents new and better ways to search these titles. Many of these works are in the public domain due to their age, and therefore there are no copyright barriers to digitizing to preserve them.

The Copyright Act of 1976 recognized libraries' need to preserve unpublished works and to replace works that had disappeared from collections. Section 108(b) applies to unpublished works in a library's collection and 108(c) to replacement of lost, damaged, deteriorating, stolen, and obsolete works. The section 108(i) exclusions do not apply to preservation and replacement, so audiovisual works, sound recordings, and such may be duplicated for preservation and replacement. In 1998, these two sections were amended by the Digital Millennium Copyright Act (DMCA).[1]

Section 108(b) permits libraries and archives to reproduce unpublished works for "preservation, security or deposit for research in another library." This section may be used either to photocopy or digitize original letters and manuscripts to prevent handling fragile works. In fact, the library may make up to three copies of these works, one of which may be digital. But the digital copy may not be used outside the premises of the library. Libraries may also replace works in their collection under section 108(c) if those works have been damaged, deteriorating, lost, stolen or obsolete, but only after the library makes a reasonable effort to obtain an unused copy of the work at a fair price. The statute defines "obsolete" as a work for which the equipment to see or hear the work is no longer reasonably available in the commercial marketplace. For replacement purposes, a library may make up to three copies of a work including a digital copy. The same premises restriction also applies to the digital replacement copies.

Section 108(h) contains an additional preservation section, which is broader than just preservation. Added in 1998 by the Copyright Term Extension Act,[2] section 108(h) applies only to works in their last 20 years of the copyright term. The section applies not only to libraries and archives but also to nonprofit educational institutions. They may reproduce, display or perform these works by print, analog or digital means for purposes such as preservation, scholarship or research. However, a library that seeks to take advantage of this statute must ascertain that the work is no longer subject to normal commercial exploitation, that a copy is not available at a reasonable price or have notice from the copyright holder that either of these conditions exists.

The questions in this chapter center on making preserved copies available to users, the meaning of particular language in deeds of gift, archiving e-mail, and digitally archiving faculty publications.

---

1   Digital Millennium Copyright Act, Pub. L. No. 105–304, 112 Stat. 2860 (Oct. 28, 1998).

2   Copyright Term Extension Act, Pub. L. No. 105–298, 112 Stat. 2827 (Oct. 27, 1998).

Q263   *Under section 108(c) a library is permitted to reproduce a lost, damaged, stolen or deteriorating work in its collection after it makes a reasonable effort to find an unused copy at a fair price. What is a "reasonable effort" and a "fair price"?*

While none of the statutory language defines these terms, there is a definition of "reasonable effort" in the legislative history. House Report 94-1476, which accompanied the 1976 Act, says this about reasonable investigation specifically in relation to section 108(c):

> The scope and nature of a reasonable investigation to determine that an unused replacement cannot be obtained will vary according to the circumstances of a particular situation. It will always require recourse to commonly-known trade sources in the United States, and in the normal situation also to the publisher or other copyright owner (if such owner can be located using the address listed in the copyright registration), or an authorized reproducing service.

While this definition is not particularly helpful, it does provide some guidance. It really means that a library should do the normal things it does to replace an entire volume and to exercise independent judgment about what constitutes a reasonable investigation for the particular type of work involved.

There are two published definitions of "fair price" related to this issue. Both give some guidance, one from the viewpoint of the copyright holder and the other from the users of copyrighted works. The first comes from a booklet published by the Association of American Publishers in 1978 dealing with nonprofit library use. It states that the fair price of a work is: (a) the suggested retail price if available from the publisher; (b) if not so available, the prevailing retail price or (c) if an authorized reproducing service is used, the normal price charged by that service. A 1995 American Library Association publication, *The Copyright Primer for Librarians and Educators* (Janis H. Bruwelheid, 2d ed., p. 27) defines fair price as:

> The fair price of a reproduction is the price as close as possible to manufacturing costs plus royalty payments. . . . If the original format was multivolume and single volumes are not

available, it could be argued that the full set price is not a fair price for a single volume.

• • •

Q264 *Both sections 108(c) and (e) require a library to make a reasonable effort to acquire an unused copy of a work at a "fair price." But section 108(h) specifies a "reasonable price." What is the difference?*

There appears to be no functional difference. Section 108(h) was a 1998 amendment to the statute and it uses "reasonable price." Maybe it was sloppy legislative drafting. There is nothing in the legislative history to account for the difference, and there has been no litigation to provide guidance.

• • •

Q265 *A book is no longer in print, unavailable from used book sellers and unobtainable from the book's author. Further, the book was previously owned by the library but it has been withdrawn from the collection. Under these circumstances, is the library allowed to photocopy the book after borrowing it from another library?*

In fact, there is no requirement even to look for a used book. Under section 108(c), a library may reproduce a lost, damaged, stolen, deteriorating or obsolete copy of a work after it makes a reasonable effort to obtain an *unused* copy at a fair price. Since the library once owned the title, it may borrow it from another library and reproduce it to replace the copy it no longer has.

• • •

Q266 *May a library make backup copies of audiovisual works and CD-ROMs in order to preserve them? They are easily damaged, quickly out of print and replacing them often is impossible.*

While the practice of making backup copies makes absolute sense to a librarian, the Copyright Act does not permit it except in very narrow circumstances. For CD-ROMs one must look at the underlying work that is on the CD. If the CD-ROM contains a computer program, section 117 allows the owner of a copy of a computer program to make a backup copy. Unfortunately, this permission does not exist for audiovisual works or music.

The only other instance in which a library may make a copy of a published audiovisual work is under section 108(c) to replace a lost, damaged, deteriorating, stolen or obsolete copy. This is after the work has become damaged or lost, not before. An obsolete copy is defined in the statute as one for which the equipment to see or hear the work is no longer reasonably available in the commercial marketplace. Even then, the library must first try to purchase an unused replacement copy at a fair price before it can duplicate the work. So, the answer is no, without permission of the copyright holder.

• • •

Q267 *Now that the library is receiving many CDs that accompany books, is there a problem with making backup copies to keep in technical services for replacement should the originals disappear from the back of the books? The practice has been to make copies of disks that accompany books, place the copies with the books and keep the original disks as archival copies. Since these copies are not for general distribution, but rather as a safeguard in case of loss, is this fair use?*

Although some libraries have routinely made backup copies of many types of nonprint works, the statute is clear. One may make a backup copy only of computer programs without permission from the copyright holder under section 117 of the Copyright Act. There is no provision for backup copies of other types of works. So, if these CDs contain software, then a backup copy is permissible. Fair use is unlikely to apply since the practice involves duplicating an entire work and copyright holders will gladly sell the library two copies so one can be used as a backup copy in case of accidental damage or loss to the other copy.

A library certainly could seek permission for duplicating other CDs as a way to guard against accidental loss or destruction, but such permission is unlikely to be granted without a fee.

• • •

Q268   *A music library is evaluating the feasibility of a CD preservation program and is considering the following to preserve its existing collection of CDs proactively but is concerned about whether these actions infringes copyright. (1) Create a single duplicate copy of CD holdings and store these copies in a secure dark archive. (2) Continue to circulate the originals as normal, but if an original becomes lost or damaged beyond usability, first conduct a search to see if a replacement copy can be found in print or otherwise available on the market at fair market value. (3) If no such replacement can be found, create a new copy from the duplicate in the dark archive and use that for future circulation.*

To some extent, the answer depends on whether these are purchased music recordings on CD. Assume first that they are. While the plan makes sense as a preservation matter, some of the actions do infringe the copyright.

(1) The only backup copies for libraries that are permitted are under section 108(b), and that is limited to unpublished works. CDs, and music CDs in particular, typically are published. Reproducing these CDs to create backup copies without permission is infringement. What the library can do is to purchase two copies of each CD and place one in a dark archive.

(2) This follows the requirements of section 108(c) for replacement copies and would comply with copyright requirements.

(3) If no replacement copy can be found at a fair price, then the library is permitted to make a replacement copy which could be made from the purchased CD in the dark archives. Even if the Copyright Act were amended to facilitate further library preservation, it likely would permit copying for preservation only if the work were at immediate risk of loss or destruction. Purchased recordings on CD are not considered to be so fragile. If the CDs are recordings of student perfor-

mances of musical works, the guidelines on the Educational Use of
Music permit schools to make a single copy of the recording for critique and to retain it.

• • •

Q269 *An instructor has an old 16mm film published by Southern
Bell Telephone and Telegraph Company. He wants to put it on videotape or DVD to use for his class, and to preserve it. Is this infringement? Should he contact the AT&T archives?*

According to the Copyright Act, only a library or archives may convert the format of a work for preservation purposes. Before that may
be done, however, section 108(c) dictates that the library first attempt
to purchase a copy in the desired format at a fair price. If it is not available, then for preservation, a library may reproduce the film. The library should contact Southern Bell to try to obtain another copy since
it appears to be the publisher, and if a VHS or DVD copy is not available, the library may then reproduce a copy in a newer video format.

• • •

Q270 *If a library is the repository of the only copy of a work
that was ever produced, do the rules governing digital preservation
apply? Does the original format of the work make any difference?*

The same rules for preservation and replacement of works digitally apply, even if the library owns the only copy of the work. From
the question, it is not clear whether the work was published or not.
This is the classic section 108(b) situation, however, where a library
owns the only copy of an unpublished work but likely does not own
the copyright in that work. Section 108(b) permits the library to make
up to three copies of an unpublished work in its collection. If one of
those copies is a digital copy, that copy cannot be used outside the
premises of the library. Presumably, however, the library could also
make a printed copy and circulate that copy as one of the three permitted copies. If the work is a published work, then section 108(c)

applies to works that the library owns but which are now lost, stolen, damaged, deteriorating or obsolete. Before the library can duplicate the work, it must first make a reasonable effort to purchase an unused copy at a fair price. If there is no other copy available, then the library may make up to three copies of the work. Again, if one of the copies is digital, that digital copy cannot be used outside the premises of the library.

• • •

Q271 *If a CD-ROM becomes damaged and unplayable may the library replace it by making another copy from the original or making a copy from another library's original?*

Assume that the CD is a published work. Under section 108(c), the library may reproduce a lost, stolen, deteriorating, damaged or obsolete work only if the library first determines by reasonable investigation that an unused copy cannot be obtained at a fair price. If no such copy is available, then the library may make another copy from the original, obtain a reproduction from another library or borrow the CD from another library and physically make the replacement copy.

• • •

Q272 *The library has a book with a particularly nice book jacket; unfortunately, this dust jacket has been damaged. May the library reproduce the book jacket to replace the damaged one?*

Under section 108(c) of the Copyright Act libraries are permitted to replace lost, damaged, deteriorating, stolen or obsolete items after the library has first made a reasonable effort to purchase an unused replacement at a fair price. Thus, the first step is to contact the publisher to see if it will supply a new book jacket to replace the damaged one. If not, then the library is entitled to reproduce the damaged cover. In order to retain the colors, the library may decide to locate a copy of the book jacket on the web and download and print it to use as a replacement, rather than photocopy the damaged cover.

Q273 *When a library has two copies of a subscription to a journal, one for the print copy and the other a license for the online version, may it use the online digital version to print out an article that is missing from the printed version and tip it into the bound volume?*

It is the license agreement for the digital version that controls, but typically replacing missing pages in the print journal with copies made from the online version to which the library subscribes would not violate the terms of the license agreement. Most licenses for online journals restrict the use to members of the campus community or other defined user group, and replacing a copy of an article in the bound volume would be such internal use. The library should consult the individual license agreement in question.

• • •

Q274 *In order to save space, each year a corporate library that has an Annual Copyright License from the Copyright Clearance Center for photocopying has its journals microfilmed by a library microfilming house, which either uses the hard copy the library provides or provides film from its own collection. It does not seem to be a problem when the microfilm is received and the hard copies are destroyed. The library considers the microfilm version to be a different format of information that has already been purchased, and the microfilm is used in place of hard copy by document delivery staff and scientists.*

Actually, this is a problem. The library is reproducing the journals cover to cover, and such reproduction requires permission of the copyright holder. If the publisher offers a microfilm edition of the journal, it is unlikely that it will grant permission for an individual library to make its own microfilm version, but the library certainly may ask. It is possible that the "library microfilming house" has a license for such reproduction and is paying royalties, but the corporate library should inquire before continuing this practice as well as consult its CCC license.

Q275 *Should journals be stored on CDs instead of microfilm? Aside from the issue of whether CD technology will be around the next few decades, there is interest in exploring this idea of replacing the older microfilm by having them converted to CDs by a jobber. The library would then load the CDs on a server or network them for access from the desktops by users. Would networking the CDs and making them accessible by one person at a time at a workstation change anything?*

It changes things considerably. While microfilming, as described in the previous question, may be infringement, at least only one analog copy is made by such activity. Digitizing a journal and burning it onto CD in order to network it without a license to do so, either through a CCC Annual Copyright License or by a license directly from the publisher, is multiple copying in digital form which is infringement. The library should contact publishers and seek permission before making a CD version of a copyrighted journal purchased on microfilm and making it available throughout the company digitally.

• • •

Q276 *A library has a rare 1773 map showing early landowners in the county. Is there a copyright problem if the library has the map scanned so the image may be saved to a Master CD for preservation purposes? Patrons have asked for a copy of the map as it shows where many of their ancestors were living in 1773. The original size of the map is quite large, and the library has never previously made copies of it (1) May it now copy the image from the CD to another CD for patrons and even sell copies of the map to them? (2) Could the library take the CD to a printer and have copies printed for sale? (3) May the library put the map on a website?*

Good news! Copy away in any format. Due to the age of the map, it is in the public domain. Therefore, anyone who has access to it may reproduce and distribute the map and even sell copies. The library may have the only copy of the map, and it does not have to grant access to others. But, the library does not hold copyright in the scanned version of the map either since scanning does not create a new copyright. Therefore, if the library sells copies of the map and someone duplicates a purchased copy and then offers those copies for sale or posts them on the Internet, there is no infringement. The map, whether the original, printed or scanned copies, is in the public domain.

• • •

Q277 *If a for-profit library sets up vertical files on subjects, areas of interests, trends in the industry, and so forth, may it photocopy journal and newspaper articles and place them in the vertical file?*

Section 108 does not mention the issue of copying for vertical files. Section 108(f)(4) indicates that libraries also have fair use rights, and making single copies for a vertical file is probably a fair use. A court would apply the four fair use factors (purpose and character of the use, nature of the copyrighted work, amount used, and market effect) to make this determination. There is one thing that might lead a court to find that vertical file copying is not fair use, however, and that is because there were vertical files in libraries prior to the advent of the photocopier. Libraries used to put original copies of articles torn from journal issues and actual clippings from newspapers into their vertical files. But photocopies are preferred by libraries because they do not destroy the original journals and newspapers. It is probably fair use, however.

If the company has an Annual Copyright License from the Copyright Clearance Center, then copying works covered by the license for the vertical files is permitted under the terms of the license.

• • •

Q278 *A public library is interested in scanning business articles from the local newspaper essentially to preserve them and to replace the vertical file. The scanned articles would be on an intranet and restricted to in-building use only just as the contents of the traditional vertical file were so restricted. Is this permitted?*

Newspaper articles are copyrighted just as are other text works. Because of the high level of interest in business articles that deal with the local community, it is easy to understand why a library would be interested in scanning them. While section 108 of the Copyright Act does not mention photocopying for vertical files as an exception to the exclusive rights of the copyright holder, making occasional single photocopies of articles from local newspapers for the vertical file likely would qualify as a fair use. Scanning in lieu of photocopying may also be fair use, but it could be seen as more systematic than is photocopying. Further, placing the articles on terminals for in-library use is still wider distribution than old vertical files.

Another solution would be to seek blanket permission from the local newspaper to scan business articles and make them available for in-library use as a local resource. In fact, the newspaper might be willing to expand use beyond the library, so asking the paper could result in even broader permission and, for example, post them on a library website.

• • •

Q279 *Suppose a library purchased a microfilm copy of a copyrighted work published a number of years ago. It has since been discovered that the type of film used by the publisher is unstable and could deteriorate rapidly as well as hasten, if not cause, the deterioration of other films in the collection. Thus, it is a "deteriorating" copy as required by the statute. Consequently, the library wishes to remaster this and other films of this same type to a more stable, durable type of film and destroy the original. Does section 108(c) justify this action? What if the library could obtain an unused replacement copy but only in the same unstable format?*

As is often the case, there is no black and white answer to this question. Section 108(c) permits the library to reproduce a work after it makes a reasonable effort to find an unused copy available at a fair price. The term "unused copy" indicates that it is not only a copy that has not been previously used, but also a copy that is usable, i.e., one that is stable. If the only format that is available for purchase at a fair price is another unstable microform, then that copy is not usable. Likely, the library should be able make a stable copy.

•••

Q280 *How useful has section 108(h) been to libraries and archives?*

Designed to ameliorate the effects of term extension, section 108(h) was added to the Copyright Act in 1998. It is an interesting provision that allows libraries, archives and nonprofit educational institutions to reproduce, distribute, perform or display copyrighted works during the last 20 years of their terms if certain conditions are met. So, at this point, the author has already been dead for 50 years. A library may not take advantage of this exception if: (1) the work is subject to normal commercial exploitation; (2) if a copy can be obtained at a reasonable price or (3) the copyright owner provides notice that either of the other two conditions are met.

The benefit is that under section 108(h), a library may digitize a work and put it on a publicly accessible website. In other words, there is no premises restriction as in sections 108(b) and (c). The U.S. Copyright Office created a process by which publishers could electronically provide the notice in (3) above. Unfortunately, not one single copyright owner has utilized this process for notification.

•••

Q281 *How long should a school archive its e-mails? Do e-mails that contain copyrighted material subject the institution to liability for infringement due to the archiving?*

Each organization or institution should have a record retention policy which includes how long it will archive e-mail. For state-supported institutions, the length of time should take into account the state government record retention requirements. For private institutions, the length of time may be based on the statute of limitations for bringing suit that would be based on any e-mail. In any event, most libraries do not stand alone but are a part of a larger institution or organization, and their policies should be those of the libraries' parent organizations.

On the other hand, a library might be responsible for archiving e-mail of a particular individual or entity as a part of a general archival project, in which case the length of retention would be the same as for other items it archives for research. The retention policy might be "forever" if the e-mails are to be archived and made available to future researchers.

The copyright infringement issue is much easier to answer. Even if any archived item contains any infringing material, the institution is not likely to be liable under section 512 of the Copyright Act, the online service provider liability provision. In offering e-mail services to its staff, faculty and students, the institution is considered to be a passive provider, and it would not be liable for the infringing activity of a user of the service if certain easy to satisfy conditions are met such as: the institution neither selects the contents nor the recipients of e-mail and receives no financial benefit from a user's infringing activity. Once the institution is aware of the infringing activity of a user, however, it has a responsibility to take disciplinary action and could even cancel the user's access to the e-mail service.

$$\bullet \, \bullet \, \bullet$$

Q282 *In old deeds of gifts to libraries for manuscripts, the term "literary rights" or "literary property rights" reserved often appears. What does this mean?*

Authors and their heirs have what is called the right of first publication. This means that for an unpublished work, the author and her heirs retains the right to publish that work or to determine whether it will be published at all. It is only the physical copy of the manuscript that is being donated and not the copyright. Thus, the library would have the right to publish the work either in print or by posting it on a web page only after the work has entered the public domain or if the copyright owner grants permission. This would occur 70 years after the author's death except for works created before 1978 which remained unpublished through the end of 2002. For those works, the term is life of the author plus 70 years or the end of 2002, whichever is greater. Thus, many of these works are already in the public domain.

• • •

Q283   *If the author of a personal letter owns the copyright in the letter but the recipient owns the only copy of the letter, what can the owner of the copy do? What are the rights of the author's heirs?*

The owner of the copy cannot publish the letter if it is still protected by copyright because that right belongs to the copyright holder. The recipient may dispose of that copy by donating it to a library or archives or may even sell the letter to a dealer or collector. After the author's death, the heirs own the same rights that the author had: reproduction, distribution, adaptation, performance and display for 70 years after the author's death. Then the work passes into the public domain.

• • •

Q284   *If an author of a work conveys by deed of gift the rights to their work, what does that include? Does the library then own the copyright?*

It depends to some extent on the exact wording of the deed of gift. Assume that the donor author says "I transfer to the archives all my rights in my work." This language means that the library owns the copyright. But if the deed of gift says "I transfer the copies of my work as detailed, "then the library does not own the copyright and must seek permission to reproduce the work, etc. The library would own the copy but not the copyright in this instance.

• • •

Q285   *Faculty member publications present particular problems for archival collections. If a library obtains only a photocopy of faculty produced works for deposit in the archives as opposed to a hard* *copy, may archives researchers make another copy of the photocopy without copyright concern? Suppose that the work is a photocopy of a letter or other miscellaneous document instead?*

There are two initial questions that have to be answered assuming that the faculty publication is still under copyright. The first is whether the faculty member owns the copyright in the work or not. If the work is a book, the answer is likely to be yes. If the work is a journal article, the answer is probably no. It depends on whether the author assigned the copyright in the works to the publisher. The second question is how the archival collection acquired the reproduction of the work. Assume that the work is a book and the faculty member owns the copyright. If the reproduction of the work came from the faculty author, then the archival collection is bound by the transfer agreement from the faculty member. If he gave permission for the archives to use the reproduction and make it available to other researchers, including to right to reproduce it, then, clearly, there is no problem in doing so.

But if the work is a journal article for which the faculty member transferred the copyright to the publisher, and if the faculty author or a third party delivered a photocopy or digital copy of the article to the archives, the archives has no reproduction rights. If the library owned a copy of the journal itself, then the library may make copies under the conditions specified in section 108. The photocopy could be used by researchers and it might even be fair use for that researcher to make a copy of the copy. Section 108 does not grant the archives itself the right to make copies from the photocopy, however.

Letters and other unpublished documents present a different situation entirely. Unpublished works are still covered by copyright, but, section 108(b) permits libraries and archives to reproduce unpublished works for purposes such as preservation, security or deposit for research in another library. So, if the archival collection has a photocopy of the unpublished work, how was that reproduction obtained? If from the author, the author's transfer agreement to the library prevails. If it came from another library that holds the original, the assumption is that it was a copy deposited under section 108(b) and that for fair use purposes, a researcher could duplicate the photocopy.

Q286 *How should a library deal with copying correspondence from its manuscript collection at the request of patrons?*

Correspondence should be treated as any other unpublished work. There is no reason for a library to refrain from making a single copy of correspondence at the request of a user who intends to make a fair use of the letter unless the deed of gift requires confidentiality or contains some other restriction. Some archival collections require users to certify that they intend to use the unpublished work for scholarship and research. The library may want to indicate to scholars that it does not hold the copyright and if the user intends to publish the work, she must seek permission from the author of the letter. If the library owns the copyright, then it may give or withhold permission for reproducing a letter in the book the scholar is writing.

CHAPTER 12

Digitization

A s libraries of all types have increasingly adopted computer technology, the potential to make digitized content available to library users has become more attractive. Library users are requesting digital copies of works more than ever before. At the same time, copyright questions about digitization have also increased. Digitizing has become much easier to accomplish, and all types of libraries are interested in the issue for various projects, for specific types of works, and for particular uses of copyrighted works. Some of the library digitization projects are to create whole digital collections, which the libraries intend to make available on the web. Other digitized content is not intended to be so widely available, and could even be housed in a dark archive. A library may want to digitize portions of its collections as a space-saving measure; others seek to preserve works via digital means. As the questions and answers that follow indicate, the reasons for such digitization vary considerably.

Many projects involve public domain works, and libraries may proceed without concern about copyright. However, librarians are often unclear about the copyright status of a work and when to seek permission. There may be instances when a library decides to go ahead and digitize works, post them on the web, and simply assume the risk, because making the works available on the web is so important to that community. Librarians should be cautious, however, and realize that just because it has become technologically easier to digitize copyrighted works, it does not mean that it can be done with impunity. Despite the fact that a library may have a very good purpose in mind when digitizing the work, such purpose alone unlikely insulates the library from infringement claims. Digitizing copyrighted works reproduces them just as does photocopying. It also affects other exclusive rights of the copyright owner besides reproduction (for example, distribution and public display when the work is displayed on a computer terminal in a public area in a library).

The wide range of questions that have been addressed in the *Against the Grain* "Questions & Answers—Copyright Column" indicates the importance of copyright issues to digitization. Questions in this chapter focus on digitizing particular types of works, such as photographs, textbooks, college yearbooks, and book illustrations. Another important issue is whether a digital copy of a work creates a new copyright. The number and complexity of questions in this area are bound to increase as individual libraries tackle more and more digitization projects.

• • •

Q287   *A corporate library is developing a web-based repository for its departmental documents and supporting literature. This may include current articles stored as PDF files, available to a limited audience with access controlled by a password. Are there copyright concerns in this situation? If the company needs permission from the copyright holder, is there a particular process that should be used?*

Whether permission is required from rights holders depends on the articles themselves, whether they are copyrighted, if they are from journals licensed to the company, and so forth. If corporate departments are duplicating licensed articles to put into this system, the license agreement may well permit the duplication, but the license agreement will control. If the company has an Annual Copyright License from the Copyright Clearance Center, then the CCC license determines whether such activity is covered by the license for CCC-covered journals. For articles copyrighted from unlicensed journals and not covered by the CCC license, however, permission is required. The limited access and controls really do not matter much, unless the company has a license from the publisher.

The only way to obtain permission is to contact the copyright owner, who is typically the publisher. There is no particular process to seek permission other than contacting the copyright holder in writing or by e-mail and retain the correspondence. Unfortunately, there is no requirement that publishers even respond to the inquiry, and failure to respond cannot be interpreted as an affirmative answer

• • •

Q288   *Patrons often request digital copies of photographs that are in the library's collection. Are there restrictions on supplying digital copies? For libraries and archives, section 108(i) of the Copyright Act states that the rights of reproduction and distribution do not apply to a musical work; a pictorial, graphic, or sculptural work; or a motion picture or other audiovisual work. Does this include photographs?*

Yes, photographs are pictorial works and are part of the section 108(i) exclusion to section 108 library copying. Under section 108(d), libraries may reproduce copies of works for patrons upon request, such as an article or a book chapter, but this general permission for libraries does not include "standalone" photographs. On the other hand, if a photograph is part of an article, according to section 108(i) it may be reproduced for a user along with the article. The photo could be digitized under sections 108(b), (c), and (h), but sections (b) and (c) do not permit copies to be made for users. If the digital photograph is public domain, then there is no problem with providing digital copies. The library may be able to provide a copy under fair use, but that is not clear.

• • •

Q289   *A school issues tablet computers to all students and wants to use the tablets to reduce the weight of backpacks for students by* *providing digital copies of their textbooks so that students can use the digitized copy of the book at school and leave the hard copy of the book at home. An added advantage is the note-taking features of the tablet PC. Since it does not harm the publisher, is it infringement to digitize textbooks in PDF format for students if one copy of the printed textbook is purchased for each student? Or does the TEACH Act permit this activity?*

Sometimes when thinking about digitizing works, it is useful to analogize it to photocopying. Suppose that the school purchased one print copy of all the textbooks it uses for each student. It decides that students should have a copy of each textbook at home as well as at school, so it photocopies each textbook and provides a photocopy to students so that each has both a purchased copy and a photocopy. Is this infringement? Certainly, because the publisher lost a sale for each of the photocopies made. Moreover, there is no exception that permits multiple copying of entire works for students.

Publishers are unlikely to give permission for a school to photocopy textbooks when published copies are available. The same is true for digitizing textbooks—permission of the copyright owner is required. The school needs permission to digitize the textbooks, even if there is no digitized version available. Digitizing does harm publishers since they may either already offer electronic versions of the textbook or may wish to market the digitized version in the future. Copyright protects potential markets as well as existing ones.

The TEACH Act applies to works that are performed (e.g., music and movies) and those that are displayed (e.g., charts and photos). It does not generally apply to the reproduction of works, except that it does allow a school to digitize a portion of a movie if no digital version is available, and a few pages from a textbook for display, but not an entire textbook.

• • •

Q290   *A library has old journals in storage and wants to digitize them. If a journal is still being published today, are the back issues in the public domain? Or is the publication still protected?*

Back issues are not necessarily in the public domain even if the journal has ceased publication. Works that were first published in the United States before 1923 are now in the public domain. Those published between 1923 and 1964 were protected for 28 years and then had to be renewed for copyright, but it is highly possible that the owner failed to renew the copyright. If the works were renewed for copyright, then they received a total of 95 years of protection, regardless of whether they are still being published. For journals published after 1964, it is no longer necessary to renew the copyright, and those works automatically received 95 years of protection. So, whether a journal volume is in the public domain depends on the publication date. The library can engage the U.S. Copyright Office to search the pre-1978 registration records to determine whether the work was renewed for copyright. The post-1978 records are publicly available online and library staff may search the records directly.

In short, digitizing back volumes published before 1923 is no problem since they are in the public domain. For volumes published between 1923 and 1964, it depends on whether the copyright was renewed. Those published after 1964, however, definitely are not in the public domain and digitization would require permission. The publisher itself may offer digital versions of back volumes.

• • •

Q291 *Professors often ask librarians why the library does not just go ahead and digitize the entire collection. How should one respond to this?*

With loud guffaws, perhaps? Faculty members appear to think that the only reason they do not have digital access to everything is laziness on the part of librarians. They are usually unaware of the major copyright concerns that would accompany such an effort. In fact, Project Gutenberg and other digital projects have had more difficulty with copyright than anything else. The Google Books Library Project is a prime example that highlights the problems.

A more serious answer to the faculty is that it would take an enormous amount of funds for the digitization project itself, including funds required to obtain the necessary permissions, and even larger ongoing funds to pay the copyright royalties. Few copyright owners would be willing to permit digitization and continued use of those digital copies by library users for a flat fee. Owners likely would charge a per use royalty or an annual fee. Moreover, some publishers would absolutely refuse to grant permission to digitize under any conditions. Thus, library collections probably will never be solely in digital format, or at least, not in most of our lifetimes.

• • •

Q292   *A local historical society is considering putting back issues of the local history magazine that it publishes online. Some of the issues date from the 1940s, and many of the articles were written by volunteers, but some by professional writers. How can the society get permission from the original authors for the online version? The copyright notice in the issues simply says "Copyright, X Historical Society" and then includes the year.*

The first question is the whether the authors transferred their copyrights to the society or whether there were other agreements in place to ensure society ownership. The copyright notice indicates society ownership but that would be for the compilation (the magazine issue). If the copyrights were transferred to the society, no permission would be necessary from authors prior to 1978. Depending on the publication dates, it is possible that some of the magazine issues are no longer protected by copyright. The first question is when the various issues of the magazine were published. Before 1978, copyrighted material received 28 years of protection. At the end of that period, the society would have had to apply for a renewal of copyright, or the issues of the magazine would have entered the public domain. If renewed, they received a total of 95 years of protection. Even if the issues were registered for copyright when originally published, it is unlikely that the local society applied for a renewal of copyright, so prior to 1964, the issues are more than likely in the public domain. The society could decide to assume the small risk and go ahead and put these issues online.

Issues published after 1978 are protected by copyright whether registered or not, however. The magazine issues now receive 95 years of copyright protection, so the society would need to seek permission of authors to place those articles online. For issues published between 1964 and 1977, renewal of copyright was automatic, and instead of 28 years, the renewal term is 67 years, for a total of 95 years of protection. So permission is needed for these articles too. Even if authors transferred the reproduction and distribution rights to the society, based on the *Tasini* decision, *New York Times v. Tasini*, 533 U.S. 483 (2001), an author must specifically transfer the electronic rights to the publisher in order for the publisher to own those rights. Thus, contacting the authors for permission is important. The difficulty, of course, is that many authors and their heirs from the earliest years in this range probably are deceased or are very difficult to locate.

The best advice for the society is to try to locate the authors and to post a notice on the society's website asking for authors to contact the historical society staff. Each article placed online for which the author has not been located should be noted along with a plea for anyone reading the article to help locate the missing author.

• • •

Q293   *If a library has old public domain documents (published in the United States before 1923) is a new copyright created by microfilming or digitizing the documents?*

No. Several years ago it was presumed that the image (i.e., the microfilm) produced a new edition that was separately copyrightable. Courts have now made it clear that a reproduction, such as a microfilm, is a simple reproduction. So, the microfilm or digital version of a public domain work does not create a new copyright. If the microfilm version has additional material added, such as editorial comments, indexes, or annotations, then the new material is eligible for copyright protection provided that it satisfies the originality requirement, but the underlying work is unchanged and remains in the public domain.

Q294   *The library is engaged in a process to digitize items in the public domain and put them on the web. Does the library own the copyright in these digital works? Does it make a difference if they are reproduced on a CD-ROM as opposed to being posted on the web?*

Public domain works are not protected by copyright. Most often that is because the copyright has expired. Digitizing the work does not create a new copyright. The only thing in which the library could claim copyright is any new material that it adds. For example, if the library creates a new index to the work, or adds a new preface, it may claim copyright in the newly added material, but the contents of the original work remain in the public domain. The library might also have a copyright in the collection of these digital materials as a compilation, but the library cannot stop anyone else from digitizing the public domain work—only from copying the newly added material or the entire compilation. Whether the public domain works are on CD or are posted online makes no difference since they are copyright free and the original contents remain in the public domain.

• • •

Q295   *A librarian is in charge of her college's archives, and the library is planning a digitization project that will include college yearbooks published between 1923 and 1977. Some of the yearbooks were published without notice of copyright. Others contain a copyright notice with an owner (sometimes the editor and sometimes the business manager specified). Do these individuals listed as the owner own the copyright, or does the college? There are no institutional records to clarify the ownership situation.*

Yearbooks are treated just as any other copyrighted work. For example, assume that the 1933 yearbook contains a copyright notice. It received 28 years of protection, but the copyright would have had to be renewed in 1961. If the renewal took place, then it is still protected by copyright until 2028 (95 years after 1933). If the renewal did not occur, and frankly, it is unlikely that the work was renewed for copyright, then the yearbook is now in the public domain. The only way to be sure about renewal is to (1) contact the copyright holder (although the company may now be out of business) or (2) contact the U.S. Copyright Office and pay for a search of the records. Electronic records exist for works registered from 1978 to the present, and those can be reviewed online directly by the public at no charge. To search the pre-1978 records, the Copyright Office will perform the search for a fee, but the search should not take long to complete.

The yearbooks published without a copyright notice before 1978 are in the public domain because notice was required in order to perfect the copyright. Even for the yearbooks that contain a notice, it is actually unlikely that they were renewed for copyright. Although 80 to 85 percent of works were renewed for copyright, those tended to be works that were still being marketed at that time. Typically, the market for yearbooks is only the year of publication.

The notices of copyright indicate that the editor or business manager owns the copyright. If the college was the owner, usually its name would appear in the copyright notice. However, without records, it is difficult to determine any ownership beyond that found in the notice. If the business manager was a college employee, his or her name as the owner meant that the college owned the copyright in those. It is possible that the business manager was an employee of the publisher, however, and the question does not specify business manager of what. Today, institutions are much more likely to negotiate for copyright ownership than they did during the specified years.

Because of all of this, the library may well decide to go forward and digitize the yearbooks and simply assume the risk that no copyright owner will come forward and complain. It might be useful to determine in advance what strategy will be employed should an owner ever come forward, however.

• • •

Q296 *An academic library is participating in a scanning project to put pre-1923 U.S. imprints on the Internet. It wishes to expand the project to include non-U.S. imprints as well, but has found conflicting information about copyright. One source said that pre-1923 was still a valid date, even for non-U.S. imprints. Another source said that it* *was a legal date, as long as distribution was limited to the United States. What is correct about scanning foreign publications?*

One cannot depend on a pre-1923 date for foreign publications. Copyright law is determined country by country, although international treaties have helped to harmonize those laws today. So, the status of pre-1923 foreign imprints depends on the country of origin of the work and its copyright law. Most European countries had life plus 50 years as the copyright term for many years before the United States adopted it in 1978; now the term is life plus 70 years both in Europe and in this country. So, it is difficult to establish a specific year as a cutoff, unless it is something quite early, such as 1850. In other words, it is highly unlikely that an author living in 1850 who published a work would still be alive even in 1925 much less in 1995, 70 years after the author's death. The pre-1923 date applies only to works published in the United States. The library may want to choose an early date and use it to mark when works are in the public domain, even in Europe.

• • •

Q297   *The library is considering a project that involves several stages: (1) scanning lists of illustrations contained in selected art books, (2) scanning the actual images themselves, (3) mounting the scanned images on a publicly available website, (4) arranging the images so that they can be retrieved via the scanned lists of images, and (5) creating a link from the catalog record for the book to the scanned illustration list. The purpose of this project is to help students and faculty determine from the library catalog what illustrations are contained in a particular book and then to provide access to those images. Typically, catalog records do not provide this information and capability. The scanning approach is favored because it would require less labor than keying the list into some sort of contents note in the catalog record.*

This is a great example of a project with a good purpose but which may be problematic. Scanning the list of illustrations and including the list in the catalog record is likely to be fair use since it is factual and is in the nature of a finding tool. Scanning the actual images, however, may go beyond what is permitted under the law. *Kelly v. ArribaSoft*, 280 F.3d 934 (9th Cir. 2002), permitted the use of thumbnail images by a visual image search engine, and it is possible that a library's use of thumbnail images to direct users of the catalog to websites where images are lawfully posted would be found to be non-infringing. But scanning the images from the art books is not likely to be considered lawful reproduction. If, however, the library has licensed access to digital images, the license may permit mounting the images in a database, but it is doubtful that making it truly publicly available, as opposed to available only to students enrolled in a particular course, would be allowed under the license.

• • •

Q298   *A donor recently gave the library a collection of newspapers from the 1960s, but they are in bad condition. If the library digitizes the newspapers, what permissions are required? Is there is a difference if the purpose of the digitization is preservation of the newspapers?*

The first question is whether the newspaper issues are still protected by copyright. If they were published before 1964, they received 28 years of protection and could be renewed for an additional 28 years. If not so renewed, they are now in the public domain. If they were renewed, then they get a total of 95 years of copyright protection. Those published from 1964 forward would still be under copyright since no renewal is required for the extended term of 95 years from date of first publication. If the library wanted to make the digitized newspapers available on the web, it would need to have permission from the newspaper publisher, even though no permission was required to digitize the work (i.e., make the copy).

Under section 108(c) of the Copyright Act, the library may preserve the copyrighted newspapers digitally, after it first makes a reasonable effort to acquire unused copies of the works. If such copies are not available at a fair price, then the library may take advantage

of section 108(c) to replace the deteriorating copies either with photocopies, with microfilm, or by digitizing them. The print or microfilm
copies may be used just as any other work, but the statute restricts the
digital copies to in-library use. In other words, the digital copy may
not be used outside the premises of the library.

• • •

Q299   *A librarian who is also an audio engineer maintains a
website that many engineers worldwide use as a reference concerning audio issues. The now-defunct audio trade publication*
Record Engineer & Producer *was a treasure trove of information
about analog recording. People often ask about finding back issues, which would be useful to help educate today's digital-savvy
but analog-ignorant audio engineers. Someone has now offered 22
years of back issues to the website owner. May the website owner
scan some of the various articles from this magazine for the website? Or can he make articles available to folks who request them
on an individual basis? The magazine ceased publication in the
early 1990s.*

The first determination deals with the publication dates of the
magazine. Issues published before 1964 are very likely in the public
domain. If they are in the public domain, then digitizing those articles for the website would be no problem. Before 1964, publishers
registered the issues and then received 28 years of copyright protection. At the end of that period, the copyright had to be renewed and
they received a total of 95 years of protection. But many publishers
of small magazines did not renew their copyrights, which meant that
those issues entered the public domain after the first term of copyright. Thus, determining whether the issues were registered initially
and then whether they were renewed for copyright is necessary to
make the determination about whether pre-1964 works are still under copyright.

Issues published between 1964 and 1977 still had to be registered
for copyright. But Congress automatically gave them a total of 95 years
of copyright protection through a series of amendments to the Copy-

right Act, and no renewal of copyright was required. So, the answer to the question about digitizing articles from the journals is dependent on the copyright status of those individual issues.

Even if the issues of the defunct magazine are still under copyright, there may not be anyone around to complain about any infringing activity. The website owner could just decide to go ahead and make them available online, although it would be infringement. On the other hand, if there is no one around to enforce the rights, the potential benefit in making the articles available may lead the website owner to assume the risk. If the website owner takes this view, it might be useful to include a disclaimer on the website that asks copyright owners to come forward and identify themselves, and volunteer to remove the article from the web if the owner of the copyright objects to its availability on the website.

It probably would be fair use to provide single copies of articles to individuals who request them occasionally, but even libraries that do this have some restrictions, including that the reproduction and distribution may not be systematic.

• • •

Q300 *An individual scholar is interested in republishing some eighteenth- and nineteenth-century books from a nearby research library and converting them to digital text. Is explicit permission from the library needed to scan these older books, convert them to text, and republish them?*

If the work was first published in the United States prior to 1923, the copyright has expired and no permission is required from the copyright holder to digitize the work or to republish it because it is in the public domain. The research library could refuse to lend its copy for this digitization project because of concerns about potential damage to the artifact, but the library does not hold the copyright. Thus, the scholar does not need permission from the library for republishing, but does need its permission to use library book copies in the manner described in the question. The library's interest is in preserving the physical integrity of the copies of books it owns.

Q301 *For a library digitization project of documents published by the university, is copyright permission necessary? The library will make these documents available on the web.*

The answer is yes, but it very easy to get permission if the library is a part of the university in question. In fact, the library should contact the university president or his or her designee and seek permission to put these documents on the web. Permission can be obtained for all documents with just one request. In other words, rather than seeking permission for each individual title, the library can make a single request for all documents published by the university. For state-supported universities, the documents may be copyright free based on state law, but for good campus relations, asking the president may be prudent.

• • •

Q302 *A university library is interested in digitizing handbooks that the university published in order to make them available to the general public. A chapter in one of the handbooks contains the following footnote: "Reprinted and adapted from* Group Leadership *by Robert D. Leigh, by permission of W.W. Norton and Company, Inc. Copyright 1936 by the publishers." It is unclear whether the copyright for* Group Leadership *has been renewed. Assuming that the copyright in this publication has not yet expired, does the university have a duty to contact the copyright owner of the work in order to digitize the handbook?*

Yes, the university should try to contact the publisher or its successor. The original rights granted did not include the digital rights. But this depends on whether the copyright was renewed, and the question indicates that renewal information is not available. The copyright in the 1936 work would have expired in 1964 and a renewal would have given it the term of life of the author plus 70 years of protection. The safest course is to contact Norton or its successor company for permission. But, even if the copyright was renewed, the university may be willing to accept the risk that the publisher of the 1936 work will not complain when the university library digitizes the handbooks and makes them available on the web. Talk with the university's counsel to help make this decision.

• • •

Q303 *A liberal arts college is being asked to put digital copies of student theses on a server. If the theses contain copyrighted images, standardized tests, and the like, is permission needed? Or should access be by password only? Is there any disclaimer that the college should use if the digitized theses are posted on the web?*

Whether the theses are available on the open web or on a password-protected site makes considerable difference in this situation. In the print world, for published theses and dissertations, student authors were required by the publisher to get permission to include copyrighted photographs and other materials. When the thesis or dissertation was placed only in the library collection, however, seldom did a student seek permission for incorporating copyrighted material since it was not going to be published. Posting on the web, however, is a type of publication with one difference—the college is the publisher, and a copyright holder whose works are infringed in a thesis is more likely to blame the college than the individual student for any infringement. Making theses available on a password-protected website is more akin to having the typewritten ones available only in the library. However, students and others who have the password can access the images and can download them from a thesis, so the college should make some effort to discourage downloading.

While a disclaimer on the web might make college officials feel better, it is unlikely to have any legal effect. On the other hand, a notice on a password-protected site stating that downloading images is not permitted would be useful and would demonstrate efforts to discourage infringement by authenticated users.

If the college decides that it wishes to proceed with putting theses on the web, then student authors should be charged with the responsibility of seeking permission for the use of copyrighted images and materials before web publication.

Q304 *A college library has a large number of student theses in its print collection. (1) In order to digitize the collection, must the library obtain permission from the former students? (2) Is there a difference in terms of what the library can do if it makes the electronic files viewable by the college-authorized user group only versus by the entire world? (3) For pre-1923 theses, are they considered to be in the public domain and therefore could be digitized in any case? (4) Do the same answers apply to bachelor's essays or papers?*

(1) Most colleges have graduate students sign a form when they begin a graduate degree agreeing to make their theses available to the library, which may use the theses for interlibrary loan. The first step is to check whether any such agreement for graduate students is required and then determine when the agreement form began to be used. Students are the authors and own the copyright in their work. If there is no agreement, then digitizing these theses requires permission of the students if the library plans to post the papers on the web. The library should get this written agreement in place for all new graduate students so that future papers can be digitized with no problem.

(2) Restricting access to digitized theses to the campus community certainly reduces the likelihood that former students will complain, but it does not change the copyright status of the work. The college may be willing to assume the risk that no student will complain, and if someone does complain, the library can then disable access to that thesis.

(3) For theses published before 1923, no problem. They are in the public domain and may be digitized with no permission. For unpublished theses produced before 1978, however, the copyright expired at the end of 2002 or life of the author plus 70 years, whichever is greater. So, the death date of the student author is critical.

(4) Whether the work is an undergraduate essay or a graduate thesis is irrelevant for copyright purposes and the above applies.

• • •

Q305 *If a library has a large collection of old sheet music that is deteriorating, may it digitize the collection and make it available on the web?*

The term "old sheet music" does not really define whether the music is in the public domain or is still under copyright. Assuming that it is still under copyright, then via section 108(c) of the Copyright Act, a library is permitted to reproduce deteriorating works, but only after it makes a reasonable effort to purchase another unused copy at a fair price. The library may make up to three copies of the work after this effort. One of these copies may be digital, and the library may make it available within the library but only on a library intranet. It cannot make the material available on the web without permission of the copyright owner.

CHAPTER 13

Miscellaneous Issues

There are a number of questions about copyright issues important to librarians, faculty members, authors, and publishers that do not fit into any of the other topical chapters. Those questions have been gathered into this final chapter. Because of the wide variety of questions in this chapter, it is not easy to introduce them.

There are questions about the nature of fair use, whether public libraries qualify for the exceptions that are available to nonprofit educational institutions, whether for-profit schools may take advantage of the nonprofit educational institution exceptions, and the meaning in section 108(a) of the Copyright Act of "open to the public." Other questions focus on the difference in musical works and sound recordings, the use of abstracts and the impact of the Americans with Disabilities Act1 on copyright rights and exceptions. There are also questions on copyright litigation, ranging from the statute of limitations for copyright actions to compliance with court orders, from statutory damages to abandonment of copyright. Questions about whether copyright and patent should be included in the same policy and if fair use is a defense to copyright infringement or a right are also included.

Librarians are often involved in the drafting and adoption of copyright law policies for their institutions and organizations. They are

---

1   42 U.S.C. § 12101–12187 (2006).

concerned about the personal liability of librarians for copyright infringement by patrons, as well as a librarian's level of responsibility to explain copyright law to users. The role and job duties of scholarly communications officers are also discussed.

• • •

Q306 *What should an independent business research firm do when its clients request monthly digests or synopses of news developments on various topics? This could include monitoring competitor activities that are covered in the news media or tracking issues and trends. The clients then want to distribute these summaries and synopses widely within their companies.*

This question indirectly raises the problem of using author- or publisher-produced abstracts versus doing one's own work. Published abstracts are separately copyrighted as adaptations of the original work, and the copyright belongs to the author, or it may have been transferred to the publisher.

Gathering information, summarizing the factual content, and producing a report for a client is a fair use as long as the work the research firm does is original and does not copy extensive portions of copyrighted works. To some extent, this may be the difference in an annotation and an abstract. The annotation describes the work rather than extracts the research results. It uses phrases such as "the author indicates that . . ." and "there are four pie charts illustrating. . . ." Such summaries are fair use as long as they do not supplant the market for the original. Therefore, a client that distributes them within the company should not present problems. The research firm may want to place some notice on the summary to indicate that the research product is not to be used outside the client's business.

If either the firm or a client company has an Annual Copyright License from the Copyright Clearance Center, it may cover using such abstracts for clients. The best course of action is to talk with the firm's CCC representative to explore coverage.

Q307 *An online news service produces abstracts of copyrighted articles and stories and publishes them online. (1) Does a content owner have any legal grounds on which to prohibit abstracts of that content, whether the work is available online or in print? (2) Does it make a difference if the news service is provided free of charge and for noncommercial purposes, plus includes appropriate attribution of the original source? (3) Could the service simply include a link to the site on which the item originally appeared, even if access to some of these requires a subscription fee?*

(1) Abstracts that are condensations or relatively full summaries of the contents of a copyrighted work probably do require permission since, as summaries or condensations of the original work, they are derivative works. If, however, the abstract is merely descriptive of the contents, then there is no problem. For example, "This article discusses these four topics, has a chart on X that appears on page Y, and is written by this expert."

(2) The fact that the online news service is not for profit is important, but it is not the deciding factor since even commercial use may be fair use. Attribution of the original content is important but does not excuse copyright infringement. Attribution is a plagiarism issue rather than a copyright problem.

(3) To link to an online article that the news service abstracts, no permission is required under the conditions described in the question. The fact that a link to the content on a publisher's web page requires a password to access the content is no problem. Many such lists of links include password-protected links; the user at least knows that the item is online and can decide whether to subscribe in order to obtain the full-text content.

• • •

Q308 *How does the Americans with Disabilities Act (ADA) affect copyright? What about a university library that reproduces a dissertation in a large-print or digital version for use by a visually impaired student?*

Congress has never done anything to harmonize the Copyright Act and the ADA. However, section 121 of the Copyright Act permits "authorized entities" to make copies of nondramatic literary works in specialized formats for the blind or others with disabilities. The definition of "authorized entity" is somewhat problematic in this situation. The statute defines authorized entity as "a nonprofit organization or a governmental agency that has a primary mission to provide specialized services relating to training, education, or adaptive reading or information access needs of blind or other persons with disabilities." Many academic and public libraries produce large-print or digital copies of works for the use of individual patrons who have disabilities. One can argue that if such a version does not exist, reproducing the work in a format that the patron can use falls under section 108(e) of the Copyright Act, which permits libraries to reproduce a substantial portion of a work or even an entire work after the library has tried to obtain a copy of the work at a fair price for the patron to use. The copy must become the property of the user, the library must have no notice that the work will be used for other than fair use purposes, and the work must contain the notice of copyright. Although currently the Copyright Act is silent about making a digital copy of a work in lieu of a photocopy, many libraries are doing so under the same conditions as they produce photocopies for users.

• • •

Q309 *The school has acquired the Kurzweil system, which can scan text and read it back to a student who has visual learning problems. The license agreement for the Kurzweil product appears to put the burden for compliance with the law back on the consumer. Why is this? This is a quote from its "Notice of Copyright Responsibilities and Exceptions."*

> *Some commentators believe that creating a computer-readable version of a copyrighted work for a visually or reading-impaired individual who owns a print copy, especially where the publisher does not itself make such versions available, is a fair use of that work. These guidelines are provided to help us-*

ers understand that there are important legal issues involved when scanning print material. . . . It is the responsibility of the user to be sure that his or her use complies with the law.

Copyright compliance is always the burden of the user and not of the producer of equipment. Kurzweil could not realistically do otherwise than to put the burden on the user, because the company could not possibly know all of the uses to which the system might be put by a consumer. Further, the equipment likely has non-infringing uses as well.

On the other hand, scanning the text using the Kurzweil software for learning-disabled users appears to be a fair use. While a digital copy is made in order for the work to be read aloud, a court likely would find that this is fair use. If the copy is retained, it should be retained by the individual student and not by the library. Moreover, section 121 of the Copyright Act permits authorized entities (those with the primary mission of providing services to the blind or other people with disabilities) to reproduce and distribute copies of works in specialized formats exclusively for use by the blind or other persons with disabilities.

• • •

Q310 *What is the difference between the composer's rights and royalties, those of the music publishing company, and the recording company?*

Under U.S. copyright law, the copyright in a work initially vests with the author (i.e., the composer). The author is the owner of the copyright and is entitled to the exclusive rights provided under the Copyright Act: reproduction, distribution, adaptation, performance, and display. If the work in question is a sound recording, the owner also has the right of public performance via digital transmission.

The composer usually transfers to the music publisher only the rights of reproduction and distribution for the composition. The publisher then collects royalties for sales of copies of the sheet music and pays a share of the royalties back to the composer. Generally, the composer retains all of the other rights, such as public performance, and so continues to collect royalties for the public performance of his or her music. The composer typically signs a license with one of the performance-royalty-collecting agencies: the Association of Composers, Authors and Publishers (ASCAP), Broadcast Music Inc. (BMI), or SESAC Inc. They collect royalties for public performances of music and distribute them back to the composer.

A sound recording of the performance of a musical composition embodies at least two and sometimes three separate copyrights: the underlying musical composition, the recording of the performance of the music, and the arrangement of the music for the sound recording. The performer, who may or may not be the composer, normally transfers the copyright in the performance of the music to the recording company that collects royalties for the sale of the recordings. The composer is compensated for the sale of recordings through the mechanical license, a compulsory license under the statute. The composer normally continues to own the copyright in the musical composition, however.

When music is played on radio or television, royalties are paid to the composer in the form of a blanket license with the performance royalty organizations. There are no performance rights in sound recordings except for digital transmission. So, traditionally, the recording company makes its money from the sale of records and not from performance. But both the recording company and the performers share the royalties for digital transmission of sound recording (e.g., from webcasting).

• • •

Q311 *A university produces a series of materials in which it owns the copyright. Later there is litigation (not over the copyright), during which the defense attorney asks for copies of the material. Must the university comply with the court order?*

An institution must comply with a court order or it is guilty of contempt of court. Sometimes legal counsel may challenge the validity of a court order, but absent that, there is no wiggle room on compliance with the order.

Q312 *May someone redraw a painting from the library collection and use his drawing for a brochure advertising the library's special collections without infringing copyright? The drawing would not be an exact replica, just similar. The original painting is still under copyright.*

A reproduction in any medium is still a reproduction. While librarians understand that a photocopy or a digital copy is a reproduction, it is easy to forget that a drawing of a painting is also a reproduction. If, when the library obtained the copyrighted painting it also obtained the copyright in the work, then no permission would be needed except from the library. The library would have had to receive a written transfer of the copyright since physical ownership of the painting does not presume ownership of the copyright. If the painting was produced before 1978 and was not protected by federal copyright, some courts have held that transfer of the physical object also included transfer of the copyright.

Since the question states that the painting is still under copyright, unless the library owns the copyright, the library should seek permission to use the drawing of the copyrighted painting in a brochure.

All of the above presumes that the drawing is substantially similar to the painting. Should the drawing simply use the ideas from the painting but not copy it, then there is no problem with the drawing. The library could decide that even though the drawing is substantially similar to the painting, it is a fair use. Should there be litigation, a court would analyze the drawing using the fair use factors.

• • •

Q313 *Librarians must often explain copyright law to patrons, including students and faculty. How should this be done?*

Educational institutions should have adopted a copyright policy that the library can distribute on its website and also have available as printed copies to share with users. A number of books and pamphlets have been developed to explain the law to various user groups. A good one is *Campus Copyright Rights and Responsibilities: A Ba-*

sic Guide to Policy Considerations, published in December 2005 by the Association of American Universities, the Association of American Publishers, the Association of American University Presses, and the Association of Research Libraries. It is available for purchase in multiple copies and also as a free download at http://www.arl.org/bm~doc/campuscopyright05.pdf. (In the interest of full disclosure, I was one of the authors of this booklet.)

• • •

Q314   *Why there is a debate over whether fair use is a defense or a right, and does it makes any difference?*

This is one of the central debates in copyright law, and there is not an absolute answer (sort of like, "What is the meaning of life?"). In law, a defense is something that may be raised by a defendant to defeat the claim made by the plaintiff in a lawsuit. In section 107 of the Copyright Act, in order to determine whether the use is a fair use, courts are directed to evaluate the particular use in relation to four factors (purpose of the use, nature of the works copied, how much is used, and market effect). This makes it clear that fair use is a defense to copyright infringement, because a court is involved only in the context of litigation. So, fair use certainly is a defense to a claim of copyright infringement, but it is also more. Often fair use is referred to as an affirmative defense, which is defined as a new fact or set of facts that operates to defeat a claim even if the facts alleged by the plaintiff in the claim are true. In other words, the defendant did make the copies of a protected work, but the purpose of the use, amount of the work copied, and so forth are such that a court would find that the use is a fair use, and this defeats the infringement claim.

But is fair use also a right? There is a significant difference between a right and defense. A defense is raised only in the context of litigation—in other words, someone has been sued for copyright infringement and then raises the defense of fair use. By contrast, a legal right is a power, privilege, demand, or claim possessed by a person by virtue of law. So, a right exists under the rules of a legal system, such as the law of a country. Sometimes fair use is defined as a privilege rather than a right, but this simply presents a circular argument since *Black's Law Dictionary* defines a right as a privilege and a privilege as a right.

Individuals who argue that fair use is a right are those who want expanded ability to use copyrighted works without permission of the copyright owner. Copyright holders, however, want to restrict fair use to a defense only. The difficulty in the copyright law is that the statute actually uses the term "right of fair use" in the library provision, section 108(f)(4). It is difficult to know if this was intentional on the part of Congress or was inadvertent, but it certainly has furthered the debate on this issue. This contrasts with section 107's direction to courts and serves to enhance the confusion even further.

Does the difference between a defense and a right make a difference? Perhaps or perhaps not, but the problem is this: If fair use is a right, then one gets to assert it as a matter of law, so that an infringement claim would not even be filed. Maybe the answer is that fair use falls somewhere in the middle between a defense and a right. To some extent, this is the essence of an affirmative defense. The debate over whether fair use is a right or a defense is likely to continue, and unless the U.S. Supreme Court or Congress speaks definitively on the matter, no clear answer is possible.

● ● ●

Q315 *What rights does a library in a for-profit educational institution have concerning reproduction and other exceptions to the Copyright Act?*

Many of the exceptions detailed in the Copyright Act are available only to nonprofit educational institutions. For example, the classroom exception found in section 110(1) and the distance education provision in section 110(2) are restricted to nonprofit institutions. Also, the negotiated Guidelines on Multiple Copying for Classroom Use and the Guidelines for Educational Uses of Music apply only to nonprofit educational institutions. Neither the library exception nor fair use is so limited, however. The reason for this restriction to nonprofit educational institutions is statutory recognition of nonprofit education as a public good.

Section 108, the library exception, contains criteria that a library or archive must satisfy in order to qualify for the exception, but nonprofit status is not one of them. A library must (1) receive no direct or indirect commercial advantage from the reproduction of copyrighted works, (2) be open to the public or to researchers conducting specialized research, and (3) ensure that copies reproduced under this exception contain the notice of copyright.

Fair use is not limited to nonprofit educational institutions, but it is generally thought to be less robust for for-profit entities. One interesting development is that copyright owners do not appear to charge higher royalties for permissions to for-profit educational institution libraries. Thus, the royalties for electronic reserves, course packs, and the like seem to be the same for both types of schools.

• • •

Q316 *Are public libraries considered educational institutions? What criteria are used to determine whether an organization is a nonprofit educational institution as part of the fair use exception?*

For copyright purposes, the question is not whether an institution is educational in nature but whether it is organized under the U.S. tax code as a nonprofit educational institution. Nonprofit educational institutions have certain privileges and exceptions that apply to them in copyright that are not available to for-profit educational institutions or to other nonprofit organizations.

Libraries are not necessarily educational institutions. To some extent, the answer depends on the type of library. A library in a school, college, or university is a part of an educational institution, and therefore it qualifies. A corporate library, even in a nonprofit corporation, is not an educational institution. A public library, while it definitely has an educational mission, is a nonprofit library, but it is not a nonprofit educational institution. The Copyright Act contains no criteria for determining what constitutes a nonprofit educational institution, but the common understanding among most lawyers is that the status is determined by how the institution is organized under the U.S. tax code.

Q317 *Academic libraries often subscribe to publications that they retain for only a few months and do not bind. Is there a problem in giving discarded issues to another department on campus? For example, the library subscribes to* Paris Match, *which it retains only for three months. The foreign language department wants the discarded issues.*

It is perfectly permissible to give another department discarded materials. The Copyright Act states in section 109(a), the "first sale doctrine," that anyone who has a lawfully acquired copy of a work may dispose of that copy in any way. The library subscribes to journals, purchases materials, and receives other materials as gifts. It may lend these items to users, give them away, sell them, and so forth. Royalties go to the copyright holder only for the first sale (i.e., the library's subscription). The first sale doctrine does not permit the reproduction of those copies, however.

• • •

Q318 *Are there any copyright rules about corporate employee donations of personal or professional association journals to the private corporate library?*

Generally anyone who has lawfully acquired a copy of a copyrighted work may dispose of that copy even by donating it to a corporate library. The real question is whether the library can then use the journal just as it does a purchased subscription. If the publisher offers only one subscription rate for that journal, then there should be no problem. But if the publisher has a separate institutional subscription rate for the journal, then the library really should not use that donated subscription except to replace missing issues for binding. It should subscribe at the institutional rate that permits multiple readers, copying, and so forth.

• • •

Q319 *If a university is drafting a copyright policy, is it better to create it as a part of the patent policy or as a separate policy?*

Although copyrights and patents are both types of intellectual property, they are very different from each other. The statutes are separate (Title 17 U.S. Code for copyright and Title 35 for patents), and the qualifications for protection, duration of protection, rights afforded, and remedies are different for each. In academia, every faculty member is affected by copyright: All faculty use copyrighted works for teaching, and in institutions that expect research and scholarship, faculty produces copyrighted scholarly works. By contrast, only a few faculty members are likely to produce patentable works or be in a position to infringe a patent, and typically those faculty members are in science, medicine, engineering, or computer science.

Universities generally are much more interested in patents than they are in copyrighted works since patent royalties produce considerable income for the institution. Usually, there is a royalty sharing arrangement between the university and the faculty inventor. On the other hand, most institutions permit faculty authors to own the copyright in their works. Few copyrighted scholarly works produce much income, as opposed to patented inventions.

The concern for including both copyright and patent in one policy is that copyright is likely to take a backseat to patent, and the default position could become university ownership for copyrights as it is for patents. Because of the money at stake with a patent, universities will consider them more important, despite the fact that many fewer faculty members produce patentable inventions than produce copyrighted works. So, a separate policy is preferable.

• • •

Q320 *What is the personal liability for a librarian who writes copyright guidelines for faculty when faculty members either do not understand the guidelines and infringe or simply do not comply with them?*

Under section 108(f)(2) of the Copyright Act, it is the direct infringer and the institution that would be liable for infringing copyright in violation of the policy or guidelines, not a librarian who drafts guidelines for the institution. The librarian who drafts the guidelines is doing so at the request of a college or university official as a part of his or her job duties. Librarians are not responsible for ensuring that every faculty member and student follow the policy or the law down to the nth degree. While an unhappy copyright owner could initially name the librarian in a suit against the institution, as well as the faculty member, it is likely that the suit would be dropped against the librarian, who was not responsible for the infringing conduct.

• • •

Q321 *A campus is drafting a copyright policy and has asked the librarian who should be on the committee to produce the policy.*

When drafting a policy, it makes sense to include faculty members, librarians, staff, and even students on the committee so that all viewpoints are represented. A member of the legal counsel staff also should be on the committee. While faculty, librarians, and even students are bound by the policy, in order to protect itself and its faculty, staff, and students, an institution is responsible for seeing that its policies are followed. Representatives of each group should be responsible for "selling" the policy to their groups. The policy should be posted on a campus website in draft form so that comments can be gathered, and the draft altered as necessary. Then the final policy should be posted.

• • •

Q322 *What is the purpose and meaning of the requirement in section 108(a)(2) of the Copyright Act that a library be open to the public in order to enjoy the library exceptions found in section 108?*

The purpose is to exclude libraries in the for-profit sector and libraries in nonprofit entities, such as private clubs, that are not open to the public. This is recognition of the public good of public libraries and similar libraries that serve the public even if open to nonaffiliated users only by appointment. The House Report 94-1476, which accompanied the Copyright Act, indicates that this would prohibit a purely commercial enterprise from calling itself a library. Only libraries that meet the requirement of being open to the public or to researchers doing research in a specialized field may take advantage of the exceptions for preservation, copying for users, interlibrary loan, and so forth under the Copyright Act. Another commonsense reason for the requirement is that it asks copyright holders to bear the cost for that exception or to forego royalties that they would otherwise receive. If a library is not open to the public, why should copyright holders bear these costs for another for-profit entity?

• • •

Q323 *Many academic institutions now have copyright or scholarly communications officers. What do these people do?*

Colleges and universities have begun to recognize how important copyright is to its faculty, staff, and students. While university attorneys are there to advise the institution on all legal issues, including copyright, they typically are not able to provide services and assistance to individual faculty and staff. A copyright officer is typically required to hold a law degree, and often also a library degree. The duties of a copyright officer may include the following: (1) developing educational materials, online instruction, and websites about copyright for the institution; (2) offering copyright education and training programs for faculty, students, and staff; (3) assisting the library by reviewing licenses for copyrighted materials; (4) answering questions for individual faculty members about the use of copyrighted works in their teaching and scholarship; (5) advising faculty about copyright transfers for their publications; (6) coordinating activities with the campus office of legal counsel; (7) participating in policy development; and (8) serving as an *ex officio* member of the campus copyright committee.

Additionally, campus copyright officers often develop relationships with other copyright experts around the country to share information and materials. Some officers also have responsibility for developing testimony in various hearings.

Q324 *Articles and books about copyright often refer to statutory damages. What are statutory damages? How do they differ from other types of damages?*

Statutory damages are those detailed in the statute. In copyright there are two types of damages available to the prevailing plaintiff: (1) actual damages and profits and (2) statutory damages. In order to recover actual damages and profits, the plaintiff would have to prove the amount of actual damage incurred because of the defendant's infringing activity. Proof of actual damage is difficult and includes such things as actual lost sales. Courts seldom award the defendants profits unless the conduct has been particularly egregious (such as a software pirate with a warehouse full of pirated software). However, sometimes a plaintiff has no choice but to seek actual damages and profits. If the work in question was not registered for copyright with the U.S. Copyright Office prior to the defendant's infringing activities, statutory damages are unavailable. This restriction should encourage copyright owners to register their works.

Statutory damages are available to a plaintiff who proves infringement, and unlike with a claim for actual damages and profits, the plaintiff does not have to prove the degree of harm suffered. Over the years, the statute has been amended to increase the limits on statutory damages; currently they range from $750 to $30,000 per act of infringement. The range is very broad to permit the judge or jury to determine what is needed to make the plaintiff whole again. They can also take into account the potential for future harm should the practice become widespread. If the infringement is innocent infringement, the damages may be lowered to $200; likewise, the damages may be raised to $150,000 if the infringement is determined by the court to be willful. If a work infringed contains a notice of copyright, an infringer may not claim that although it did infringe, it was good faith infringement and therefore damages should be reduced to $200. On the other hand, if the infringer had reasonable grounds to believe that the use made of the copyrighted work was fair use; and if the infringer is an employee of a nonprofit educational institution, library, or archives and is acting within the scope of employment; damages may be remitted entirely.

• • •

Q325 *What is the statute of limitations for filing a lawsuit for copyright infringement? How long does someone have to discover the infringement before the statute of limitations begins to run?*

According to section 507 of the Copyright Act of 1976, the statute of limitation for civil actions is three years and for criminal actions is five years. A 1999 amendment to the Act increased the damages but did not alter the statute of limitations. There are two schools of thought about when the statute of limitations starts to run. In the Seventh Circuit, if the wrong is a "continuing wrong" then the three or five years start to run when the last act occurred. The second view is the tolling statute of limitations theory, which says that the plaintiff may look back for three years for damages after the date that the suit is filed. This is the Ninth Circuit approach, and it is the preferred view.

• • •

Q326 *In the past, libraries have been required to place a copyright notice on self-service photocopiers under 37 C.F.R. Ch. 2, Sec. 201.14. Was this notice requirement eliminated by the Digital Millennium Copyright Act (DMCA)? The copiers here in the library no longer have the notice. Did this happen accidentally when the library obtained a new copier contract or has the law regarding these notices changed?*

The DMCA did not change the section 108(f)(1) notice requirement at all. That section requires libraries that offer unsupervised reproduction equipment to post a notice that making a copy may be subject to the copyright law. Absent such notice, the library may be liable for the infringing reproduction activities of patrons on that equipment. Thus, the problem may be one of oversight, and the library should ensure that the requisite notices are posted. Any language may be used for the notice, but most libraries appear to use the copyright warning from the Code of Federal Regulations (CFR).

• • •

Q327 *If an author abandons copyright or makes an item available under a Creative Commons (CC) license, can the heirs try to enforce the copyright after the author's death?*

Abandonment of copyright is difficult to prove; it almost takes some written, affirmative statement by the copyright holder that he or she is abandoning the copyright in that particular work. If the work truly is abandoned though, then neither that author nor the heirs have any further rights in it.

If the author has made the work available with a CC license, that license is governed by state law. The heirs cannot enforce the copyright against anyone who used the work as permitted under the CC license, although they are free to release the work under a new license to others.

EPILOGUE

Emerging Challenges in Copyright

The questions and answers in this book indicate that there are many copyright issues that are still being debated by librarians, archivists, publishers, and authors, as well as legislators, attorneys, and members of the public. For many information professionals, copyright is frustrating because answers to their questions too often begin with "It depends." That is the nature of a law that so often requires interpreting a statute that is unclear and outdated, examining prior case law and the facts of a particular situation, and then doing one's best to arrive at the answer. Librarians often follow what they believe to be best practices, and when there is no answer to their questions, in the end, they do a risk assessment to determine whether the use they want to make of a copyrighted work outweighs any risk of infringement.

As this book goes to press, there are a number of issues that are the subject of recent legislative discussions and litigation that will provide answers to some of the questions to which currently there is either no answer or an incomplete one. Questions addressed in the epilogue are (1) The Google Books settlement; (2) orphan works legislation; (3) the *Author's Guild v. HathiTrust* case; (4) the Digital Public Library of America; (5) the *Georgia State* case; (6) the JSTOR copying indictment; (7) the first sale doctrine to foreign-made copyrighted works, *John Wiley & Sons v. Kirtsaeng*; (8) *Pearson, Cengage and Bedford, Freeman & Worth v. Boundless Learning*, which deals with the protection of textbooks in the electronic environment; and (9) the Section 108 Study.

• • •

Q328 *An academic librarian asks about the judge's rejection of the Google Books Settlement 2.0 proposal. What has happened since then? Are library users disadvantaged by this decision?*

In March 2011, Judge Denny Chin for the federal district court, Southern District of New York, rejected what many termed an over-reaching settlement proposed by a number of publishers and Google that would have granted Google the unprecedented ability to reproduce copyrighted works, index them, and license their use, as well as to manage orphan works. (*See* http://thepublicindex.org/docs/amended_settlement/opinion.pdf for the full text of the judge's order.) Doubtless, scholars would have benefited from the availability of this huge corpus of scanned books, but some copyright owners have pointed out that people would benefit from bank robberies if the proceeds were distributed to those in need. In other words, in their views, both represent a taking of property without compensation, and the argument is that it is justified because of the public good. Most librarians have mixed feelings about the settlement, recognizing the tremendous benefit the Google Books project would offer to libraries and to scholars. On the other hand, giving a monopoly to Google for making, storing, and providing access to the digital copies of these works is problematic.

Judge Chin highlighted problems in the proposed agreement, ranging from the attempt basically to rewrite U.S. copyright law, to the settlement's opt-out system rather than opt-in for copyright holders, to the monopoly it would create for Google, to the private management of orphan works. There are several potential next steps, some of which could occur simultaneously. First, the parties could appeal the judge's ruling. Or, the parties could go back to the drawing board for a third time to redraft a settlement agreement. There was some attempt to do this. Another possibility is that the litigation challenging Google's scanning of materials could go forward should settlement prove impossible. Another potential outcome is that other entities such as the Internet Archive, the proposed Digital Public Library of America, another nonprofit entity, or a coalition of these organizations create digital libraries of millions of books with similarly excellent search capability. The settlement rejection could spur congressional action, especially for orphan works legislation, but also for public funding of a national digital books project. It is too soon to know with certainty what will happen next, however, but these are a few of the possibilities.

On May 31, 2012, Judge Chin rejected Google's motion to dismiss the Authors Guild suit as an association plaintiff and granted the Guild's motion for class certification, which permits it to sue Google for the scanning on behalf of the country's writers as a group. Google opposed, claiming that an association had no standing to initiate the suit but instead that the plaintiffs had to be individual writers. The judge stated that it would be unjust to require authors to sue Google individually since Google did not engage in individual evaluations of their works before scanning. How long the litigation will continue is not clear, but likely for many months.

• • •

Q329 *A few years ago, there was much in the press about orphan works and it was expected that the copyright law would be amended to deal with orphan works as do the laws of several foreign countries. What has happened to orphan works legislation?*

An orphaned work is a copyrighted work with no identifiable parents. More specifically, it refers to works for which the copyright holder is unknown or whose owner is difficult or impossible to locate. Under the 1909 Copyright Act the problem was often solved by the renewal requirement. After the first 28 years of copyright protection, a copyright holder had the opportunity to extend the copyright an additional 28 years, but he or she had to apply for a renewal. Failure to renew meant that the work entered the public domain after the first term of copyright. Most orphaned works passed into the public domain after the first term due to failure to renew, but it was difficult to know for sure about a particular work. With the extension of the copyright term to life of the author plus 70 years, or 95 years after date of first publication for works of corporate authorship, the problem is even more acute.

The Register of Copyrights recognized that it may create an inappropriate burden on the users of copyrighted works to try to obtain permission to reproduce orphaned works since it is virtually impossible to do so. In 2005, she initiated a study of the problem caused by these orphan works and reported to Congress in January 2006 (*see* http://www.copyright.gov/orphan/orphan-report.pdf), calling for legislation to amend the copyright law to provide protection for anyone who uses an orphan work. In order to take advantage of the provision, a user would have to conduct a reasonable search to locate the copyright owner. After such a search, the user then would not be responsible for any damages for that use should the copyright owner later come forward. However, the user would be responsible for damages for use after that time and would have to negotiate future royalties with the owner in order to continue using the work.

It appeared that the legislation would move swiftly through Congress, but it met a roadblock when media photographers raised strong objections. The proposed amendment languished after that point. An easy solution to the roadblock might have been to permit the legislation to go forward but exempt photographs from its provisions. This has not been proposed, however.

During the Google Books settlement talks, however, interest in orphan works again surfaced. In the Google Books settlement, there were some proposals that would have, at least partially, solved the orphan works problem. Many legal scholars, librarians, and, ultimately, the judge criticized the proposed settlement's handling of orphan works and opined that this should be left to federal legislation and not to private ordering among parties to the Google Books suit.

On October 25, 2011, the new Register of Copyrights, Maria Pallante, issued a document that contained her three-year priorities for the U.S. Copyright Office. Among them is orphan works legislation (*see* http://www.loc.gov/today/pr/2011/11-204.html). Because of all that has transpired since the 2006 report, it is likely that the Copyright Office will review that report and make changes to the earlier proposed legislation. There is also a need to couple orphan works legislation with a study of collective licensing for mass digitization of works that are still in copyright, perhaps similar to that used in Nordic countries.

• • •

Q330   *HathiTrust is an organization that will preserve works digitally and make them available to researchers. Why has the Authors Guild sued the HathiTrust? What is the likely outcome?*

On its website, the HathiTrust is defined as "a partnership of major research institutions and libraries working to ensure that the cultural record is preserved and accessible long into the future." (*See* http://www.hathitrust.org/about#.) Open to institutions around the world, the HathiTrust is made up of more than 60 partner libraries.

It is estimated that HathiTrust members have scanned more than seven million copyrighted works to date for the repository. In June 2011, the University of Michigan announced that it would make available to its students and faculty for access and download works from the corpus that it had determined were orphan works. The university had a protocol for searching for an author and posting the name of a work for 90 days in order to determine whether it would deem the work to be an orphan. Several other schools joined the project. In September 2011 the Authors Guild filed suit, claiming that it had strong leads to authors and estates that hold copyright to the first 167 works listed by Michigan as orphan candidates. Then Michigan announced that it was suspending the program of determining which works were orphans, but it continues to host the seven million digitized works.

This litigation is proceeding with the same question as discussed regarding the Google Books settlement (*see* Q328): whether an association can sue on behalf of its author members. Authors groups from the United Kingdom, Canada, Norway, and Sweden have now joined as plaintiffs. While many U.S. universities participated in the Google Books project, including Harvard, Princeton, and Stanford, most allowed only books that are in the public domain to be scanned. Only a few schools have allowed Google to scan copyrighted works. Defendants countered, asking the federal judge to hold that the HathiTrust project is a fair use. The Library Copyright Alliance filed an amicus brief in the case (*see* http://www.infodocket.com/2012/04/24/library-copyright-alliance-files-friend-of-the-court-brief-in-the-authors-guild-v-hathitrust-case/). The Authors Guild has responded that the reproduction of seven million works is not permitted by any statutory exception to the rights of the copyright holder. The litigation will be watched by informational professionals around the world.

• • •

Q331 *The Digital Public Library of America (DPLA) is such a great idea. Why is it not progressing more rapidly? What problems has it encountered?*

The aim of DPLA is "to make as much of the learning and cultural patrimony of the United States in the humanities, the sciences, the social sciences, and other areas of knowledge free and accessible to the citizens of the United States and around the world" (*see* http://www.nypl.org/blog/2011/11/07/digital-public-library-america). It is similar to the Google Books project, but it plans to be more comprehensive and unimpeded by commercial motives. One problem with DPLA is that it has not yet articulated a consistent and concise statement of its scope, but it is closer to developing a mission statement. It will begin with making available public domain works and digitized works from the Library of Congress and the National Archives. It will collaborate with Europeana (*see* http://www.europeana.eu/portal/), the digital library project that is aggregating some five million digital objects from European research libraries. The Sloan Foundation and Arcadia Fund have contributed five million dollars toward the DPLA. A version of DPLA is slated to be rolled out in April 2013.

While there are other problems that the DPLA is encountering, copyright is the major legal issue. Another aim of DPLA is to digitize cultural works that are still under copyright protection but which are out of print. It is the digitizing of copyrighted works that is causing most of the problems. DPLA has created a number of work streams, and one is the legal work stream that will deal with copyright. Whether the project can proceed beyond public domain and U.S. government publications will depend, in part, on what happens with orphan works legislation. The DPLA also is encouraging the Register of Copyrights to address mass digitization projects.

• • •

Q332 *Why did publishers sue Georgia State University (GSU), claiming that it has infringed copyright? What is the status of the litigation?*

Cambridge University Press, Oxford University Press, and Sage Publications filed suit against GSU in 2008, alleging that the university infringed their copyrights by creating electronic course packs, posting portions of their books in course management software, and reproducing their materials in the library's electronic reserves (e-reserves) system without seeking permission or paying royalties. In the past GSU had paid royalties for print course packs, but when it converted to electronic course packs, it ceased paying royalties. Publishers claimed that they repeatedly tried to work with the university but that officials and librarians refused to talk with them. The university had a copyright policy that was far more liberal toward fair use than the policies of most colleges, and during the pendency of the suit it revised the policy.

The publishers claimed that even with a revised policy, GSU implemented it in such a way that GSU invited disregard for basic copyright norms by delegating difficult copyright decisions to faculty without guidance, having no meaningful review mechanisms in place, and providing no funds to pay for permissions when necessary. Publishers claimed that this threatened their businesses and incentives for scholars and publishers to develop materials for students, and that the university could seek permission on a case-by-case basis, or obtain the Copyright Clearance Center campus-wide license. In the suit, plaintiffs stated that a CCC license for GSU's over 30,000 students would be about $3.75 per student per year. GSU defended the suit on the basis of fair use.

The federal district court issued its 350-page opinion on May 11, 2012. While it may best be described as a somewhat mixed opinion, it did find that 69 of 74 claims of infringement were fair use. Other claims did not reach the decision stage because the publisher did not offer a digital license for the work at the time of the suit, because it could not prove ownership of the copyright, or because there was no evidence that students had ever downloaded the work despite its availability in the course management system or in e-reserves.

Specific holdings that favor GSU include the following: (1) the Guidelines on Multiple Copying for Classroom Use are not relevant for this digital copying (the court said that they are not compatible with the language and intent of section 107 of the Copyright Act); (2) the one-semester rule is an impractical and unnecessary limitation; (3) despite some problems with GSU's 2009 Copyright Policy, it represented a good faith effort to assist faculty in interpreting fair use; and (4) if digital copies of works are not available through a license, libraries may make expanded uses of these works. Holdings that favor the publishers are as follows: (1) although GSU is a state-supported institution, the case qualified for an exception to Eleventh Amendment immunity from suit since the only remedy sought is an injunction (as opposed to monetary damages); (2) digital copies of works on e-reserve are not transformative use; and (3) if the copyright owner earned significant income from license fees, the court was less likely to find that a small excerpt was fair use. Further, the judge was somewhat dismissive toward community best practices in determining whether something is fair use. It should be noted, however, that the ARL Code of Best Practices in Fair Use for Academic and Research Libraries was published after the case had begun and was not considered by the court (see http://www.arl.org/pp/ppcopyright/codefairuse/index.shtml).

One holding appears to favor neither side. The judge converted the third fair use factor—amount and substantiality of the portion used in comparison to the work as a whole—into a bright-line rule rather than a flexible rule of reason. According to the opinion, using an excerpt in e-reserve or course management systems of 10% of a work, or a single chapter, is fair use. Beyond that, it is not. This is less flexible than GSU wanted and is a greater amount than the publishers sought as a limitation.

The case has now moved to the remedial stage for the judge to craft an injunction. After the injunction, it is certainly possible that the case will be appealed. One important limitation of this case is that it deals only with books and not with journal articles, poetry, audio-visual works, or other media used in course management and e-reserve systems.

• • •

Q333 *Recently there was a news story about an individual who was indicted for misappropriating more than 4.8 million articles from JSTOR. He reportedly obtained access illegally through the library at MIT and has been charged with abusing computer networks at MIT and with disrupting the servers at JSTOR. He could be sentenced to 35 years of imprisonment. In response to this situation, some librarians and scholars have indicated they believe that access to scholarly articles should be free, which is apparently what this individual was attempting to accomplish. How likely is it that this will happen?*

Journal publishers license JSTOR to provide electronic access to their journals and back issues. JSTOR's own website (*see* http://www.jstor.org/) states that it is "a not–for–profit service that helps scholars, researchers, and students discover, use, and build upon a wide range of content in a trusted digital archive of over one thousand academic journals and other scholarly content." Many publishers rely on JSTOR to provide electronic access to their back files. Even though JSTOR is nonprofit, it must support itself through license fees and through fees for the downloading of individual articles by non-licensed users.

The indictment may be found at http://publicintelligence.net/u-s-district-court-of-massachusetts-aaron-swartz-jstor-downloading-indictment-july-2011/. Aaron H. Swartz, the co-founder of Reddit, was charged by the U.S. Attorney for Massachusetts with wire fraud, computer fraud, unlawfully obtaining information from a protected computer, and recklessly damaging a protected computer. He apparently settled with JSTOR, but federal criminal charges continue. The latest indictment was on November 17, 2011; a grand jury indicted Swartz on charges of breaking and entering, larceny of electronic data, and unauthorized access to a computer network for the illicit downloading of millions of academic articles. Some of the charges are based on the fact that Swartz violated MIT and JSTOR user policies, which raises some concerns for the academic library community.

It is not very likely that access to back runs of journals will be free. Despite the fact that Larry Lessig and others have stated that the price JSTOR charges for providing access to these articles is too high, copyright law is totally contrary to the idea that this valuable property will be made available free unless the publisher (owner) so decides. The United States is a capitalistic country, and publishing is a business. What publishing companies produce are articles, books, and the like, and these are valuable property that they sell and/or license. Owning the copyright in these articles is critical for these publishers.

Certainly more and more scholarly articles are going to be available free as scholars avoid traditional publishers and post them directly on the web. But users of these articles and papers also lose something important—quality control. Publishers have organized peer reviewing and offered some assurance of the quality of the articles. Direct publishing on the web by authors has no such assurance. Libraries and scholars will trust the work of some authors, but for others, they may be unable to verify the authors' credentials, the accuracy of their work, and so forth. Like it or not, journal publishers provide this for the articles published in their journals.

The suit has had one good effect. In September 2011 JSTOR announced that it had released the public domain content of their archives for public viewing and limited use. According to JSTOR, staff has been working on making those archives public for some time, and the recent controversy involving this case made it move forward with the initiative.

$$\bullet\ \bullet\ \bullet$$

Q334 *Will the recent case involving the first sale doctrine and foreign-made works have any impact on libraries?*

The case is *John Wiley & Sons v. Kirtsaeng,* 654 F.3d 210 (2d Cir. 2011), and involves what is referred to as "gray market goods." The court ruled that Kirtsaeng infringed Wiley's copyrights when he imported and sold in the United States cheap foreign editions of the publisher's textbooks sent to him by his family from Thailand. Two sections of the Copyright Act are relevant in this case. Section 602(a) says that importation into the United States without the authority of the copyright owner of copies of works acquired outside the country is an infringement of the exclusive right of distribution. However, the first sale doctrine, section 109(a), permits the sale, lending, and so forth of lawfully acquired copies. So, the question is whether these copies are "lawfully acquired." The Second Circuit held that section 109(a)'s first sale doctrine does not apply to works manufactured outside of this country, which means that publishers can prevent their importation.

Publishers often produce cheaper copies of their works using less expensive paper and binding, then sell them abroad at a reduced price. This holding represents a disagreement among the circuits concerning application of the first sale doctrine to foreign works. The Ninth Circuit earlier held in *Omega S. A. v. Costco Wholesale Corp.*, 541 F.3D 982 (9th Cir. 2008), that a producer could prevent importation of their works, but only if the works were manufactured abroad. This case holds that the first sale applies, no matter where the work is manufactured and regardless of where the sale takes place.

Costco had an exception for libraries, and the decision should not restrict the first sale doctrine for books manufactured abroad and imported into the United States. *Kirtsaeng* contained no such exception. The U.S. Supreme Court has granted certiorari and will decide whether copies of copyrighted works made and legally acquired abroad, which are then imported into the United States, are covered by the first sale doctrine. Should the Second Circuit decision be upheld, libraries are concerned that the first sale doctrine is at risk. After all, that doctrine is how libraries lend work in their collections. If a publisher wants to control application of the first sale doctrine, it could move manufacturing offshore, which would have the effect of eliminating the doctrine for libraries. Thus, the potential impact on libraries is enormous.

• • •

Q335 *Why are textbook companies objecting to the production of electronic textbooks? There was a news report about a case involving this.*

In March 2012 there was a report of a suit filed in the Southern District of New York for copyright infringement by three of the largest textbook publishers in the United States (Pearson Education, Cengage Learning, and Bedford, Freeman & Worth Publishing Group) against Boundless Learning (*see* http://dockets.justia.com/docket/new-york/nysdce/1:2012cv01986/393501/). Boundless is representative of the open education movement, which intentionally injects materials into the public domain so that they may be used freely by teachers and students. Boundless raised approximately $10 million and began to develop and make available basic textbooks. The publishers claim that Boundless is creating and distributing free replacement copies of their works that mirror not only the substance but also the organization, selection, and layout of popular college textbooks.

The case will turn on whether the authors of the published textbooks created original works since textbooks are compilations. The originality bar is set pretty low in U.S. copyright law, so publishers must exhibit selection, organization, and presentation of facts in a sufficiently creative and unique way. Boundless is defending on the basis that the content of its replacement textbooks are factual and come from open education resources. Publishers disagree and claim that there is enough creativity to qualify for copyright protection, which includes the decisions about the information and topics to include, the order of presentation of the topics, and the manner in which the textbook emphasizes and presents the topics.

• • •

Q336 *A few years ago there was a study and a report on section 108 of the Copyright Act of 1976. What has happened with the recommendations for amending the statute?*

To address concerns about libraries, archives and museums, and digital copies, the U.S. Copyright Office and the Office of Strategic Initiatives at the Library of Congress assembled a group of knowledgeable individuals to study section 108 of the Copyright Act and make recommendations about whether it should be amended to reflect the changes that these institutions have experienced due to the digital revolution, and to permit them to use digital technology, while not unduly impacting the rights of the copyright holder. The Section 108 Study Group was made up of nineteen people who met over a three-year period to address these issues and develop recommendations on changes needed in the law. The Group met from April 2005 to March 2008 and its report was issued in March 2008 (*see* http://www.Section108.gov/docs/Sec108StudyGroupReport.pdf). Recommendations relate primarily to eligibility and preservation.

In its report the Study Group recommended that museums be added to the list of institutions that are eligible for the section 108 exceptions. Further, it recommended that an additional functional requirement be added to the definition of eligible institutions, such as possessing a public service mission, employing trained library or archives staff, providing professional services normally associated with libraries and archives, or possessing a collection comprising lawfully acquired and/or licensed materials. The Group also recommended that libraries be permitted to outsource section 108 activities if certain conditions are met.

Most of the recommendations related to preservation, however. The Study Group recommended that the three-copy restriction in section 108(b) and (c) be removed because it is impossible to specify the number of copies that can be made for preservation since it is unknown exactly how many copies may be needed to preserve a particular work in digital form. The Group suggested that a more appropriate measure is a "reasonable" number of copies to accomplish the preservation. Additionally, it suggested that for published digital works, establishing a "preservation only" exception would ensure that these works are not lost to society. Another recommendation was to add the term "fragile" to the triggers for replacement copies (lost, damaged, deteriorating, stolen, or obsolete). Finally, the Group recommended that a new preservation activity be added to the statutory exception—the ability to curate and preserve websites and other publicly available Internet content that have no access controls. Despite all of the work of the Study Group, it was not able to reach consensus on making preserved copies available to users off site.

For a number of reasons, the Study Group report has languished in the U.S. Copyright Office since its completion. The new Register of

Copyrights has put the recommendations on her three-year priority list (*see Report on Orphan Works*, available at http://www.copyright. gov/orphan/orphan-report.pdf), and she recently invited members of the Group to Washington to discuss the recommendations and changes since 2008. She has announced that she intends to recommend amendments to section 108 based on these recommendations and any new ones developed by the Copyright Office. (In the interest of full disclosure, I was the co-chair of the Section 108 Study Group.)

APPENDIX

When U.S. Works Pass into the Public Domain

DATE OF WORK	PROTECTED FROM	TERM
Created 1-1-78 or after	When work is fixed in tangible medium of expression	Life + 70 years[1] (or if work of corporate authorship, the shorter of 95 years from publication, or 120 years from creation[2]
Published before 1923	In public domain	None
Published from 1923–63	When published with notice[3]	28 years + could be renewed for 47 years, now extended by 20 years for a total renewal of 67 years. If not so renewed, now in public domain
Published from 1964–77	When published with notice	28 years for first term; now automatic extension of 67 years for second term
Created before 1-1-78 but not published	1-1-78, the effective date of the 1976 Act which eliminated common law copyright	Life + 70 years or 12-31-2002, whichever is greater
Created before 1-1-78 but published between then and 12-31-2002	1-1-78, the effective date of the 1976 Act which eliminated common law copyright	Life + 70 years or 12-31-2047, whichever is greater

1   Term of joint works is measured by life of the longest-lived author.

2   Works for hire, anonymous, and pseudonymous works also have this term. 17 U.S.C. § 302(c).

3   Under the 1909 Act, works published without notice went into the public domain upon publication. Works published without notice between 1-1-78 and 3-1-89, effective date of the Berne Convention Implementation Act, retained copyright only if efforts to correct the accidental omission of notice were made within five years, such as by placing notice on unsold copies. 17 U.S.C. § 405.

Notes courtesy of Professor Tom Field, Franklin Pierce Law Center, and Lolly Gasaway.

Last updated 11-5-03.

INDEX